The Royal Priesthood of the Faithful

AN INVESTIGATION OF THE DOCTRINE
FROM BIBLICAL TIMES TO THE
REFORMATION

CYRIL EASTWOOD

WIPF & STOCK · Eugene, Oregon

Wipf and Stock Publishers
199 W 8th Ave, Suite 3
Eugene, OR 97401

The Royal Priesthood of the Faithful
An Investigation of the Doctrine from Biblical Times to the Reformation
By Eastwood, Cyril
Copyright©1963 Epworth Press
ISBN 13: 978-1-60608-731-2
Publication date 4/27/2009
Previously published by Epworth Press, 1963

Copyright © Epworth Press 1963
First English edition 1963 by Epworth Press
This edition published by arrangement with Epworth Press

CONTENTS

CHAPTER		PAGE
1	BIBLICAL BASIS: THE OLD TESTAMENT	1
2	BIBLICAL BASIS: THE NEW TESTAMENT	26
3	THE EARLY CHURCH	56
4	ST AUGUSTINE	91
5	THE MIDDLE AGES	102
6	THE IDEA OF PRIESTHOOD IN ROMAN CATHOLIC THEOLOGY	138
7	MARSIGLIO OF PADUA AND JOHN WYCLIF	163
8	THE MONKS AND FRIARS	179
9	THE MYSTICS	195
10	CONCLUSIONS AND REASSESSMENT	225
	BIBLIOGRAPHY	251
	INDEX OF SCRIPTURE REFERENCES	257
	INDEX OF SUBJECTS	260
	INDEX OF NAMES	262

To
HARVEY EASTWOOD
a Local Preacher of the Methodist Church
and my first teacher in Christian Doctrine

CHAPTER ONE

THE BIBLICAL BASIS

Old Testament

THE Old Testament presents us with three important patterns of thought: the People of God, the Servant of the Lord, and a Kingdom of Priests. The People of God are called and chosen by God to a priesthood of which sacrificial service is the characteristic feature. In the final consummation they, together with all peoples, will be presented before God as a Kingdom of Priests. The Old Testament, therefore, shows that the doctrine of the universal priesthood[1] is closely related to Election, Servanthood and Eschatology, and that it can be properly interpreted only in the light of these concepts. It is our purpose to consider how these concepts developed in the history of Israel and then to ascertain whether or not they are important and determinative for the life and thought of the New Israel.

THE PEOPLE OF GOD
Israel are the People of God by divine revelation

Sinful man is entirely dependent upon divine grace. Man is not aware of his need of divine grace apart from revelation. Yet even when the revelation is given, it is not always understood. This is due to human pride which does not easily take a second place. By his sinful nature man is ever self-assertive, yet God demands the death of self and sin. The story of religion is the attempt to resolve this paradox. Unless God speaks, man cannot understand his condition or hope for a cure. Man does not know himself unless he knows God. But he cannot know God unless God makes Himself known.

He makes Himself known by a revelation of grace. Man's dilemma, however, is increased by the fact that God reveals Himself freely

---

[1] The phrases 'The Royal Priesthood of the Faithful' and 'The Priesthood of All Believers' are used interchangeably, the former being prominent before the Reformation, the latter after it.

and lovingly. Because of this, man is always in danger of confusing the means of revelation with its meaning.

In ancient Israel the temptation was to make the people through whom the divine revelation was mediated the end of the revelation. In a sense, the error is understandable but it is not excusable. It is understandable because a people had emerged where there had been no people, and this miracle bestowed upon Israel an incomparable privilege: it is inexcusable because they had been taught that the words, 'I will be your God' must always precede, 'Ye shall be my people.' It was this essential priority which Israel invariably overlooked. The privilege is unmistakable: 'Ye shall be unto me a kingdom of priests, a holy nation' (Exod. xix. 6). It is a privilege which may easily be misunderstood. It is always forfeited when the distinction is lost between the divine revelation itself and the means which God uses to mediate it. The reason why this situation is dangerous is because it invariably means that the people become less concerned about the Holy One than about the holy things connected with His appearance. Perhaps the privilege was too great for them or too difficult to understand. In any case, there is no doubt that the elaborate paraphernalia of temple worship tended to obscure its vital purpose. There were three important lessons for them to learn: that they were recipients of a revelation of grace, that it was a revelation to the whole of Israel, and that it could be forfeited by disobedience and self-will.

Divine initiative, leadership and sovereignty were recognized by the Hebrews from the beginning, and even when the people thought that God was active through human intermediaries, there was never any doubt about the supremacy of Jehovah. With remorseless consistency the prophets stressed the oneness, holiness and almightiness of God's character. The idea of God's coming to deliver man does not originate in man but in the mind of God. It was not man's sin which brought God into contact with man, but God's love which always wills to redeem. The story of divine revelation begins with God. From this beginning there follows an eternal activity of grace.

It was unlikely and indeed unnecessary that they would immediately understand all that the revelation meant, but it was necessary that they should recognize that it was a revelation from God and respond to it. Nor was it sufficient for one towering mind only to grasp the significance of God's dealings with them. God wanted a nation which was willing to become the instrument of His will. The King of all the world demanded a kingdom, but just because he was a righteous King he required a kingdom of priests—men who were obedient, holy and faithful. Yet all this was conditioned by their willingness to enter into a relationship with Him. The whole of Israel stood in a priestly relation to God, but how could they know this?

If Jehovah was as great and wise as they believed Him to be, He was wise enough and great enough to devise a means whereby they might enter into a full relationship with Him as well as understand its meaning and implications. A noble title, therefore, was bestowed upon them: they were to be 'a kingdom of priests' (Exod. xix. 6). A kingdom, because God had chosen them as the instrument of His purpose; priests, because they were to become servants of His will by revealing His purpose to the world. Every member of the kingdom of priests was privileged to draw near to God in dedication, worship and service, so that they might learn how their mission to the world was to be fulfilled.

> Israel is a priestly people, and ideally no Israelite has any privileges over another in drawing near and presenting offerings before Jehovah. Throughout the history of Israel we find this privilege largely taken advantage of. Any Israelite felt himself entitled to offer sacrifice before the Lord.[1]

These privileges belonged to the Lord's people and not to any exclusive class. Again we see the significance of the words: 'Ye shall be my people' (Lev. xxvi. 12), for, as Jeremiah wisely observed, the history of the Hebrews from the deliverance from Egypt to his own day, was simply the realization of that promise (Jer. xi. 4).

At the same time, it should not be forgotten that this revelation of grace which was made to Israel as a whole could be forfeited. It was forfeited when it was divorced from the righteousness of God and the corporate duty of Israel. Israel's mistake was in regarding it as a right instead of a privilege. Just because they thought the revelation was their right, they were able to think of it as something entirely independent of their attitude and conduct. They believed that their rights could be protected and their religious duties performed by a special class of men which had been set apart for this

[1] A. B. Davidson, *The Theology of the Old Testament*, p. 307.

purpose. This class eventually became an hereditary caste and was largely restricted to certain priestly families. The result was that a cleavage appeared in the nation between those who fulfilled the religious duties and those who had neither the right nor the desire to do so. More serious still, the attention of the people was focused upon holy persons, holy things and holy places instead of upon the Holy One. To a people who had adopted this twofold travesty of religion Jeremiah brought the astonishing news that it would do no good to boast of 'the temple of the Lord' as being theirs, for because of their evil ways the Lord reveals that 'I will cast you out of my sight' (Jer. vii. 15). The nation that He had created for His own had become 'a nation that obeyeth not the voice of the Lord their God, nor receiveth correction: truth is perished, and is cut off from their mouth' (Jer. vii. 28). All this did not alter in any sense the basic truth that the people to whom God revealed Himself were elected to be His people, called to a distinctive service on His behalf.

Israel are the People of God by divine election

The world is God's creation. 'God formed the earth and made it' (Isa. xlv. 18). But the world is a setting in which a people might be brought into being. The second miracle is no less remarkable than the first, and the Old Testament is preeminently the story of Jehovah and His people. Israel were to be not only *a* people but God's people. Wherefore, 'I will be your God' (Lev. xxvi. 12) is the fundamental and recurring theme of Old Testament religion. This absolute assurance of God's presence was implicit in their election. They were convinced that all blessings came from God and that there was no other source of blessing. Salvation belonged to God and to Him alone. God's presence with His people was the chief end as well as the beginning of Hebrew religion. God's presence was at once the proof and the symbol of their election. 'If Thy presence go not with me,' cried Moses, 'carry us not up hence' (Exod. xxxiii. 15). The covenant was regarded as the assurance of His presence and of the salvation which He bestowed. 'God', 'People', 'Covenant', in these three words the whole history of the Hebrews is enshrined.

This election involved their sanctification. They were to be separated from others, separated unto God, and separated unto a specific task. Even at Sinai they were called 'a people' not 'a nation'.

Later (1 Sam. viii. 5) *they* wanted to become a nation, for they clamoured for a king like the other tribes. But they were not like the other tribes, for they had been chosen. It was not for them to work out the manner and method of their own destiny, but by obedience to God's will to fulfil the destiny already appointed for them. For this reason it is a mistake to regard the idea of the Jews as a *religious* community as the product of historical development. The idea of a natural development—Abraham, a family, a religious community—is not in accordance with the facts. They *were* a religious community. They did not grow into one, for they were an elect race, and truly God's people. Prof. D. J. Watts declares: 'Before Israel became a nation it was a people—the people of Jahweh. This fact is basic and determinative for the study of the Old Testament conception of the people of God.'[1]

This election of a people was not based upon their merit, prestige, power, or will, but solely upon God's mysterious grace. It is this fact which reveals the uniqueness of Israel's God as well as the uniqueness of Israel. It is this which distinguishes their God from all the gods of natural, cultural and philosophic religions. Professor Snaith has drawn attention to four important truths which emerge out of this election-love: that Jehovah existed before Israel; that if He once existed without them He could do so again; that if He chose them, He could also reject them; and that He was different from other gods in the demands He made upon His people.[2]

There is, therefore, a divine dimension about the calling of Israel which arises from the character of the God who called them. Their story is not to be understood as the inevitable emergence of a religious community which was brought about by some humanly contrived scheme, but as the apprehension of the truth that they were God's elect people. His presence was their portion, and their heritage was His gift. But a gift must be recognized and received, it cannot be merited and won.

Difficulties arose when the Hebrews began to look upon the heritage as something which could be won by their own efforts, by temple ritual, sacrificial rites, ordinances and the setting up of shrines. The importance of this deviation for later Hebrew history cannot be overstressed. It implied an entirely different kind of

[1] *Expository Times*, LXVII, No. 8, p. 233.
[2] See N. H. Snaith, *Distinctive Ideas of the Old Testament*, ch. IX.

religion. Ceasing to be regarded as a revelation of grace, religion came to be regarded as the observance of law. The unbalanced emphasis upon temple priesthood and sacrificial cultus quickly followed, and the result could only be that God's presence became conditioned and regulated by factors other than grace. This meant extraneous factors limited and controlled the approach of God to man, and religion, instead of being a revelation of grace, became the manifestation of ceaseless good works largely performed on behalf of the people by the sacrificing priests. Men sought by their own efforts to win their way into the presence of God when, in fact, His presence was offered freely to them all. This situation was due, almost entirely, to a misunderstanding of God's covenant-love.

Israel are the People of God by a divine Covenant

We must, therefore, examine the general meaning of the word 'covenant' so that we may understand the meaning of God's Covenant with Israel. Now when a covenant is made one thing is assigned to another as his personal possession. It always implies an offer which God makes to man. This offer is prompted by divine love. Covenant-love, by its very nature, implies a direct relationship. Yet God and man never meet on equal terms. God graciously offers to man a relationship with Himself, a relationship which man cannot alter, or change, or annul, for it rests solely on God's eternal grace. The terms of this relationship could not have been made by man and cannot be altered by him. As Dr Flew has written, the dominant meaning is: 'unilateral enactment: an arrangement for the people of God depending on God's initiative and issuing from His gracious will'.[1] This divine offer is not something elicited by man's need, it was the inevitable expression of divine love. As Barclay puts it: 'The very word *diatheke* has in it the inescapable truth that "all is of God".'[2]

That is the general meaning of 'covenant', and we must now consider God's Covenant with Israel in the light of it. Israel under the Old Covenant is an 'elect race', and a 'people of God's own possession', inasmuch as it has been selected out of all the peoples of the earth to be at once the recipient and the instrument of God's saving purpose. It is a people set apart and dedicated to God, and

[1] R. N. Flew, *Jesus and His Church*, p. 100.
[2] W. Barclay, *A New Testament Wordbook*, p. 32.

therefore a 'holy nation'; and because it has been set apart and dedicated for special service to God and man, it is a 'kingdom of priests'. That at any rate is what Israel was intended to be; that is the purpose of its election, and that is what God promised it should be when through Moses He established the Old Covenant (Exod. xix. 5–6).

In one sense, the keeping of the Covenant is a certainty for it is rooted in the unconditioned, disinterested love of God. Dr Snaith has drawn a distinction between *'ahabah'* and *'chesed'*. Both mean love, but *'ahabah'* is unconditioned love, not limited by the conditions of the Covenant but only by the will or nature of its Author. *'Chesed'*, on the other hand, is conditional upon there being a Covenant, for without the prior existence of a Covenant there could never be any *'chesed'* at all. The first implies election-love and the second covenant-love. The first is the cause of the Covenant, the second, the means of its continuance.[1]

If, on the divine side, the keeping of the Covenant was certain, why should there be a Covenant at all? It was necessary for Israel's sake. The spiritual relationship had to be established by a concrete, contractual agreement. It was all the more necessary if their unity as a nation was to be guaranteed. They belonged to Jehovah by election, consecration and mission. The Covenant was the irrevocable seal of this threefold privilege.

The Hebrews were so sure of this covenant-love that they thought it excused and exonerated them in times of disobedience. Moreover they sometimes forgot that for their own sakes there were conditions attaching to the Covenant. The conditions are the ten words given at Sinai. The immense significance of these moral and ethical precepts was not realized all at once. Later on, however, the prophets were unanimous in regarding the constitution of Israel as a moral constitution, and in their conception of it a very small place was given to ritual and ceremony. In other words, the people were expected to accept and obey the authentic words given at Sinai, and to acknowledge that disobedience unquestionably implied the forfeiture of their Covenant relationship. That the Covenant demanded not ritual and ceremony but obedience, is stressed in the following passage:

> Thus saith the Lord of Hosts: put your burnt offerings unto your sacrifices, and eat flesh. For I spake not unto your fathers, nor commanded them in the day that I brought them out of the land of Egypt,

[1] See N. H. Snaith, *Distinctive Ideas of the Old Testament*, pp. 94 ff.

concerning burnt offerings or sacrifices. But this thing commanded I them, saying, *Obey My voice*, and I will be your God, and ye shall be My people. (Jer. vii. 21-3).

Jeremiah's emphasis on the inwardness of the Covenant should not be isolated from his general teaching. He exposed the futility of external service and material symbols. The kind of reform which only served to engender national pride could not, in Jeremiah's view, be regarded as true reformation. His cry was: 'Circumcise your hearts,' which shows that he was much more interested in inner regeneration than in outward reform. He knew that it was sin that had to be dealt with, and that ceremony alone was quite ineffectual.

Jeremiah's teaching is all the more significant because spiritual religion had almost disappeared in Judaism and materialism had taken its place. This materialism which resulted in the glorification of the state led the prophet to emphasize another vital truth, namely, that the state may vanish but that Jehovah and the individual remain. Viewed against this background, Jeremiah's conception of the inward Covenant is an amazing achievement. He grasped more clearly than any of his contemporaries that a covenant, if it is to be adequate to the people's need, must possess a threefold significance: it must be spiritual, it must concern individuals, and it must answer the problem of sin. This was indeed an adequate Gospel, but it could only be made effective by a means which Jeremiah could see only from a distance. Dr Flew has shown that this teaching differed from the old idea of covenant in three respects: 'First there was inwardness: "I will put my law in their inward part"; second, individualism: "All shall know me"; third, forgiveness of sins: "their sins will I remember no more".'[1] No man in the pre-Christian era came nearer to the New Testament doctrine of justification than Jeremiah with his idea of religion as a spiritual, individual relationship with God based on forgiveness of sins. It needed something more or, more accurately, Someone else, to make it real, effective and abiding, but there is no doubt that the germ of true religion is here revealed.

All this, however, refers to the inestimable privilege bestowed upon Israel—their unique calling and the trust which God had placed in them. They were in this threefold sense the people of God,

[1] R. N. Flew, *Jesus and His Church*, p. 102.

THE BIBLICAL BASIS—OLD TESTAMENT

by a revelation of grace, by divine election and by Covenant-love. Alongside this notion there emerged in Israel another concept, equally important, which revealed to them the *purpose* of their election and the nature of its fulfilment. This concept is the 'Servant of the Lord' and to an examination of its meaning we must now turn.

THE SERVANT OF THE LORD

We may best consider this phrase by drawing attention to four aspects of its meaning: its corporate, sacrificial, 'royal' and universal significance.

The Servant idea has a corporate significance

The following passages set forth the character, sufferings and mission of the Servant of the Lord: Isa. xlii. 1-4; xlix. 1-7; l. 4-9; lii. 13-15; liii. 1-12. It is true that sometimes they have been given an individual and mythological as well as a collective meaning. When interpreted in the individual sense it has been said to refer to Deutero-Isaiah himself, to a member of the Davidic dynasty, possibly Zedekiah or Jehoiachin, and to the prophet Jeremiah.

When the phrase is given a mythological interpretation, Israel is regarded not as an actual nation but as it existed in the mind of God. The personified Israel idealized is still the Servant of God. More often than not, however, the Faithful Remnant is envisaged rather than the whole of Israel.

According to the collective interpretation, Israel's peculiar mission is held to be first to teach the whole world the knowledge of the true God (Isa. xiv) and then to bring the whole world under the rule of God (Isa. xlix). Israel is called not to a ministry which can be carried out by one outstanding individual, but to one in which the whole nation is involved. Israel as a nation is the instrument whereby God will accomplish His design. Israel's suffering is regarded as redemptive and implies also a missionary vocation. Even the ten apostate tribes must be won in order that they may share the messianic salvation. The Servant therefore incorporates in himself all the Israelite people. The same idea is expressed by Jeremiah who hears Rachel weeping for her children (Jer. xxxi. 15), but she is weeping not only for Joseph and Benjamin (her own children), but for all the northern exiles. All the children of Israel are incorporated in her as all the people are incorporated in the figure of the Servant.

It must be admitted that it is impossible to keep the thoughts expressed in these interpretations permanently apart; they overlap at several points. A People, for instance, may function through one or more of its members as representatives. Again, the ancestor, the prophet, the priest, the king, are sometimes regarded as corporate personalities. All the same, there are one or two broad conclusions which may reasonably be drawn from the ideas which underlie the Servant conception.

The sharp antithesis between the individual and collective interpretations is no longer tenable. Recent sociological studies have shown that the idea of corporate personality does not necessarily mean the absorption of individual personality. Moreover, a people may be regarded as an entity which embraces past, present, and future, and this is a conception which transcends those limitations which are attached to any individual personality. Further, modern psychology has shown that there is a racial consciousness as well as an individual one, and that some individuals are more powerfully aware of this racial consciousness than others. It is possible for one individual to be vividly conscious of the weaknesses as well as the potential triumphs of the whole race. Perhaps here is a pointer to the meaning of the Incarnation. At any rate the following verse should be viewed in the light of it: 'As in Adam all die, even so in Christ shall all be made alive' (1 Cor. xv. 22).

There are certain ruling thoughts which are invariably associated with the Servant figure. Four principal motifs may be suggested: Corporate personality; the role of the prophet; the idea of sacrifice; and the idea of the dying and rising god. The last three arise out of the master-motif of corporate personality. From this basic motif there arise the prophetic, priestly and kingly ideas respectively.

Another broad conclusion which may be drawn is this: the Servant idea forms a part of the whole pattern of Hebrew theology and should not be separated from it. The Servant's duty is bound up with his covenant responsibility.

> In Deutero-Isaiah the assurance of a new covenant reposes on two great conceptions—the universalistic conception of Jahweh as God, and that of the invincible power of the knowledge of the true God once implanted in the heart of mankind; . . . and this idea of the true knowledge or word of the true God implanted in Israel, incarnated in the seed of Abraham, and personified into a Being is the Servant of the Lord. . . . His (the Servant's) cause was that of Jahweh, and though

he stood *contra mundum*, he would surely prevail, 'I know that I shall not be put to shame' (Isa. 1. 4-9). So the Servant becomes a covenant of the people.[1]

Here is a notion which is too sublime and far-reaching to be contained in a single individual. The field was the world and not just a part of the world, and God's all-embracing purpose could be grasped and revealed to others only by a responding nation. It could not be fulfilled by one person but only through the response of the nation as a whole. Whatever might be said about the destiny of other nations, there is no doubt that as far as Israel was concerned she would only fulfil her true destiny and understand its meaning if she accepted the role of Servant. Once she accepted this role, the terrible and terrifying consequences of it became at least bearable. The truth is that Israel realized herself when she realized her Servanthood.

The Hebrew meaning for the word 'servant' is 'an honourable, voluntary and priestly service to God' (HDB IV, p. 468). In the voluntary acceptance of this role, and by her submission, sacrifice and service, Israel pointed unerringly to a way of salvation for the whole world. But this meant that politically and socially she had to be ready to accept whatever was in store for her. She must not measure herself by political or social ideals, nor by humanistic ideals of any kind; her true destiny carried with it a spiritual dimension.

It was essential, therefore, that her religion should not become externalized. Yet this is what happened. Their well-developed institutions became their stumbling-block. They were bedevilled rather than helped by the elaborate organization of their religion. When they were asked, why did God choose us? invariably they answered:

> Because we are Abraham's children; because we keep the covenant; because we keep the sabbath; because we are circumcised; because we make the proper sacrifices; because we keep the Law.... The salvation motif has disappeared, and nothing of God's saving work remains. The emphasis has come to be on what Israel was and what Israel did.[2]

They could not be God's peculiar Servant and at the same time fall into the perilous externalism of the surrounding tribes.

---

[1] Hastings, *Dictionary of the Bible*, I, p. 514, art. 'Covenant'.
[2] N. H. Snaith, *Hymns of the Temple*, p. 63.

It was essential also that her religion should not become fossilized. The servant-concept is not a static one, it is apocalyptic in character. It is the continuous uncovering of the divine purpose, and the more we see of it the more clearly is revealed the tragic element in it. At the same time, it is characterized by a perennial hope. For when the people became lethargic, indifferent, self-satisfied and self-centred, the prophets enjoined them to listen for the authentic word from the Lord, to look for the coming Messiah, and to remember the eternal inheritance which had been promised them. If the cultus stultified, the prophetic word inspired.

It was essential too that their religion should not become sacerdotalized. Yet as they became more and more enmeshed in a religion of works they tended to leave religious duties to the experts, and this was perilous. It meant that the corporate sense of vocation was jeopardized. If they were corporately the Servant of the Lord, there was no reason to leave their religious duties in the hands of a few, for each had a responsibility with the collective whole. Moreover, all the vicarious acts of the priests could not excuse the moral and spiritual obligation of the nation as a whole. Israel was God's Servant and the accompanying obligation was inescapable. A further insight was revealed to them: Israel was the Suffering Servant of the Lord.

The Servant idea has a sacrificial significance

A new note is sounded by Deutero-Isaiah; it is that there can be no redemption for Israel or for any other nation apart from humiliation and suffering. This new insight is in the sharpest contrast to the mighty imperialistic policies of Assyria, Egypt, Babylon and Persia. Israel is not called upon to ape them but to *lead* them, for Israel is not the pawn of the mighty nations but their pattern. Israel was not to be their rival but their saviour, and as there is no salvation without suffering, the path which lay before the Servant was clear. Israel learned this lesson as the custodian of truth for the whole world.

Suffering, therefore, is inevitably bound up with the Servant's mission. It is in this concept that the priestly and prophetic ideas of the Old Testament are combined. The prophetic word and the priestly task are one. Salvation in the Old Testament means fellowship with God, and inasmuch as the prophetic word enshrines the hope of salvation, and the priestly sufferings provide the way of salvation, the Servant is both word and priest, and therefore the promise and pledge of salvation for all nations. Although the Servant's sufferings are undeserved, he bears them on behalf of others, for 'the Lord hath laid on him the iniquity of us all' (Isa. liii. 6).

The Servant is, above all, the Servant of the divine will, and if his suffering can be viewed in the light of that will, even though it is against his inclination and desire, it will be tolerable because it is God's will. 'It pleased the Lord to bruise him'; knowing this the Servant faces and bears his appointed vocation of suffering, for in so doing he is the mediator of the supreme blessing. His suffering is effective in restoring others to fellowship with God: 'With his stripes we are healed.'

It must be noted, however, that although the divine plan is the paramount consideration, it is essential that it should be voluntarily accepted by the Servant. If the idea of compulsion is introduced, the Servant concept is destroyed. This is the relevance of Professor Butterfield's observation:

> For any reconciliation to be achieved, it requires to be assumed, at this point in Old Testament thought, that the nation has great spiritual resources and recognizes a Divine plan in history, recognizes also that it has a mission in that scheme, a mission which, though prescribed by God, must be accepted as self-assumed.[1]

This is true of the Servant Israel whose repentance and voluntary acceptance of suffering mediate restoration. Eventually it will be made clear that this suffering had the divine sanction and that it was effective in restoring the people to God, for, as the prophet says: 'They shall look unto me whom they have pierced' (Zech. xii. 10).

The certainty of the Servant's triumph through suffering is never forgotten, and his part in Jahweh's final victory is always brought to the fore by the prophets. He thus speaks to the Servant: 'I will preserve thee and give thee for a covenant of the people, to raise up the land, to make them inherit the desolate heritages' (Isa. xlix. 8). Yet this final restoration is effected not in any external way in the sense that Cyrus was called God's servant, but by the inner awakening of a new faith and a new spirit within the people. The condition of restoration is repentance and this comes with the consciousness of servanthood.

[1] H. Butterfield, *Christianity and History*, p. 86.

It is generally recognized that certain patterns of thought in the New Testament are prefigured in the Old Testament. Sometimes, however, this method is used to make light of Old Testament concepts, and frequently to contrast them with those of the New. When the concept of servanthood is considered, it is the similarity not the contrast which strikes us. As we have seen, Israel is designated the People of God by revelation, election and covenant-love, and in considering the Servant concept we have found that the corporate aspect persists, and that to it is added and exemplified the function of the Servant which is voluntary, sacrificial and vicarious. Now when these two ideas are combined we see that Israel is called and chosen to fulfil a corporate, priestly function, which not only prefigures the coming King, Priest and Servant, of the New Testament, but also the kingdom, priesthood and servanthood which He initiates. For it is plainly stated in the New Testament: 'And He made us to be a kingdom, to be priests unto His God and Father' (Rev. i. 6). Moreover, our Lord explicitly refers to his followers as servants: 'It is enough for the disciple that he be as his master, and the servant as his Lord' (Matt. x. 25). The very words which our Lord uses to describe His people were used to describe the People of God in the Old Testament. Wheeler Robinson draws attention to the priestly element in the Servant concept:

> If the Israel of the future is to share in the prophetic consciousness (Jer. xxxi. 31ff), so also she is to be named 'priests of Yahweh' (Isa. lxi. 6), 'a kingdom of priests' (Exod. xix. 6). There is a priestly element, as well as a prophetic, in the portrayal of the suffering Servant of Yahweh (Isa. liii. 4–6).[1]

Lindhagen emphasizes that the ultimate fulfilment of the Servant concept is nothing less than the Christian Church: 'The fulfilment of the Servant-prophecy in Christ, in which—for the first time—the equation Servant-Messiah takes place, has a collective aspect, the Church.'[2] Indeed it may justifiably be argued that Servant-Messiah, Priest-King, the sacrificial-eschatological, are ideas which only stand clearly revealed when the Servant of the Lord becomes the 'Servant-Lord'. The emphatic statement that the Servant idea

---
[1] H. W. Robinson, in *A Companion to the Bible*, ed. T. W. Manson, p. 324.
[2] *Expository Times*, LXVII, No. 9, p. 282.

THE BIBLICAL BASIS—OLD TESTAMENT 15

is determinative for an understanding of the priesthood of the whole Church is made by Torrance:

> The conception of the Suffering Servant is the great characteristic of the Church's ministry, and it is that which above all determines the nature of priesthood in the Church. That applies to the Church's threefold participation in Christ's prophetic, Priestly and Kingly Ministry, for the Church is engaged in all these as servant bearing the Cross like the man of Cyrene (Matt. xxvii. 32). It is indeed in terms of the suffering-servant-ministry that we are to see the basic unity in the Church's prophetic, priestly and kingly functions.[1]

The Servant idea has a royal significance

In this connection we must consider the Servant's anointing, and also in what sense he is Servant King.

The Servant's Anointing. In a passage that is closely associated with the Servant Songs we read: 'The Spirit of the Lord God is upon me; because the Lord hath anointed me . . .' (Isa. lxi. 1). Again, in one of the Servant Songs we find the words: 'I have put my spirit upon him' (Isa. xlii. 1). A similar word is spoken of the future Messiah: 'The Spirit of the Lord shall rest upon him' (Isa. xi. 2). Now anointing was usually reserved for kings and priests, and this anointing means three things: (*a*) that Israel is marked out as the Servant of the Lord; (*b*) that a divine gift is bestowed upon Israel in order that she may fulfil her mission; and (*c*) that Israel is of the seed-royal and of the holy seed of the priesthood. It is for this reason that the Servant may be called the Royal Priest. But the symbolism is deeper than that implied in the anointing with oil, for he is anointed with the Spirit of God. He is, in fact, the Servant of the Word.

> The only instrument which the Servant employs is the word of the Lord. This word is powerful, because it is not a mere dead letter; the Lord Himself is in it. . . . The Servant does not so much wield the word of God, he is rather an impersonation of it: 'He made my mouth a sharp sword. . . . He made me a polished shaft, and said unto me, Thou art my Servant' (xlix. 2). The Servant is the word of the Lord incarnate in the seed of Abraham.[2]

The immense significance of this anointing of the Spirit should not be overlooked. The Spirit is given not as a temporary enabling in time of emergency but as a permanent endowment, for the Spirit

---
[1] T. F. Torrance, *Royal Priesthood*, p. 87.
[2] A. B. Davidson, *The Theology of the Old Testament*, pp. 394-5.

rests upon him. It is true that the Spirit has previously endowed certain individuals, but in such cases it was in order to accomplish a limited task, sometimes sacred, sometimes secular. But this endowment was different: Israel's task was so great that the Spirit is given without measure—the Spirit rests upon the Servant and is not to be withdrawn from him. So Israel is not only the word of God incarnate in the seed of Abraham, but the proclamation of that word also. By the anointing of the Spirit, Israel is God's royal servant. It is interesting that our Lord is regarded as both King and Priest by the writer to the Hebrews, where He is spoken of as a Priest after the order of Melchizedek, King of Salem. Yet this fact in no way derogates from the word addressed to Christians in 1 John ii. 20: 'And ye have an anointing from the Holy One.' If the Old Israel have an anointing, so also have the members of the New Israel and by their anointing they are made kings and priests unto God.

Further, the study of the Servant Songs makes it difficult to avoid the conclusion that the Servant King is portrayed. In Isaiah xlix. 7 to the speechless servant an astonishing vision appears: a Servant-King before whom kings and priests stand up and then prostrate themselves. The Servant is the Chosen One of God, who fulfils his promise because He is the All-Faithful. Here is a glimpse of that mystery so long hidden away in the eternal counsels of God that to the Suffering-Servant-King victory was assured.

Perhaps it is going too far to suggest that the Servant and Messiah may be equated,[1] yet the fact that such a theory may be even contemplated lends strength to the idea that the Servant concept bears a royal significance. It is, however, possible to think in terms of the messiahship of the Servant without equating the two.

W. Manson's theory has much to commend it, namely, that the Servant motif is a phase of the Messianic idea.[2] The function of Israel is surely that of a Servant-King: He will bring forth judgment to the Gentiles (Isa. xlii. 1) his reign will extend to the ends of the earth: 'I will give you as a light to the nations that my salvation may reach to the end of the earth' (xlix. 6) RSV. His supremacy shall be recognized even by the kings of the earth: 'My Servant shall prosper, he shall be exalted and lifted up and shall be very high ... kings shall shut their mouths because of him' (lii. 13, 15). Yet the Servant-King will fulfil his task in a way they could not

---

[1] See Oesterley and Robinson, *Hebrew Religion*, pp. 306–7.
[2] See W. Manson, *Jesus the Messiah*, p. 174.

have expected. He accepts meekly and without rebellion the responsibility that is placed upon him and there is grace and tenderness in his words: 'The Lord Jehovah hath given me the tongue of disciples, that I may know how to comfort with words him that is weary. He opened mine ear and I was not rebellious' (l. 4-5). All this presents a picture of Israel whose character and function can best be described as Servant-King.

The Servant idea has a universal significance

The Servant is divinely commissioned to restore all nations to Jehovah. The notion slowly dawned that other nations were related to God no less than Israel. Nearly two hundred years earlier Amos had emphasized the same truth:[1] 'Have not I brought up Israel out of the land of Egypt and the Philistines from Caphtor?' (Amos ix. 7). And Isaiah, facing a more powerful Assyria than Amos ever knew, contemptuously dismisses the great empire as but the rod of Jahweh's anger, and sees the prescribed limit to its power (Isa. x. 5). So Jeremiah hears Jahweh speaking of 'Nebuchadnezzar, my servant' (xxv. 9), and Deutero-Isaiah calls Cyrus who does not know the hand that girds him, 'the anointed of Jahweh' (xlv. 1). The idea that Jahweh was ruling and controlling all nations was widely accepted. It is, however, the peculiar glory of the Servant concept, that through it Israel was seen to be reconciled to the role of submissive obedience whereby the nations of the world should realize that Jahweh ruled. The Servant now accepted not only the mission but the cost which it involved. In short, Israel's priestly service is to create the conditions in which the idea of universal priesthood may be realized. There is no suggestion in these passages that God was doing all this for the sake of Israel alone. On the contrary, Israel's privilege consisted in the fact that she had been chosen in order that through her all nations might be brought into a knowledge of God. So the Servant's priestly mission was no less than a universal vocation. We may now reasonably affirm that the dominant idea of the Servant concept—its corporate, sacrificial, royal and universal significance—provides a strong basis for the idea of the Servant-Priest of the New Testament, and the royal priesthood which arises from it.[2]

[1] The Servant Songs of Deutero-Isaiah belong to the sixth century.
[2] For a full account of the Servant idea see C. R. North, *The Suffering Servant*, chaps. IV and V; and a more recent study: *Jesus and the Servant*, Morna D. Hooker.

A KINGDOM OF PRIESTS

Original priesthood

There was a time at the beginning of Hebrew history when no priestly class existed. In those early days the head of the Hebrew household was the equivalent of a priest. Although he had certain priestly duties, he was in no sense an official priest. It is important to notice that soon after the setting aside of individuals to serve as priests in an official capacity, there was strong resistance from some of the people. If Korah's rebellion is now seen to be defective, it is only so in its method rather than in the principle it sought to affirm. The principle was right: 'All the congregation are holy, every one of them, and the Lord is among them' (Num. xvi. 3); it was the subsequent attack upon the persons of Moses and Aaron that was wrong. Three truths stand out clearly in early Jewish teaching on this subject:

(*a*) The priestly prerogative of the whole community.

Korah referred to the status of the whole community and the prestige they enjoyed. How often had Moses stressed this very point! His constant endeavour had been to raise the whole community to the level of holiness and to stimulate their consciousness of the constant presence of the Divine in their midst. Moses set himself the task of creating a holy congregation. He never said that only a few selected individuals were to be deemed worthy of this status and that the rest were to be mere onlookers. 'Would God that all the Lord's people were prophets' (Num. xi. 29) he had once exclaimed, and this was truly indicative of his desire and mission.

(*b*) The priestly duties of the whole community.

At that stage the Hebrews did not encourage the creation of a hierarchical class or sect such as a priesthood, which should be endowed with greater privileges than the so-called layman. There were no 'holy orders', nor were some men vested with powers distinguishing them from their fellow-Jews. In ancient Israel even the offering of sacrifices was not the exclusive prerogative of a priesthood. A man not a member of the priestly caste could perform sacrificial rites— as the patriarchs had done (Gen. xxii. 12; xxvi. 25), and as Gideon and Manoah did (Judges vi. 26; xiii. 19)—although he might prefer to avail himself of the services of a priest if there were one at hand (Judges xvii. 7).

Three demands were made of Jews in general: that all should be learned in the Law, that all should minister in the sanctuary of the spirit, and that all should devote their minds and hearts to the doctrines of the Jewish Faith.

(c) We must also note the individual responsibility of each member for the spiritual welfare of the whole community. The uniqueness of Judaism is seen at its best when it is reduced to the lowest common denominator. Upon each man devolves the responsibility of conducting his domestic affairs in an atmsophere of priestly sanctity. The father is the teacher of the child and the mother is the guardian of the sanctuary. The family unit is the dominant factor in Judaism, and not the pomp and ceremony which surround public display. Thus each Jew becomes a teacher, priest and minister in his own domestic sanctuary, and by this means he is also a witness to those outside it. It is his duty to equip himself for that sacred office. Surely if each member of the House of Israel became aware of his unique privilege, then everyone of them would be holy and the Lord would be in the midst of them. It is along such lines that the original idea of priesthood in Israel is to be understood. It includes holiness of character, knowledge of the Law, and the duty of witnessing to the Faith by example and teaching. It is interesting and not a little surprising that this interpretation of priesthood has so prominent a place in modern Jewish teaching. The absence of any sacerdotal tendency is significant, and the knowledge of the Law and the teaching of the Faith have remained essential characteristics of Judaism.

The Teaching Priesthood

Even when individuals were set apart, teaching was their most important function. Moses himself was the first priest and his successors derived their authority from him. It is true that the first thing he did was to consecrate as priest his brother Aaron, but Moses himself remained the mouthpiece of God, the interpreter of the will of God, and the undoubted spiritual leader of the community. It may help to assess the place of the priest in Hebrew religion if we state the duties which were allotted to him.

The priest as guardian of the temple[1]

He was the guardian of the sacred vessels and the supervisor of the worship of the altar. 'And ye shall keep charge of the sanctuary, and the charge of the altar: that there be wrath no more upon the children of Israel' (Num. xviii. 5). These duties are further extended in Deuteronomy x. 8 where the priest is described as bearing the ark of covenant of Jehovah, standing before Jehovah to minister to Him, and blessing the people in His name.

It soon became clear, however, that they possessed special privileges as representatives of the people. As the Chronicler puts it: 'It appertaineth not unto thee, Uzziah, to burn incense unto the Lord, but to the priests the sons of Aaron, that are consecrated to burn incense' (2 Chron. xxvi. 18). Moreover, the priestly blessing is that with which the sons of Aaron are commanded to bless the people: 'Speak unto Aaron and unto his sons, saying, On this wise ye shall bless the children of Israel; ye shall say unto them, the Lord bless thee and keep thee . . . . So shall they put my name upon the children of Israel and I will bless them' (Num. vi. 23-7). There are, then, these four facts that we know about the priests: first, they are appointed from the house of Aaron; second, they are associated with a shrine; third, they are to ensure that God was approached in a proper manner; and fourth, they are representatives in a twofold capacity, representing God before the people and the people before God.

The priest as interpreter of God to the people

The priest is the mouthpiece of God. God speaks. This is fundamental to an understanding of Hebrew religion. God speaks to those who listen and to those who enquire of Him. 'He spake by the prophets' but this was later. His first messenger was the priest. Before the prophet became such a powerful force in Israel, he was distinguished from the priest in two ways: the priest was attached to a local shrine, whereas the prophet was an itinerant; moreover, the priest usually received his message through an oracle, whereas the prophet received his message through an ecstatic vision. These differences are of more than casual importance; they indicate two firm principles of Hebrew religion. God was not to be identified

---

[1] See N. H. Snaith. 'The Priesthood and the Temple' in *A Companion to the Bible*, ed. T. W. Manson, pp. 418 ff; H. W. Robinson, *Inspiration and Revelation in the Old Testament*, pp. 200 ff.

with any local shrine, and He is One who speaks to whom He will. The neglect of these two principles ultimately led the Hebrews to religious practices which their doctrine did not warrant. They were prone to forget that Jehovah was a 'God who spake at sundry times and in divers manners in times past unto the fathers', and their later attempts to regulate His dealings with men and to canalize His revelation into particular channels had disastrous results. The fact is that the real function of the priests and prophets was to repeat what God had said. It was their duty to convince the nation that God had spoken. The close association between the prophetic and priestly functions may be gathered from the following two passages: When Moses pleaded inadequacy, 'The Lord said unto Moses, See I have made thee a god to Pharaoh, and Aaron shall be thy prophet' (Exod. vii. 1). Again, we read that God said to Moses: 'I will teach you . . . and he shall be to thee a mouth, and thou shalt be to him as God' (Exod. iv. 15-16). So Aaron was to act as priest to Moses in that he was to speak the words which Moses put into his mouth. At that time, this was the primary duty of the priest.

The teacher of the ways of God

The mouthpiece of God must teach the ways of God. Indeed, for their knowledge of God's ways the people were dependent upon the priest. This knowledge made them His people. They were not a people when they were ignorant of God's ways. Hence the eternal pathos in the Lord's cry: 'Israel doth not know, my people doth not consider' (Isa. i. 3). In so far as the priest did not fulfil his function, the nation was, to that extent, in danger of disintegration and destruction. Micah emphasizes this particular function of the priests when he says: 'The heads (of Jerusalem) judge, the priests *teach*, and the prophets divine' (Mic. iii. 11).

The discerner of the will of God

The Hebrews had no doubt that God spoke, but they were not always able to interpret His will even when His words were made known to them. When they were in doubt they appealed to the priest, whose duty it was by the method of Urim and Thummim to divine God's will. The furniture of the sacred lot was in the care of the priest and only he was permitted to use it. In this threefold sense, therefore, the priest was the servant of God: he was the servant of the Word of God, the Law of God, and the Will of God.

The sacrificing priesthood

The transition from the didactic function of the priest to the sacerdotal function was a gradual one. As long as his functions were didactic, the means of communication was the spoken word, but when his office became more and more sacerdotal, the means of communication became a visible offering. It was his duty to dedicate the gift and to see that the offering was made according to the prescribed ceremonial. Eventually, however, greater attention was given to the precise fulfilment of the regulations than to the purpose of the offering.

(*a*) What were the reasons for this transition from the teaching ministry to the sacerdotal ministry? In the early days of nomadic life the priest's duty was to teach. This is easy to understand because the religion of the wilderness was simple in character and expression, and did not require expert priestly assistance. In Canaan, worship became much more elaborate and mysterious, and the priesthood became a necessary institution. This settled existence meant that there were permanent temples and not merely temporary shrines to be looked after. Moreover, the priests were heavily occupied in rebutting the claims of rival gods like Chemosh and Baal. There is no doubt that the priesthood became more and more sacerdotal as it incorporated into Hebrew religion the offerings which were common in a land of numerous agricultural deities.

(*b*) The change from a nomadic to a settled existence was not the only reason, however, for the rise of sacerdotalism. The rise of the written tradition meant that much of the priest's work was taken over by the Levites and Scribes. As long as tradition was mainly oral, the word and teaching of the priest were final, but with the rise of the written tradition, interpretation was undertaken by others. It follows that the office of the priest became less and less didactic and more and more sacerdotal.

(*c*) Further, the perfect holiness of God led the people to approach Him by certain stages, and immediate but occasional access to the Holy of Holies was only possible to the High Priest. The sons of Aaron were permitted to minister directly before God, but only if they observed the most rigid rules of purification. As for the layman, although he was conscious of the transcendent holiness of God, the increasingly complex ritual made it even more difficult for him to approach God. Consequently, the offering of sacrifice became a virtual monopoly of the priesthood. The layman could not approach God without the mediation of a priest.

Between the transcendent holiness of God and a keen awareness of their own sin-stained condition, stood the priest as the people's representative before God. But even the work of the priest is limited. He has to face the endless tedium of repeatedly offering sacrifices which bring only a partial expiation, and it is emphatically the greatest single weakness of Hebrew religion that it made payments of a debt which was never entirely wiped out. Yet this very fact established the strong position of the Aaronic priesthood in Judaism. As long as the people were aware of their sin the sacrifices were essential, and as long as the sacrifices were ineffectual to do what had to be done, the necessity for the official priest remained. This meant one thing: the functions of the priest had undergone a complete change. Instead of being the interpreter of the Word and the Law and the Will of God, he became the indispensable intermediary between men and God, and Judaism became a theocracy ruled by a hierarchy.

It should be noted, however, that there were several other factors which enormously increased the power of the temple priesthood. By the time of the Judges the priesthood had settled down into families and heredity became the deciding factor. For example: Eli at Shiloh and Zadok at Jerusalem. Again, the temple priesthood was considerably strengthened by the centralization of worship at Jerusalem. A further sacerdotalizing of Jewish religion took place after the exile when there was no king, and the priests assumed much greater power. From this time religion finds expression in the idea of a theocracy administered by a priestly hierarchy. All the same, 'a recollection of the earlier liberty with regard to the exercise of priestly functions always remained',[1] and it is true to say that the ideal priesthood was never eliminated from Hebrew thought.

The Idealized Priesthood

In order to understand the meaning of the ideal priesthood which recurs in Hebrew thought, we must examine more closely the phrase: 'a kingdom of priests'. The idea that the People of God should be a kingdom of priests was not a convenient human arrangement nor

[1] Harford and Stevenson, *Prayer Book Dictionary*, p. 563.

was it the product of the minds of men, it was God's will. The statement is crystal clear: 'Ye shall be unto me a kingdom of priests' (Exod. xix. 6). But this is only possible if the terms of the Covenant are observed. Now God's Covenant with Israel was a royal Covenant, and through it the People of God were to find their true destiny as the royal priesthood to all the nations of the world.

The very fact that they were included in the Royal Covenant meant that they were God's possession. No reason or explanation is given why Israel in particular should be chosen; it was a holy mystery but it was also an inescapable fact. To be 'God's possession' meant something that was withdrawn from the general property as a special donation. In other words: Israel is a given people, a people already offered. This means that their priesthood as a people must not be thought of as metaphorical or symbolic, but as an experience through which they must pass. Israel is called to be God's instrument, and this involves something more than the conferring of title upon Israel, it means a priestly experience. Israel is set apart and dedicated for special service to man as well as to God. She has a special service to God in that she is chosen as the instrument of His purpose, and a special service to man in that she is also the realization of this purpose and a guide to all nations.

Moreover, they are to be a *kingdom* of priests and this means that they are at the immediate disposal of the king, appointed by the king in a secular environment. The obvious inference is that all the people of Israel stand in an identical and immediate relationship to God as His pledged servants, and it is an intrinsic part of their service to bring all nations to an awareness of their spiritual destiny. Once they lost sight of this universal aspect of their calling, they forfeited the privileges they had received. But this involved a long, hard struggle, and it must be admitted that Israel learned some vital lessons on the journey. All the same, there were questions to which Israel did not know the answers. For if they were to be instrumental in turning the thought of the kingdom of priests into fact, and thereby bringing all nations into a true relationship with God, it was essential that they should be sure of the ground of their own relationship. But it was at this crucial point that they were themselves uncertain. Micah's question haunted them all: 'Wherewith shall I come before the Lord?' (Mic. vi. 6). Were they to come with the traditional sacrifices of the cultus or was there another and a better way? To be sure, illumination was given them. 'Sacrifice and offering thou hast no delight in' (Ps. xl. 6). In such ways it was made clear to them that God required justice, mercy, obedience, faithfulness, thanksgiving and penitence (Mic. vi. 6-8; 1 Sam. xv. 22; Ps. xl. 6-8; l. 14; li. 17). The realization that God required spiritual sacrifices was a long step forward, but there still persisted in the minds of the people as a whole the idea that invisible, spiritual sacrifices were not quite sufficient and that they needed to be supplemented by material ones. And just because traditional sacrifices were unacceptable to God, and because their faith was by no means strong enough to rely entirely on spiritual sacrifices, they left unanswered the question, 'Wherewith?' Questions, however, which could not be answered under the Old Covenant could perhaps be answered under the New. The New Testament answer to the question 'Wherewith?' is that man comes before the Lord through Jesus Christ.

There is, of course, a difference between the priesthood of promise and the priesthood of realization, and this is brought out clearly in the tenses of the verbs in the following passages: We note the future tense in the Old Testament: 'And ye shall be unto me a kingdom of priests' (Exod. xix. 6) 'But ye shall be named the priests of the Lord' (Isa. lxi. 6); and the Psalmist says: 'Her priests also will I clothe with salvation' (Ps. cxxxii. 16), for in the ideal kingdom of priests the mark of priesthood is salvation. The use of the future tense with reference to the kingdom of priests in the Old Testament clearly indicates Israel's promised destiny. But significantly the tenses in the New Testament are different, and this is because something has taken place which has turned the promise into realization. In Revelation i. 6 we read: 'And He made us to be a kingdom, to be priests unto God.' The use of the aorist tense indicates that an event has taken place once for all whose consequences are unlimited. We must notice also that in 1 Peter ii. 9 it is not the future tense that is used: 'Ye shall be . . .' but the present: 'Ye are . . . a royal priesthood.' It is on the ground of the New Covenant that the idealized priesthood of the Old Testament is transformed into the realized universal priesthood of the New. The concepts of the People of God, the Servant of the Lord, and the kingdom of the priests, are not superseded or displaced but are fulfilled in the People of the New Covenant, the Servant-Priest, and the Royal Priesthood.

CHAPTER TWO

THE BIBLICAL BASIS

New Testament

THE PEOPLE OF THE NEW COVENANT

(a) *The New Revelation*

WE have already seen that God made Himself known to His people in His creative acts, in the prophetic word, and in His election and Covenant Love. By such means facets of His nature and phases of His purpose were revealed. But the full and final revelation of God Himself is only to be found in the Incarnate Word. The Incarnate Word reveals the Redeemer. It is true that the Hebrews had seen glimpses of redemptive and restorative love by their deliverance from Egypt and Babylon, but only the Redeemer brings redemption from sin. It is passing strange that those who had already received a foretaste of redeeming grace should remain apparently indifferent when the Redeemer Himself appeared. The author of the Apocalypse pointed out that their true heritage could be claimed and their true priesthood realized only through the redemption which Christ had wrought: 'Unto Him that loved us and loosed us from our sins, and made us to be a kingdom, to be priests unto his God and Father, to Him be glory . . .' (Rev. i. 6). It is true that they had already known themselves to be an elect and redeemed people, but the nature of their redemption was changed by the Incarnation of the Redeemer.

Their failure to recognize their Redeemer was linked up with their failure to understand the purpose of their election. St Peter's words must have had a familiar ring in Jewish ears, for what was new to Christians was only a reminder for the Jews: 'But ye are an elect race, a royal priesthood, a holy nation, a people for God's own possession, that ye may show forth the excellencies of Him who called you out of darkness into His marvellous light' (1 Pet. ii. 9). Israel's signal failure, then, was a failure to realize that their election was an election to service. They failed to realize this because they did not perceive that the coming of Christ involved a radical change in their conception of redemption. They did not learn to sing: 'Hail to the Lord's anointed, Great David's greater Son.' All this meant that they were unable to fulfil their priestly service to the world.

There was another reason for this extraordinary lapse: they did not realize that the Lord's coming was a *new* revelation. So much stress had been placed upon the means of God's revelation—the Law, the Covenant and the Cultus—that when the final revelation appeared in Jesus Christ, it was unrecognized: 'they that were His own received him not' (John i. 11). By that time the Jewish religion was regarded as a self-sufficient and self-contained entity, and instead of realizing that they were the instrument whereby God's final revelation in Christ should be introduced to the world, they thought that the revelation had ended with them. They made the mistake of thinking that they *were* the revelation, and consequently their minds were closed to the new and final revelation of God in Jesus Christ. Temple worship, Rabbinism, and the Cultus had acquired such a sufficiency as left no room for anything else. The fact that 'the veil of the temple was rent in the midst', was significant, it seemed, for everyone except those whom it most intimately concerned. Their own importance had blinded them to the all-important fact. In this way Israel's mission was jeopardized and brought about a further misunderstanding of priesthood. Unfortunately this led the Jews to regard Jesus of Nazareth as the stumbling-block of their faith instead of the fulfilment of their hope. Failure to understand the meaning of our Lord's Sonship deprived them of the benefits of His Priesthood.

A clue to the understanding of His Sonship is to be found in Psalm ii. 7. The king, who is speaking on the day of his anointing, says: 'The Lord said unto me, Thou art my son, this day have I begotten thee.' In the New Testament the words are applied to the Lord Jesus, who is the true Son of God, by His Resurrection from the dead (Rom. i. 4); by His superiority over angels (Heb. i. 5); and by His appointment by God Himself as Priest (Heb. v. 5). The Son became Priest not because He put Himself into that office, but because the Father had chosen Him. The Son is Priest not simply because He faces death but because He overcomes it. He is enthroned far above men and angels because His work, as well as his office, transcend theirs. Here is no self-appointed Saviour, no temporary manifestation, no angelic visitor, but the Son of God. When the writer to the Hebrews combines the Sonship of Christ with His Priesthood in Hebrews v. 5–6, he is teaching us that in Christ divine Sonship and eternal Priesthood are one.

There is another way in which the Incarnation reveals the Priesthood as well as the Sonship of our Lord. As long as men thought of God as a dark mystery, it was necessary to find means of drawing near to Him so that the mystery might be solved. This was the primary concern of the Hebrew sacrificing priests. And it was all very well for a time; but God did not remain a dark mystery, and it is precisely in Christ that God has revealed Himself to man. But it was not only the mystery of the divine nature that was made clear in Jesus but the mystery of the divine purpose too. God revealed Himself to man as man, and this was necessary because it was man who had gone astray and needed to be saved. An angel or some other heavenly visitor might have impressed the world without saving it, but the Son's work was to save. God is revealed only once, but this is enough because of the completeness of the revelation. 'The only-begotten Son which is in the bosom of the Father, He hath declared Him' (John i. 18). Jesus is the Word of God from the other side. That is why He is called 'the Apostle ... of our confession' (Heb. iii. 1); sent from God He not only knows the way to God but He is the Way. Yet He is not only the revealed Word of God, He is also the responsive word of man. God will not approach man except through Him, and man cannot approach God except through Him, so that at one and the same time He is 'the Apostle *and High Priest* of our confession'. In His Priesthood we see the bringing together of His Sonship and Kingship, and this is clearly brought out in Torrance's impressive words:

> On the ground of His Sonship and His incarnational qualification He ascends into the Holies. Here we pass beyond the conception of Aaronic priesthood to priesthood of another order. He is Priest in final reality, fulfilling the Mosaic priesthood because His Word is identical with Kingly act; fulfilling the Aaronic priesthood because His offering is identical with His Person. This is Royal Priesthood, in the coincidence of grace and Omnipotence, in the identity of Person and Work. As such it is as unique as God Himself.[1]

[1] T. F. Torrance, *Royal Priesthood*, p. 14.

THE BIBLICAL BASIS—NEW TESTAMENT 29

Because Jesus is in Himself the revealed Word and the redemptive Act, the whole meaning of priesthood is changed. The Incarnation means the end of all other priestly mediations. The prophetic words about God are fulfilled in the Word of God; the sacrifices of the old Order are superseded by the Sacrifice of Christ; the old priesthood is surpassed and the new priesthood inaugurated by the New Covenant; and the Son of God has opened up a new and living way for all men. Hence, He that is holy addresses the Church: 'I have set before thee a door opened, which none can shut' (Rev. iii. 8). The way to God—and therefore to forgiveness, peace and heaven—is now for ever open, for the Priesthood of the Son has accomplished the one thing needful. The laws of the levitical priesthood were valid until Christ came; they are no longer valid because there is no further work for them to do. Their purpose was to wait for and point towards Christ. Now that Christ has come, the priesthood has changed accordingly. Christ Himself has become the Sacrifice and Mediator between God and man so there is no room for any other sacrificing priesthood. Instead of a body of priests pointing to the future, we see in the New Covenant Christ Himself who has fulfilled all expectations and brought to perfection all God's promises. And so the priesthood of the New Testament is ruled by a single Priest, Jesus Christ, the Son of God.

Moreover, the Incarnation expresses the universality of the Son's Priesthood. The sheer grandeur of this conception should not be missed. There is, of course, a world-embracing vision in the Old Testament, but its fulfilment is only to be found in Christ. His Priesthood gives Him preeminence in the sphere of nature, in the world of men, and in His Church. For it must be remembered that the Priest's redeeming work is not only for believers, not even for humanity in general, but for the entire creation. He is the 'first-born of all creation', but this does not mean that He is part of creation but that He is the first-born of the Eternal. He is also 'first-born from among the dead' (Col. i. 18), for the distinction of *this* Priest is that He has passed through death. When He speaks of sacrifice He is speaking of Himself. But creation and redemption are brought together in His Incarnation, for He is also 'the first-born among many brethren' (Rom. viii. 29). 'As the final cause of all things is the glory of God, so the final cause of the Incarnation and of the effect of the Incarnation upon man is that the Son may be surrounded by a multitude of the redeemed.'[1] If the whole universe is to be restored to God, it can only be done if the Mediator of salvation is the first-born from the Eternal, the first-born from among the dead, and the first-born of many brethren. Both our creation and our redemption are possible only through our Incarnate Lord. Just because He is Eldest-born, the rest of the redeemed family share the inheritance of the saints in light. The benefits and privileges which He wins are shared by all. By being joined to Him, all realize the destiny for which they were created. Christians possess all things 'in Him'. For He is Priest by coming from God to man, by being Himself Priest and Mediator, by restoring all things to God, and we all share His Priesthood because we share the benefits of it. In and through Him and on the ground of His Priesthood, we also are priests unto God. Watson has put this succinctly in the following passage:

> The Christian belief in God as Creator and Restorer of life is bound up with a further and still more decisive historical event, namely, the life, death and resurrection of Jesus Christ. Through Him, Christians know themselves to have been brought into a new covenant-relation to God, whereby they have been given new life and hope; and in this they see a work of boundless divine love and grace, which they cannot but confess to be sovereign over all existence and over death itself.[2]

(b) *The New Covenant*

Redemption and restoration are solely dependent upon the New Covenant inaugurated by Christ on the night that He gathered His disciples together and said: 'This is My blood of the New Covenant, which is shed for many.' This act and these words of Jesus do not only indicate the fulfilment of the prophetic word of Jeremiah, they are an assurance given to the world that God's Covenant was to be ratified and sealed by the blood of the Son of God. A mediator of the Covenant had appeared, the last and final High Priest had come, and with His act, a new and redeemed community had emerged. Now all this involves an inevitable change in the idea of priesthood. This becomes increasingly clear when we remember that the New Covenant places men in an inescapable responsibility to God. The New Covenant pre-supposes an existential relationship and this is the case

---

[1] Sanday and Headlam, I.C.C., Romans, p. 218.
[2] P. S. Watson, *The Concept of Grace*, p. 66.

THE BIBLICAL BASIS—NEW TESTAMENT

even though men do not appreciate either its privileges or its demands. Strictly speaking, men do not make a covenant with God because they have no power to do so. Certainly *diathéké* (and this is the word used in the New Testament) cannot be made between persons of equal status. Apart from the fact that man cannot initiate *this* Covenant, he can neither appreciate its meaning nor appropriate its blessings without the Mediator. He can receive its blessing but only through faith in Christ. It must be emphasized that the Covenant places man in the position of a suppliant and a recipient. 'Philo says: "A covenant is a symbol of grace which God sets between Himself who extends the boon and man who receives it. It is fitting for God to give and for a wise man to receive." '[1]

At the same time, when a covenant is made, everything is assigned to another as his possession. In Christ, and not in any other way, God assigns everything to His people. Hence the relevance of Paul's words: 'For all things are yours; ... and ye are Christ's; and Christ is God's' (1 Cor. iii. 21, 23). It is precisely because Christ is God's Son, and accepts all that this involves, that we receive all things at His hands. 'He that spared not His own Son, but delivered Him up for us all, how shall He not also *with Him* freely give us all things?' (Rom. viii. 32). This Covenant cannot be made except at tragic cost, and the circumstances in which our Lord spoke His memorable word make it the key to the understanding of His mission. 'This cup is the New Covenant *in my blood*, even that which is poured out for you' (Luke xxii. 20). This New Covenant brings forgiveness of sins (Rom. xi. 27 citing Isa. xxvii. 9). So that what the Old Covenant and its ordinances could not do, is now accomplished 'in His blood'. In the strictest sense Christ *is* the New Covenant. Jesus came in the fullness of time, stood before God with a single sacrifice, offered up Himself, and suffered death upon the Cross. From that moment true priesthood was founded upon the blood of the Son of God. As Sacrifice, Priest and Mediator, our Lord becomes the centre of a new conception of priesthood. It is for this reason that priesthood based on sacrifice must remain for ever the pattern of Christian life and service.[2]

---

[1] Quoted by W. Barclay, *A New Testament Wordbook*, p. 31.
[2] For further discussion on the 'New Covenant' see V. Taylor, *Atonement in New Testament Teaching*, pp. 173–83, and R. N. Flew, *Jesus and His Church*, pp. 99–106.

The significance of our Lord's Sacrifice is that it is representative, perfect and universal. Each of these words is important for an understanding of the universal priesthood. It is representative because He takes upon Himself the burden of the sins of others and embodies in Himself the chequered history of the whole race; it is perfect because His death and resurrection banish guilt which alone bars the way to God; it is universal because all who accept its benefits in faith become partakers of the new priesthood, although this priesthood only recognizes one Priest—Christ Himself.

(c) *The Birth of a New Community*

The New Testament writers did not hesitate to use phrases which were applied to the People of God in the Old. The Church is the 'Israel of God' (Gal. vi. 16); a 'people for God's own possession' (1 Pet. ii. 9); whose members are 'kings and priests unto God' (Rev. i. 6); it is Ezekiel's New Israel risen from the dead (Eph. ii. 4–10); the liberated people of the Second Isaiah (Rom. iii. 24); and Daniel's People of the Saints of the Most High (1 Cor. i. 2).

The least that can be said of these passages is that Christian believers were sure that they were God's people. They were His people not only as individuals but as a community. Yet these were bold claims in the light of the beliefs of the Old Israel. Yet they were God's people in a new way. They were not His people on the grounds of nationality or lineage or by the works of the Law but on the grounds of Christ's death. They had received the title-deeds of His Sacrifice, and for this reason they believed they were His people directly and not indirectly. They had one Representative before God—their Saviour. Now this was an entirely new relationship; it was a direct relationship with Christ based on His merits. When they spoke of it in its corporate sense they used phrases like 'the Body of Christ' (1 Cor. xii. 27); the 'Household of God' (Eph. ii. 19); 'an holy temple in the Lord' (Eph. ii. 21); 'an habitation of God through the Spirit' (Eph. ii. 22). As the Body of which Christ was the Head, the Church naturally shared in the priestly character of Christ. As members of the universal priesthood of the Church they were justified in claiming to be a new community. It is this idea which distinguishes the People of God in the new dispensation from the People of God in the old.

The universal significance of the People of God is only fully appreciated in the Great High Priest. Christ as our Representative embodies the whole race, and in this sense all people are His people. As W. R. Matthews has written:

> Both in the New Testament and in traditional theology the Person and Work of Christ are represented as having racial significance. Not only, we are told, is He representative Man; in some way He sums up all things, in the phrase of Irenaeus, He 'recapitulates' humanity. We remember too St Paul's contrast between the natural and the redeemed man, 'as in Adam all die, even so in Christ shall all be made alive'.[1]

Perhaps when Jesus uses the term 'Son of Man' He is recapitulating the history of the People of God. For our present purpose the phrase has a twofold significance: firstly, since it originates from and means 'the people of the saints of the Most High', it implies the solidarity of the Church in and with Christ and indicates His representative action on our behalf. Secondly, there is always a pervasive reference to the vocation of suffering which this recapitulation involves. It is always 'The Son of Man who *must* suffer, die, and rise again'.

Now the writer to the Hebrews discovered that the only way in which these two ideas of the solidarity of the People of God, and their inherent vocation of suffering, could be adequately expressed, was by using the figure of the Great High Priest, for He alone includes in Himself God's People and suffers in Himself for them. Also St Paul's great phrase 'in Christ' is to be understood not simply in the mystical sense but also in the eschatological, for Christ is the culmination as well as the Author of man's faith; and the final victory over evil, for which all creation groans, is to be seen as the final and vivid projection of the dread act of Calvary. In that act the High Priest is for ever identified with the need of man, and man in faith is identified with Christ's Death. It is only in the light of such teaching that the visionary's conception of Jesus in the Apocalypse as Alpha and Omega is intelligible. It is in the central act of the Church's worship—the Lord's Supper—that Christians are reminded of their present redemption and of the final consummation. Indeed to the eye of faith the two ideas are telescoped, and Christ's death and final victory are the same. In this way every member of the royal priesthood knows that if he is really to take his part in the priestly service of the whole Church, he must keep the Sacred Feast

[1] W. R. Matthews, *The Problem of Christ in the Twentieth Century*, p. 49.

and thereby make the full and glad response to the Self-Offering of his Lord. This *is* his priesthood—the anticipation of the great Messianic Feast beyond the grave in which the perfected Royal Priesthood will share. But the New Covenant which brings believers together in the Eucharist also inaugurates for them both here and hereafter the kingdom in which Christ alone shall rule.

(d) *The New Community in an Eschatological Setting*[1]

The New Israel emerges in the New Testament as the direct result of our Lord's resurrection. Indeed the idea of the birth of a new community is unthinkable apart from the victory of Christ. His sufferings and death are particular aspects of His kingship. Even when He stood before His judges He spoke of His kingdom. He was destined to rule. It is important that we should see His victory in its proper light. Mankind was in the grip of sin, Law and Death. As man, Jesus was subject to these powers, but His divinity enabled Him to renounce them, and His death on the Cross proved that His victory was for everyone and for all time. By taking the way of renunciation, His was the victory. The Cross is the universal abolition of evil; it is the death of sin. Sin, Law and Death are done away, and Life, Victory and Righteousness become the characteristics of the new type of creation.

It is when the New Testament writers speak of the Priesthood of Christ that they view His work in an eschatological setting. The Son has achieved the victory of righteousness, 'But unto the Son, he saith, Thy throne, O God, is for ever and ever; a sceptre of righteousness is the sceptre of thy kingdom' (Heb. i. 8). It is under Him that all thrones and powers, human and angelic, hold sway, and they exist only as they submit to His rule, although it is their privilege to participate in it. He is pictured as passing through the seven heavens of traditional Jewish thought (Heb. iv. 14), for by His conquest of sin and death, He has become ruler of heaven as well as earth. It is Christus Victor who is set at the right hand of God. 'We have such an high priest, who is set on the right hand of the throne of the Majesty in the heavens' (Heb. viii. 1). In such

[1] C. H. Dodd and R. Bultmann have emphasized 'realized' or 'existential' eschatology in contrast to the more traditional interpretation. The two views are not mutually exclusive. The New Community is the 'kingdom of priests' on earth, but it is also true that 'they shall reign with him' (Rev. xx. 6).

passages it will be noticed that victory is both the result and fulfilment of our Lord's priestly vocation.

Our Lord now ensures that His priestly work may continue in the world, and therefore he bestows upon the Church and the world the fruits of His victory. St Paul has this in mind in Ephesians iv. 8: 'When He ascended on high, he led captivity captive and gave gifts unto men.' The reference is to Psalm lxviii. 18 where the Conqueror is seated in triumph and receives homage on all hands. This receiving of homage means that all are subject to His sway and that God may now dwell with His people undisturbed in Zion. St Paul gives the whole passage a significant interpretation: Our Lord's victory, ascension and exaltation bring two gifts which only He has the power to give. The first gift is to the world and it ensures 'that the whole universe from lowest to highest might know His Presence'. (Eph. iv. 10, Phillips'). The second gift is to the Church: it is the equipping of the Church with faithful officers and leaders, and the bestowing of spiritual gifts so that His work may be continued through them. The first gift implies that God can no longer be confined to any particular race or place, for He is now accessible to all. The second means that the Church possesses those gifts which will enable her to continue her mission for ever.

Just as our Lord has made this possible, so He commissions men to make it known. Now in doing this the apostles did not only speak of a promised victory but of a victory already won. The proclamation of the Gospel on any day was also its proclamation on the last day. So that the proclamation was also an acclamation.

> After the resurrection of Christ and the outpouring of the Spirit the proclamation goes out to the ends of the earth, and when it has reached that point the end comes (Matt. xxiv. 14; Acts i. 6–8; xxvi. 23). The risen Christ is in the Gospel and comes to men in preaching. When He reaches them, they are in His resurrection; then the dead arise, and the end has come.[1]

It is at this point that the eschatological moment and the existential moment are brought together. The Church proclaims the end in the very moment that the end has come. But what authority has the Church for doing this? Instead of saying that the apostles were commissioned to take the Gospel to others, it is perhaps more true to say that Christ is all the time reaching men through the Church

---

[1] G. Windgren, *Theology in Conflict*, pp. 132–3.

and the Gospel. So the Church has a priesthood, and through it the Priest reaches out in love and power to all the world. The Church which the Priest may use for His own purpose is truly His priesthood.

The preaching of the apostles refers to an inward crisis as well as an external eschaton. Through the New Covenant the external sacrifices of Judaism are changed into spiritual sacrifices, and the external priesthood is changed into an inward spiritual priesthood. In the same way the exlusively external eschaton is changed into an inward experience. This is what von Dobschutz meant by 'transmuted eschatology'.

> I mean transmuted in the sense that what was spoken of in Jewish-eschatology as to come in the last days is taken here as already at hand in the lifetime of Jesus; transmuted at the same time in the other sense that what was expected as an external change is taken inwardly: not all people seeing it, but Jesus' disciples becoming aware of it.[1]

This change takes place on account of our Lord's consciousness of His Kingship and Priesthood. What He believed about His Kingship determined the nature of the reign of God which He came to establish, and what he believed about His Priesthood determined the nature of the priesthood which He came to inaugurate.

All Christians are included in His Rule and Priesthood because they are involved in His Resurrection and Ascension. In what sense do Christians share His rule? Flew gives an impressive answer to this question:

> Christians are a kingdom because they exercise rule. The rule is delegated to the Ecclesia by Christ. ... The 'Son of Man' represents the people of the saints of the Most High; the kingdom is their own rule over all the dominions under the whole heaven. We Christians, despised, harried, persecuted, are a community of princes and priests, 'with a great history and a greater hope'. Our connexion with Christ makes us truly imperial.

> *On all the kings of earth*
> *With pity we look down:*
> *And claim in virtue of our birth,*
> *A never fading crown.*
> (C. WESLEY.)[2]

In what sense do Christians share His Priesthood? The author of the Apocalypse (Rev. x. 9–14) refers to the fruit of our Lord's

[1] E. von Dobschutz, *The Eschatology of the Gospels*, p. 150.
[2] R. N. Flew, *Jesus and His Church*, p. 234.

victory in two respects: first, in respect of the honour which He has brought to all Christians, and second, the honour which He has brought to Himself. In creating a priestly community, He has brought to Himself endless glory. Dr Taylor explains it as follows:

> They (sacrificial ideas) are visible also in the reference to a priestly community established by the deed of Christ; for the thought of redemption is at once followed by the claim that He has consummated 'a kingdom of priests unto His God and Father', while the unique character of His deed is expressed in 'the glory and dominion' ascribed to Him for ever and ever. The testimony of the Apocalypse is its tribute to this sovereign act of Christ.[1]

The thought of victory was in the mind of Jesus even as He spoke about the New Covenant. It was this apocalyptic note which prompted the early Christians always to think of the Lord's Supper as a joyful affair. For the Master had said: 'I will no more drink of the fruit of the vine until that day that I drink it new in the kingdom of God.' (Mark xiv. 25). He inaugurated the kingdom with its final consummation in mind. The New Covenant transforms everything: there will be a new kingdom, a new priesthood, a new community, new as in the first creation.

It is perhaps for this reason that the constant theme of the Apocalypse is the *enthronement* of the Lamb. Christians take courage from this fact which is at once a present reality as well as a living hope.

> The Ascension of Jesus Christ to the throne of God was the enthronement of the Word made flesh, the enthronement of the Lamb. It was the inauguration of His Kingdom in which 'God gave him to be the head over all things to the church, which is his body' (Eph. i. 22). But until the *parousia* He holds back the epiphany of Glory; He exercises His Kingdom only through His Priesthood, bestowing His Spirit upon the Church that the proclamation of the word of the Cross may be the power of God unto salvation to all who believe (1 Cor. i. 17ff). He waits to be gracious. And so the Church on earth lives and moves and has its being in the Kingdom and Patience of Jesus.[2]

The New Community is not only inaugurated but lives in this eschatological setting. Thus all Christians, waiting and hurrying, listening and serving, in struggle and in hope, go forth to meet their Lord.

[1] V. Taylor, *The Atonement in New Testament Teaching*, p. 56.
[2] T. F. Torrance, op. cit., p. 61.

THE SERVANT-MESSIAH-PRIEST

The attempt to understand the Person and Work of our Lord involves an understanding of the Servant Christology. We have already noticed that the whole duty of the priests was summed up in the expression: 'I serve Jahweh' (Deut. xvii. 12; xxi. 5); and that the priests were servants of the Word of God, the Law of God and the Will of God. We must now enquire as to whether *the* Word has appeared from God, which is at once the fulfilment of the Law and the perfect expression of God's will. In other words: has the Servant-Messiah-Priest appeared?

In the Gospels the conception of Jesus as the Son of God is closely allied with that of Jesus as Servant. Matthew openly identifies the two. He points out that in Jesus the prophecy of Isaiah is fulfilled: 'Behold, my Servant whom I have chosen, my beloved in whom my soul is well pleased . . . he shall not strive nor cry aloud' (Isa. xlii. 1–3; Matt. xii. 17–19): Jesus Himself was conscious of the fact that His life and destiny could only be properly interpreted in His vocation as Servant: 'I am among you as one who serves' (Luke xxii. 27). Professor W. Manson has stated that although Jesus did not use the term Servant in reference to Himself, yet whenever He spoke of His life-work the thought of Servanthood was never far away: 'He who is called to be the Messiah-Son of God sees the way marked out for Him by the practice of the Servant, and teaches also that only through the humiliation and self-sacrifice of the Servant is the glory of the Son of Man to be attained.'[1] While it is true, then, that Jesus did not use the term 'Servant' as the subject of any pronouncement about His life and vocation, He did use it as the predicate. Similarly, although Jesus did not use of Himself the term 'Priest', yet when He spoke of His priestly service for mankind, He is clearly thinking of His vocation as Servant, 'For the Son of Man has not come to be served but to serve, and to give His life as a ransom for many' (Mark x. 45, Moffatt). Our Lord's relationship to God and His priestly service for mankind are combined in the term 'Servant'. Moreover, the very fact that 'the Son of Man came to serve' links the office of the Messiah with the function of the Servant.

In order to reinforce this truth it may also be observed that when John's disciples were sent to Jesus to enquire whether He was the

[1] W. Manson, *Jesus the Messiah*, p. 111.

Messiah (Art Thou He that cometh, or look we for another?), the answer of Jesus is that the *Servant's* mission is being fulfilled. 'Tell John the things which you do hear and see: the blind receive their sight, and the lame walk, the lepers are cleansed, and the deaf hear, and the dead are raised up, and the poor have good tidings preached to them' (Matt. xi. 4–5). It is almost certain that Isaiah lxi was in mind at the time—'The Lord hath anointed me to preach good tidings unto the poor,' and this is significant not only because it modifies the common view of the Messiah but also emphasizes the specific functions of the Servant.

Further, in our Lord's reply to the enquiring Greeks, which is really a discourse on His own sufferings and death, there is a striking reference to the servanthood of the disciples: 'If any man serve me, let him follow me; and where I am, there shall also my servant be: if any man serve me, him will my Father honour' (John xii. 26). It is in such passages that the Messianic nature as well as the servant function of the Church are seen to arise out of the Messiahship and Servanthood of Christ. It is also important to notice that the Father who glorifies the Son also glorifies the Son's servants.

Yet the glory which comes to the servants of Christ is not the usual idea of glory. It means facing with gladness persecution, hardship and suffering, for it is one thing to accept the idea of their Lord's appointed destiny and another and a greater thing to realize that this destiny is also being worked out in their minds and bodies. Suffering is always 'for My sake'. If suffering is the result of their own failure or misconduct, there is no honour in it, but when it is 'for My sake' it is glorious.

> Jesus, the Servant Messiah, knows that suffering will be the lot of the Servant's disciples, but bids them 'count it all joy' for the Kingdom of Heaven's sake. He does not mean that suffering *qua* suffering is blessed: he means that where persecution needs must be, the disciple has an opportunity of proving his fitness for that Kingdom:
>
> > Its king a servant, and its sign
> > A gibbet on a hill.[1]

Even so, such hardship and suffering receive their meaning from the fact that the servants of Christ are sanctified in Him. It is not merely that their *sufferings* are sanctified but that the servants themselves are sanctified. This is the purpose of our Lord's High Priestly

[1] A. M. Hunter, *Design for Life*, pp. 36–7.

Prayer. 'And for their sakes I sanctify Myself, that they themselves also may be sanctified in truth' (John xvii. 19). At the same time, persecution and suffering do not constitute their priesthood, but express something that is already theirs. They are already priests because they are consecrated in Christ—His Self-consecration is also their priestly calling. Hebrews x. 19–25 also affirms the priestly consecration of the servants of Christ. It is not without reason that John xvii. has been called 'the Consecration Prayer'. Commenting on this Hoskyns says:

> The prayer is the solemn consecration of Himself in the presence of His disciples as their effective sacrifice; it is His prayer for glorification in and through His death; it is His irrevocable dedication of His disciples to their mission in the world, and His prayer that both they and those who believe through their teaching may be consecrated to the service of God; and finally, it concludes with the prayer that the Church thus consecrated may at the end behold the glory of the Son and dwell in the perfect love of the Father and the Son.[1]

In addition to the teaching of Jesus there are certain dramatic acts which vividly remind us of His twofold calling of Messiahship and Servanthood. The first of these was the occasion of our Lord's visit to the synagogue at Nazareth (Luke iv. 16–22). He read Isaiah lxi. 1–2, and the evangelist makes the comment: 'And the eyes of all in the synagogue were fastened on Him' (Luke iv. 20). It may have occasioned some surprise that Joseph's son, one of their own, should read and interpret the Scriptures with such courage and authority. On the other hand, they may have been surprised because He omitted the usual passage from the Law and read a passage of His own choice. But it is more likely that their astonishment was due to our Lord's emphatic comment on the passage from Isaiah: 'Today hath this scripture been fulfilled in your ears' (ver. 21). The passage from Isaiah tells how God anoints His Servant with His Spirit to bring joy, freedom and good tidings to all who are in misery, but these were also the expected signs of the coming of the Messiah (see Luke vii. 19–23). Jesus, therefore, is the anointed Servant in whose work the signs of Messiahship are clearly evident. The purpose of this dramatic act was to make the people realise that they could not accept the programme without first accepting Him who carries it out. Moreover, the passage shows clearly the difference between

---

[1] E. C. Hoskyns, *The Fourth Gospel*, p. 586.

Jesus and John the Baptist. John was the prophet of doom, Jesus was the Priest of Good Tidings who stood before them offering God's gifts because He offered Himself. So the Servant-Messiah is also the Priest through whom alone all divine blessings are to be received.

The second dramatic act is the Triumphal Entry into Jerusalem. Matthew quotes the words of the prophet Zechariah: 'Behold, thy King cometh unto thee, meek and riding upon an ass' (Matt. xxi. 5). Nowhere in the Old Testament do we find kings thus mounted. Undoubtedly a military leader would have ridden on horseback but this would have been the symbol of war. One who speaks peace to the Gentiles rides on an ass. A servant might ride on an ass, a king never. So while there is much in the triumphal procession that tells of royalty, there is also something which adds: 'My Kingdom is not of this world.' The people were allowed to hail the coming kingdom of David, because, unknown to themselves, they were confessing that in Christ, as He went to His death, the kingdom of God came. Whether they realized it or not, they were, in fact, hailing the Servant-King.

The intention of the Servant-King in visiting Jerusalem is revealed in the third dramatic act. The Cleansing of the temple is concerned with the meaning of priesthood. Since Christ's Kingdom was universal, the Temple should have been 'a house of prayer for all nations'. The Jewish priesthood had made it a place of profit for themselves, a house of Mammon instead of a house of God. The coming of Christ, the true and only Priest, meant that the old order of religion with its corruptions and false ideas of priesthood should be swept away. The prophet Malachi had written: 'The Lord whom ye seek shall suddenly come to His temple; ... but who may abide the day of His coming?' (Mal. iii. 1-2). As an act of external reformation the Cleansing of the Temple may have accomplished little, but it was indicative of the universal nature of priesthood which His appearing had inaugurated.

Perhaps the most significant of the dramatic acts of our Lord is that of the washing of the disciples' feet. It was the act of one who 'came forth from God and goeth unto God' (John xiii. 3); it was therefore Messianic. The washing of the disciples' feet was pre-eminently the work of a servant; it was therefore a servant's act. The feet washing was a symbol of inward cleansing, 'He that is bathed needeth not save to wash his feet, but is clean every whit' (xiii. 10); it was therefore the priest's act.

The disciples had much to learn about their servanthood, and all that they needed to learn was here. Jesus not only spoke about being Servant (Luke xxii. 27), but acted what He said. In the very moment 'that the Father had given all things into His hands', He demonstrated that He had accepted the role of a Servant. The Messiah from God, 'knowing that His hour was come,' reveals it by taking the form of a Servant. If there was any danger of the disciples missing the lesson of this dramatic act, the words of Jesus made the lesson plain: 'If I then, the Lord and Master, have washed your feet, ye also ought to wash one another's feet' (John xiii. 14). They will fail if they do not learn to be servants of one another because they are servants of one Lord. Moreover, 'A servant is not greater than his Lord, neither one that is sent greater than He that sent him' (16). Now 'one that is sent' is an apostle, but it must be remembered that an apostle is never the Lord's substitute but His servant. Even so, because he has the honour of apostleship he must be all the more careful to reveal his apostleship in servanthood.

Is it not the case that in this dramatic act the disciples are instituted into a royal priesthood in the New Covenant? Jesus knew that as He was the High Priest over the House of God, the disciples were its priests. He knew that cleansing was necessary before they could receive the anointing of the Holy Ghost. Their supreme service was to proclaim the Word to others, carrying the sacred vessels of the Gospel and being custodians of its divine truth. And can anyone bear this priestly responsibility who has not first received the priestly cleansing? The priesthood and servanthood of the disciples were never more cogently expressed than in this dramatic act by the Servant-Priest.

The fifth dramatic act was the celebration of the Passover Meal. Now at this Meal Jesus was clearly linking the idea of the New Covenant with His Messianic fulfilment, yet He was thinking of that fulfilment in its servant form and not in its Davidic form. As Dr Moffatt aptly says:

> What made Him sit loose to the latter ideal was His higher conception of the messianic vocation in connexion with the Servant of Yahweh, rather than a preference for some more apocalyptic ideal of Messiah, or a desire to emphasize His divine (as contrasted with a

Davidic) Sonship, though we may admit that the latter thought is not entirely to be ruled out of the argument.[1]

There is, however, another reason why Jesus did not at this stage emphasize His Messiahship in its Davidic form, and that was because it had specific reference to His Davidic descent, and this was something that the disciples could not share. But they could share His Servanthood. At this point in the history of our Lord the symbol and fact of Sacrifice were hardly separated, and even though Crucifixion was not for the disciples, it was theirs through faith-participation in His dramatic act. In giving them the bread to eat and the cup to drink, He was associating them with Him in His Sacrifice. In this moment, by His will, they shared His Priesthood. Consequently the disciples rose from the table as men redeemed by the death of their Lord, and as people of the New Covenant to whom the Kingdom and Priesthood were already given.

It will be clear, therefore, that in these five dramatic acts—the scene in the synagogue, the Triumphal Entry, the Cleansing of the Temple, the Washing of the disciples' feet, and the Last Supper—our Lord stands forth unmistakably as the Servant-Messiah-Priest, and that in each act His followers emerge as members of a Kingdom and sharers of a Servanthood and Priesthood which are theirs as well as His for ever.

Nor is the evidence confined to the Gospels, for in the days of the Apostles the idea of servanthood is still uppermost in the minds of the People of God. We find Peter justifying his own position as servant and preacher at Pentecost by a quotation from Joel: 'Yea and on my servants ... in those days will I pour forth of my Spirit, and they shall prophesy' (Acts ii. 18). We find Stephen in his last sermon covering the whole range of the history of the covenant People of God, and in the end being identified by his own martyrdom with the Suffering Servanthood of his Lord. Philip finds the Ethiopian reading from Isaiah liii. 7-8, and at once preaches Jesus in the light of the Suffering Servant of Isaiah: 'And Philip opened his mouth, and beginning from this scripture, preached unto him Jesus' (Acts viii. 35). The Author of the Apocalypse looks forward to the Church Triumphant and knows no more lofty conception of heavenly bliss than that of being a servant of the

[1] J. Moffatt, *The Theology of the Gospels*, pp. 164-5.

Lamb: 'And the throne of God and of the Lamb shall be therein; and his servants shall do him service' (Rev. xxii. 3).

There is yet another picture of the Servant-Priest in the famous Kenosis passage of St Paul: 'Have this mind in you which was also in Christ Jesus, who being in the form of God, counted it not a thing to be grasped at to be on an equality with God, but emptied Himself, taking the form of a servant, being made in the likeness of men' (Phil. ii. 5–7). The passage is important for several reasons. There is the link between the Servant and the servants: 'Let this mind be in you which was also in Christ Jesus.' Paul is exhorting the Philippians to catch the spiritual attitude of servanthood from their Master. Moreover, the word *'doulos'* is used of Jesus only in this instance. It is surely significant that a word normally used of individual Christians should be applied to our Lord. There is something more than condescension envisaged here, there is identification at every point: physical, mental and spiritual. The phrase 'form of a servant' means two things: first, it signifies the reality of His Incarnation, and secondly, it signifies His qualification for Saviourhood. But the servant Christology of the passage does not depend on that one phrase. The tone of the whole passage implies that the obedience, humiliation, suffering, death and exaltation of Christ are to be interpreted in the light of His Servanthood.

The lesson had been inculcated into the mind of Saul very early in his career. There is the apt point first made by St Augustine, that although Saul had spent his time persecuting Christians, the voice on the Damascus Road said: 'Saul, Saul, why persecutest thou *Me*?' The complete identification of the Suffering Servant, Christ, with His persecuted servants could not be more forcefully expressed.

A similar instance is to be found in 2 Corinthians iv. 5 where it is seen how closely Christology is related to ecclesiology. The passage implies that the proclamation of the Gospel means to proclaim the servant-people as well as the Servant, for both 'Christ' and 'ourselves' are direct objects of the verb 'we preach' in the passage mentioned: 'For we preach not ourselves, but Christ Jesus as Lord, and ourselves as your servants for Jesus' sake.'

The writer to the Hebrews is concerned with our Lord's voluntary acceptance of suffering service for mankind. Jesus is set forth as the obedient Servant of God. 'I am come to do Thy will, O God' (Heb. x. 7). All that He did was inspired by the spirit of absolute obedience: 'He learned obedience by the things which He suffered' (Heb. v. 8). A contrast is made between Moses who was a faithful servant and Christ who rendered unique service in that He 'offered Himself' (ix. 14). It is true that even the first covenant had ordinances of divine service (ix. 1), yet under the New Covenant the people are cleansed from dead works 'to serve the living God' (ix. 14).

Inasmuch, however, as our Lord's Servanthood consists in His redemptive service, there is a sort of carry-over between His Servanthood and Priesthood. Redemptive service means obedience, suffering and sacrifice, and these are the marks of His Priesthood. The universal character of this obedience, and its importance for an understanding of our Lord's priestly action for humanity, are emphasized by Dr Taylor:

> In the New Testament Christ's representative work is one of obedience to the Father's will and of self-identification with sinners. The emphasis laid upon His Person as the Son of Man and the Son of God gives to his work a universal character. His minstry is not simply that of an individual within the race, but the service of the High Priest of our humanity, the mediator of the new covenant between God and man.[1]

It will be noticed, therefore, that those qualities which mark out Jesus as the divinely appointed Servant also characterize Him as our High Priest. Our Lord's consciousness of His Servanthood was at the same time His consciousness of His priestly mission. Not in his wildest dreams would any Israelite have conceived the idea of the priest becoming the victim, yet it is but a short step from the idea of Priest-Servant to Priest-Victim. This is what Charles Wesley meant in the following verse:

> *O Thou eternal victim slain*
> *A Sacrifice for guilty man . . .*
> *Our everlasting Priest art Thou,*
> *And pleadst thy death for sinners now.*

Since Christ has become the Sacrifice, there is no further need of any other Mediator between God and man. Priesthood in the New Testament is founded upon the Person and Work of Christ. All the same, there is a difference between His Priesthood and ours: we are servants sharing that Servanthood which He as the Servant *par excellence* creates. Divine love constitutes His Priesthood; faith

[1] V. Taylor, op. cit., p. 291.

constitutes ours. He is Priest by nature; we are priests by faith-union with His Sacrifice. His Priesthood consists in offering His life for the sins of the world, ours in sharing the inestimable benefits of His offering. While His Priesthood is incommunicable, it is nevertheless the pattern of that general servanthood and universal priesthood of those who by faith and obedience have chosen to become lowly servants of the divine will.

THE MARKS OF THE ROYAL PRIESTHOOD

Baptism

Baptism is the consecration of a new member to the royal priesthood. It is the sign whereby a member is baptized into the Death of Christ, sealed by the Spirit, endowed with the gifts of the Spirit, and given a part and lot within the total priesthood of the Church of God. There is no more dramatic expression of the real meaning of priesthood than that in which a person is baptized into Christ by the waters of baptism. To be baptized 'into His death' (Rom. vi. 3) means to participate in the priestly act of Christ at its most crucial point. With Christ buried, rising with Christ and living in Him, the believer is incorporated in the community of the Faithful. It is not only an initiation into a New Community, but a total experience in which all spiritual blessings are vouchsafed to him. It also implies the consecration of life, for the believer bears the mark of the Redeemer. Each believer has 'an anointing from the Holy One' (1 John ii. 20), for the mark of the Cross is ratified by the inward seal of the Spirit, and this indicates not only a presentation but a consecration. This is why the early Christians soon learned to speak of baptism as a 'priestly consecration'.

It must be noted that Baptism is above all the gracious act of God, and this precludes any notion of good works, since the believer relies solely on the mercy of God and the renewing power of the Holy Ghost.

> But when the kindness of God our Saviour, and His love toward man, appeared, not by works done in righteousness, which we did ourselves, but according to His mercy He saved us, through the washing of regeneration and renewing of the Holy Ghost, that being justified by His grace, we might be made heirs according to the hope of eternal life (Tit. iii. 4–7).

There is no room for good works 'which we did ourselves' but only for repentance and faith, and so we draw near 'with a true heart and fullness of faith', for this is the only way in which God's mercy may be received. Whether in the case of an infant or an adult, the faith of the believing congregation is exercised and in this act the priesthood of believers is fulfilled.

Nicodemus, as a Jew, might have thought that there was some other way of entering the kingdom of God; hence the importance of our Lord's words to him: 'Except a man be born of water and the Spirit he cannot enter the kingdom of God' (John iii. 5). John's baptism of purification and the Messianic baptism of the Spirit are a necessary preparation, even a condition for admission to the kingdom. The one purifies and the other empowers, and that is why baptism is regarded as the initiation into the universal priesthood.

Yet even in baptism there is an eschatological reference, for, according to St Paul, the purpose of baptism is the sanctification of the whole Church: 'That he might sanctify it, having cleansed it by the washing of water with the word, that He might present the Church to Himself a glorious Church . . . that it should be holy and without blemish' (Eph. v. 26–7).

One truth stands out clearly: Christians become priestly not by what they do, 'not by works of righteousness', but 'by the fullness of faith'. Through faith they die to their own works and live unto Christ. Priesthood, therefore, arises out of baptism, and although baptism is a single act, it is continually renewed by the Holy Ghost, and only so can the priestly character of the Church, which is holiness, be revealed. But true priesthood is not confined to a single act of initiation, it is revealed continuously by the sacrificial nature of the Christian life.

Sacrifice

The first thing we must notice is that, according to Scripture, the royal priesthood is dependent on the Sacrifice of Christ (Rev. i. 5–6). In verse 5 alone there are three references to the death of Christ; '*martus*' may be translated 'martyr' or one who is faithful unto death. Also Jesus is the 'First-born from the dead', and He 'loosed us from our sins *by His blood*'. It is significant that immediately after this threefold reference to the death of Christ, the writer says: 'And he made us to be a kingdom, to be priests unto His God and Father.'

Nor is this an isolated instance, for the same connexion of ideas occurs in v. 9–10: 'For thou wast slain and didst purchase unto God *with thy blood* men of every tribe, and tongue, and people, and nation, and made them to be unto our God a kingdom and priests.' Here again it is the Sacrifice of Christ which constitutes the priesthood of all who believe. The only difference between the two passages is that in the second one the author envisages the effects of Christ's death as more far-reaching than in the first. As Swete observes:

> The new song which they sing vindicates for Jesus Christ the unique place which He has taken in the history of the world. By a supreme act of self-sacrifice He has purchased men of all races and nationalities for the service of God, founded a vast spiritual empire, and converted human life into a priestly service and a royal dignity.[1]

Further, when we turn to 1 Peter ii. 5 we notice that the spritual sacrifices which are offered by the royal priesthood receive their meaning only as they are linked with the Sacrifice of Christ. 'Ye also ... are to be a holy priesthood to offer up spiritual sacrifices acceptable to God through Christ.' True worship consists in faith-identification with His Sacrifice. Shapland makes this comment on this verse:

> This becomes all the plainer when we consider the nature of this worship, which consists in the offering of spiritual sacrifices to God through Christ. The verb seems to suggest a definite act, not a series of acts: 'the once-for-all devotion of the body'. This devotion Christ offered for us upon Calvary, and age by age the Church pleads and offers that Sacrifice as the only ground of her hope. It is ours, not because we make it, but because we appropriate it by offering ourselves with it and in it.[2]

The same thought is emphasized by St Paul. Upon what grounds does he exhort his brethren to offer their bodies as a living sacrifice on the altar of God? They are exhorted to do this on account of the mercies of God which are referred to in Rom. xi. 30–3. For as God has been abundantly merciful to both Jews and Greeks, they are to offer a sacrifice to Him—a sacrifice which befits His holiness. The implication is that the whole life of the Christian must be sacrificial.

The same connexion between the Sacrifice of Christ and the

---

[1] H. B. Swete, *The Apocalypse*, pp. 8–9.
[2] C. R. B. Shapland, *First Epistle of Peter*, p. 14.

priestly function of believers is stressed by the writer to the Hebrews. What is the result of the work of Christ, the Priest? He forgives their sins (vii. 27); He enables them to draw near to God (iv. 16); He purifies their consciences and equips them for service to God (ix. 14); His people share His priestly work by their sacrifices of praise and neighbourly service (xiii. 15). It is only through the Sacrifice of Christ that believers are enabled not only to claim their priestly privileges but also to fulfil their priestly tasks.

Priestly dedication to God is not the abnormal but the normal expression of true Christian character. The true meaning of New Testament priesthood is set forth by Dr Moberly:

> Priesthood in its catholic meaning stands not only for outward functions but for the spirit of sacrifice, which is the spirit of love in a world of sin and pain, whose expression in the inner soul is priestly intercession, and whose utterance in the outward life is devotion of ministry 'for others': for others, from the Christlike point of view, as for those for whom Christ died.[1]

But the real issue for the Christian lies deeper still, for if man is fully to share the priesthood of Christ, he too must die. Death and sacrifice are indispensable factors in Christian experience. As a member of the race of Adam, man dies; as a member of the race of Christ, man lives. In conformity with the Sacrifice of Christ, he sacrifices himself unto death with Christ, and in this act he becomes a member of the royal priesthood. But his priesthood is expressed in worship and to a consideration of this we must now turn.

Worship

Worship is a function of the royal priesthood. The word *leitourgein* is sometimes used in the New Testament to mean 'a work done' or 'a service representatively undertaken', and it is generally translated quite simply as 'service'. Generally speaking, however, when divine service in the sense of worship is implied, the word *latreia* is used. St Paul looked forward to the day when the brethren would, of their own free will, offer their bodies a living sacrifice, holy and acceptable unto God, for this was their reasonable service (*latreia*). *Leitourgos* could not possibly have been used here, because the thought is of Christians offering the sacrifice of themselves and not of another doing it on their behalf. Moreover *leitourgos* had been associated

[1] R. H. Moberly, *Ministerial Priesthood*, p. 260.

with the ministrations of priests and levites, and the service offered in Romans xii. 1 is reasonable and not the offering of an irrational animal.

Latreuein is also used of the service of both priest and people and the word is used in Acts xxvi. 7 to depict the service rendered to God by the whole race. There is the lofty thought of the whole community offering service to God continually, and in the whole passage St Paul's language is as catholic as his thought. *Leitourgein* could not have expressed the continuous worship of the whole race as was envisaged by Paul.

The same applies to the interpretation of Revelation vii. 15: 'Therefore are they before the throne of God, and serve Him day and night in His temple; and He that sitteth on the throne shall dwell among them.' Commenting on this H. B. Swete says:

> Since the members of the Church are priests unto God (Rev. i. 6; v. 10; xx. 6), *leitourgein* might have been expected here and in xxii. 3 rather than *latreuein*. But the conception is that of a vast worshipping congregation, and the use of *leitourgein* would rather have suggested that of an exclusive priesthood admitted to the sanctuary, while the great majority were content to pray without. The Israelite who was not a Priest or Levite did not proceed beyond the *hieron* (sacred enclosure), one tribe only having access to the *naos* (temple itself). But in the Eternal Temple the Seer sees the whole Israel of God admitted to the *naos*, and the occasion for the *leitourgia* of a tribal or special priesthood has disappeared, all being priests and all serving in the presence of God.[1]

It is interesting to note that *leitourgos* now means simply 'a workman', and its specifically religious connotation has been considerably weakened. With *latreia*, however, the process has been different for it is now used entirely of the worship of God. The Jews have always associated it with spiritual worship, and the Rabbis declared that in the Messianic age only one sacrifice would remain—that of thanksgiving, and this will continue forever.

Although we have considered the worship and thanksgiving which are offered to God continually in heaven, we must not overlook the fact that in the Church on earth there is an unceasing offering of thanksgiving in the mystery of Holy Communion. Holy Communion is the sacrament of the royal priesthood. Members of this priesthood do not glory in what they bring to Christ but in what

[1] H. B. Swete, op. cit., p. 103.

they receive from Him. All worship is centred in the Sacrifice of Christ and priesthood consists in showing forth that Sacrifice to the world. The Eucharist is a corporate act—it is the thanksgiving of the whole Church. Christ is Host and Celebrant and there is none other. On every single occasion and all the time:

> *He pleads His Passion on the Tree,*
> *He shows Himself to God for me.*

The reality and efficacy of His Death are applied to our believing souls. Those who share in this corporate act are not regarded as isolated units, they are an adoring worshipping community. This act is the expression of the priesthood of all believers. The universal priesthood is present at every service of Holy Communion.

At the same time, it is in the Eucharist that Christians 'show forth the excellencies of God' as St Peter says. The Eucharist proclaims to all that Father, Son and Holy Spirit are eternally active in spiritual and material self-giving on behalf of all mankind. To make this known in word, worship and action is the priestly duty to which all Christians are committed. The priestly service of the believers is closely linked with eschatological fulfilment. Every service is sealed by victory, it is always 'until He come'. At the same time, this victory is continuously revealed in the witness and mission of the Church.

Mission

In 1 Corinthians ix. 14 St Paul refers to those who 'proclaim the Gospel', and in Acts xvi. 17 it is clear that the proclamation of the Gospel is the service to which all are called: 'These men are the servants of the most high God, which show unto us the way of salvation.'

How may this be done? In a sense the Church exists for nothing else. It cannot be regarded as a Church if the Gospel is not shown forth in it. Professor T. W. Manson has drawn attention to the fact that in the sending out of the Seventy 'service' is the dominant thought. The instructions they received were about the service they were to render. They served as they proclaimed the kingdom of God, and they justified their existence by this service. In the household of Stephanus (1 Cor. xvi. 15) one of the two titles to honour was that they laid themselves out to be of service to the saints. In the light of this argument it is easy to see why Professor Manson affirms that the Church is 'a continuation of the Messianic ministry (service) of Christ'.[1]

The royal priesthood is also the royal servanthood, for the Church is called to serve Christ in the world. Christ continues His ministry through the believing community. The Church does not exist for her own purpose but only as the servant of Christ. To speak of the Church as the servant of Christ is the equivalent of speaking of the Church's priesthood. This service is an obligation and no one may contract out of it. Even when the Church grows lax the obligation remains and it is always a reminder of the Church's need for penitence and vision and mission. As every believer has received the benefits of Christ's Passion and the gift of the Spirit, so every believer is bound to render to Christ that form of service for which he has been equipped. All the varied ministries of the New Testament are the expressions of one mission just as all forms of service are the outcome of one priesthood. This has nothing whatever to do with legalistic systems or official duties, it is the Christian's inevitable task. It is God's will, 'who has qualified us to share in the inheritance of the saints in light' (Col. i. 12). More and more the conception of ministry as service is being recognized as the true inheritance of the whole Church and not simply of an order within it. So Professor Greenslade can say: 'All human ministry and priesthood is a continuing participation in the ministry of Christ. The ministry and priesthood of Christ are continued and shared by the whole Church, and not limited to an ordained ministry within it.'[2]

Perhaps in the ultimate analysis the only criterion of true apostolic succession—that of apostolic faith and practice—is apostolic success. For the failure of the Church is always a failure in mission, and inasmuch as mission precedes, creates and inspires the Church, it is constitutive of her varied ministries in the world. Mission is basic, and all forms of service in the Church are related to this fact. All believers are irrevocably involved in this mission. Perhaps this is why Manson gives such a high estimate of the status of the Church member:

> We find only one essential and constitutive Ministry, that of our Head, our Lord Jesus Christ. All others are dependent, derivative, functional.... Member of the Body of Christ, partaker of His Spirit,

[1] T. W. Manson, *The Church's Ministry*, p. 25.
[2] *Scottish Journal of Theology*, IX, No. 2.

and sharer of His Ministry is not too high (a status) for any. In any case there is none higher.[1]

In so far as the Church endeavours, under the sole sovereignty of Christ, to show forth the Death of Christ as well as to show forth the Gospel, she is fulfilling her priestly task. When this is a reality rather than a hope, all priesthood will be viewed in the light of the Sacrifice, Priesthood, Servanthood and Sovereignty of Christ.

It must be confessed, however, that the view expressed here concerning the ministries within the mission, and the manifold forms of service within the one priesthood, is not acceptable to all. At the same time, it is strongly supported in the New Testament. Dom Gregory Dix has pointed out that the New Testament tends to use *diakonia* for all forms of the Christian ministry rather than *leitourgein*, and he concludes, 'There is no ground for the anti-sacerdotal deductions sometimes drawn from this fact.'[2] Nevertheless it is interesting to notice that the New Testament quite definitely preferred the *diakonia* to *leitourgia* which had sacerdotal associations. This preference can hardly be brushed aside as of no importance. After all, it would have been most natural for the New Testament writers to have used *leitourgos* which was the word for 'ministration' or 'service' in the LXX. Why then did these writers prefer *diakonia*? Because the exception in the Old Testament is the rule in the New, and this is a suggestive fact. The New Testament ministry is not one of the priest as distinct from the people; on the contrary, the exclusive class becomes a universal priesthood.

Now *leitourgein* and its correlates occur in St Paul, St Luke, and in Hebrews, and not in any single case can it be made to apply to a literal priestly function on the part of the Christian ministry. It is true that on three occasions St Paul uses it with the thought of sacrifice: one refers to his offering of the Gentiles in prayer (Rom. xv. 16); another to the Philippians who are priests and whose faith is the sacrifice (Phil. ii. 17); and the third instance is used of the sacrifice of charity for the poor saints (2 Cor. ix. 12). So even when the word is used, it does not refer to official priestly duties. The only reasonable deduction is that the New Testament writers did not bring the word into common usage because it was inadequate to express the new ideas of priesthood and ministry which had emerged. They

[1] T. W. Manson, op. cit., p. 30.
[2] K. E. Kirk (ed.), *The Apostolic Ministry*, pp. 228 ff.

used *diakonia* because they were thinking of a kingdom of priests and not of an exclusive class. Moreover this word was adequate to express Christian ministration or service of any kind (1 Cor. xii. 5; Rom. xi. 13; Eph. iv. 12) whether of an Apostle or of the humblest believer, and service of an official kind is never included in its meaning.

The royal priesthood is 'in Christ' and not 'in law'. It cannot be interpreted along narrow nationalistic lines. It is universal because the Death of Christ has broken down the barriers between Jew and Gentile, and has, as St Paul says, 'made both one' (Eph. ii. 14), so that they are united to one another as well as reconciled to God. The way of salvation is made known not only to a single nation but to all nations. This is because the knowledge of God is available to all and the dignity of priesthood belongs to all who believe.

These then are the marks of the royal priesthood—Baptism, Sacrifice, Worship and Mission revealed in varied ministries. These marks characterize the royal priesthood in every age, and although the interpretation of them varies, the theme remains.

We may now summarize the Biblical evidence which must underlie any interpretation of the doctrine of the Priesthood of all Believers. We began with an exposition of three dominant concepts of Old Testament thought—the People of God, the Servant of the Lord, and a Kingdom of Priests. We found that Israel were the People of God on three grounds: by divine revelation, election and covenant. We further discovered that the unique service to which Israel was called had a threefold significance: it was corporate, sacrificial and royal. Our interpretation of the phrase 'a Kingdom of priests' involved a survey of the idea of priesthood in Old Testament thought, and our investigation traced four definite stages of development: the original priesthood, the teaching priesthood, the sacrificing priesthood and the idealized priesthood. In the first and last of these stages we found the promise and hope of that universal priesthood which became a characteristic of New Testament religion.

Turning to the New Testament we noticed a genuine continuity of thought, and, while many Old Testament ideas were carried over into the New Testament, their meaning was tranformed and crystallized by certain important events. For instance, the elect People of God became the redeemed People of God, and the Incarnation and the Atonement gave rise to the People of the New Covenant—a New Community whose mission to the world had an eschatological as well as an ecclesiological significance. Moreover, we found that the Messianic, servant and priestly forms of the Old Testament were embodied in and transformed by the Servant-Messiah-Priest. By faith-participation with Him the New Israel emerges as a servant-hood, a kingdom and a priesthood. The marks of this new, universal priesthood in the New Testament are: Baptism, sacrificial service, worship and mission. We believe that we have here a sound biblical basis for an understanding of the theology of the Priesthood of all Believers. We must now consider how these ideas were worked out by the Early Fathers of the Christian Church.

CHAPTER THREE

THE EARLY CHURCH

Universal priesthood and Corporate worship
CLEMENT (*Bishop of Rome, end of first century*)

(*a*) *The Order of the Laity*

WHAT was the type of worship which existed in the Early Church? The following words of Clement will give us an early glimpse of the manner of Christian worship: 'Therefore they that make their offerings at the appointed seasons are acceptable and blessed, for in following the ordinances of the master they do not err. To the high priest are given his special ministrations, a special place is reserved for the priests, and special duties are imposed upon the Levites, while the layman is bound by the ordinances concerning the laity.'[1] They are exhorted to fulfil only their appointed duty for each part has an important function in the service of the whole. 'Let each of you, brethren, in his own order, give thanks to God with a good conscience, not transgressing the appointed rule of his service, in reverence.'[2] We are not told what was meant by the ordinances of the laity, but we must assume that laymen had certain essential duties to perform and that these ministrations were reserved for them alone. It is a mistake to suppose that such duties were of minor importance. We know that laymen were permitted to baptize;[3] they were also permitted to receive deathbed confession in the absence of a priest, and sometimes preaching was included in their duties.[4] Origen, for instance, was invited to preach at Caesarea in Palestine while he was still a Catechist; and when the Bishop of Alexandria remonstrated, Alexander of Jerusalem replied by quoting instances of similar invitations given by Bishops to laymen in various parts of Asia Minor.

[1] 1 Clem. ch. xl. (Here and afterwards 1 Clem. refers to his First Epistle to the Corinthians.)
[2] 1 Clem. ch. xli.
[3] See J. Wordsworth, *The Ministry of Grace*, p. 161.
[4] Ibid., p. 164.

(b) The authority of the Congregation

How were the leaders of the local Christian communities to be selected? Those who possessed spiritual gifts were selected by the Christian Community. The same custom applies on the mission field in our own day, for missionaries have no option but to appoint as elders in any particular village the first-fruits of their work. That this practice was adopted in the Early Church is shown by Clement who says: 'So preaching everywhere in town and in country, they appointed their first-fruits, when they had proved them by the Spirit, to be overseers and deacons unto them that should believe.'[1] This, then, was the initial stage. Afterwards, the responsibility devolved upon the local Christian community whose duty it was to make arrangements for their future spiritual oversight. 'For this cause, therefore, they appointed the aforesaid persons (i.e. their first converts) and afterwards gave a further injunction that if they should fall asleep, other approved men should succeed to their administration.'[2]

In the same letter we find that the congregation is the supreme authority. The letter itself is addressed to the whole Church, 'To the Church which sojourneth in Corinth' (preface); and the evil-doers are urged to do 'what is ordered by the people' (liv. 2). It is assumed that the 'gifts' of the Spirit are present in their midst and are manifest in the congregation's power of judging.

It was early recognized that there may be strife over the dignity and authority of the spiritual overseer's office, hence Clement's warning,

> Let a man be faithful, let him be able to expound a deep saying, let him be wise in the discernment of words, let him be strenuous in deeds, let him be pure; so much the more ought he to be lowly in mind, in proportion as he seemeth to be greater; and he ought to seek the common advantage of all and not his own.[3]

If they needed guidance as to the sort of person to choose as their spiritual overseer, it was there for them, and they had also the impressive description of the right person to choose in St Paul's first letter to Timothy, chapter 3.

[1] 1 Clem. ch. xlii.   [2] 1 Clem. ch. xliv.   [3] 1 Clem. ch. xlviii.

(c) *The Eucharist and the Universal Priesthood*

The conception of sacrifice which was prevalent in the first century is shown in Clement's references to the meaning of the Eucharist. As we have seen, Clement says that it was the president's duty to 'present the offerings' of the people. Professor Lindsay sums up the matter in the following words:

> The idea of a sacrifice offered in the Christian congregation was continually present, and from the beginning it was intimately connected with the Eucharist, but the thoughts suggested by the words were always evangelical. It was believed that all Christians were priests before God, and that all had to do the priestly work of sacrificing. The sacrifices of the Church, the bloodless sacrifices predicted by the prophet Malachi, were the prayers, the praises, and the worship of the believers. The Holy Supper which was the supreme part of the Christian worship, was a sacrifice because it was an act of worship, and because it combined as no other act did, the prayers of *all* the worshippers and the gifts or oblations of bread and wine which were given by the worshippers and were used partly in the Holy Supper and partly to distribute among the poor. The idea of the priesthood of all believers was firmly rooted in the thoughts of the early Christians.[1]

(d) *The spiritual sacrifices of the Universal Priesthood*

The sacrifices thus referred to were spiritual sacrifices. These consist of praise (Heb. xiii. 15), faith (Phil. ii. 17), almsgiving (Acts xxiv. 17), the devotion of the body (Rom. xii. 1), and the conversion of unbelievers (Rom. xv. 16), and even when an altar is referred to (as in Heb. xiii. 10) it refers to the spiritual services that are rendered by the Christian Church.

These sacrifices were often made, not by individuals but by the whole congregation, although it was the minister's duty to 'present the offerings' to God. It is true that this custom eventually led to the belief that the sacrifice thus made was an act of the minister who officiated, but there is no evidence that this was believed in the days of Clement. Two things emerge from this investigation of Clement's writings: first, the sacrifices were made by the whole congregation whose representative was 'the president of the brethren'. It was his duty to lead the worship and to preach. Secondly, the sacrifices which were offered through him were purely spiritual.

---

[1] T. M. Lindsay, *The Church and the Ministry in the Early Centuries*, p. 307.

This finds support in the Didache (approx. 110)[1] where it is stated that the purpose of Sabbath worship was simply to offer a pure sacrifice:

> On the Lord's Day, assemble and break bread and give thanks, having first confessed your sins that your sacrifice may be pure. If any have a dispute with his fellow, let him not come to the assembly till they be reconciled, that your sacrifice be not polluted. For this is the sacrifice spoken of by the Lord: 'In every place and at every time offer to me a pure sacrifice; for I am a great king, saith the Lord, and my name is wonderful among the Gentiles' (Mal. i. 11, 14).[2]

It is interesting to notice that the confession of sins preceded the breaking of the bread. Pardon which resulted from confession was not brought about by the sacrifice which they offered but was the condition of it. Had this fact been firmly grasped, the history of the Eucharist might have read very differently.

Another significant fact about the Didache is that it seems to use the terms 'prophet', 'teacher' and 'high priest' interchangeably.

> But every true *prophet* that willeth to abide with you is 'worthy of his food'. In like manner, a true *teacher* is also, like the labourer, 'worthy of his food'. Therefore, thou shalt take and give to the prophets every first-fruit of the produce of the winepress and the threshing floor, of oxen and sheep. For the prophets are your *high-priests*.[3]

The connexion of these two is also implied in Acts xiii. 2 where the prophetic calling of Saul and Barnabas is part of their priestly function. The latter is signified by the use of the term *leitourgein*. We read 'as they ministered (*leitourgounton*) unto the Lord'.

Universal Priesthood and the local congregation
POLYCARP (70–156)

Polycarp also is important because he wrote early in the second century. The Epistle to the Philippians is his only extant work and all our evidence must derive from that. But his letter provides early evidence of conditions in the early Church.

We notice at once that although a bishop he does not write with

---

[1] The date is assigned by most critics to the beginning of the second century. Harnack's view that it has a much later origin (150–170) has not received widespread support.
[2] The Didache, XIV.   [3] Ibid., XIII.

any conscious superiority but rather as one who is replying to their request for advice. 'These things, brethren, I write to you concerning righteousness, not because I take anything upon myself, but because ye have invited me to do so.'[1]

Moreover, whatever developments might have taken place in the following century with regard to the power invested in the bishop, there is no doubt that Polycarp acknowledges the disciplinary authority of the congregation, and such authority was to be exercised even in the case of one who had been a presbyter among them. He writes on this vital question with moderation and restraint:

> But who of us are ignorant of the judgment of the Lord? Do we not know that the saints shall judge the world? as Paul teaches. . . . I am deeply grieved, therefore, brethren, for him (Valens) and his wife; to whom may the Lord grant true repentance! And be ye then moderate in regard to this matter, and do not count such as enemies, but call them back as suffering and straying members, that ye may save your whole body. For by so acting ye shall edify yourselves.[2]

Further, in the early Church where there had not been much time to give a Christian interpretation to the place of women in society, Polycarp envisaged an order of widows in the Church. He does not hesitate to refer to them as 'God's altar'. 'Teach the widows to be discreet as respects the faith of the Lord, praying continually for all, being far from all slandering, evil-speaking, false-witnessing, love of money, and every kind of evil; knowing that they are the altar of God, that He clearly perceives all things, and that nothing is hid from Him, neither reasonings, nor reflections, nor any one of the secret things of the heart.'[3]

It is possible that he was referring to those widows who had already been enrolled in the order and had been given certain duties to perform. They are 'God's altar', the medium, that is, through which the sacrifice of alms is offered to God.

Polycarp concludes the letter with a prayer that Christ, the High Priest, may bestow upon all of them a lot and portion among the saints, for they have their indisputable place in the life of the Church. 'But may the God and Father of our Lord Jesus Christ, and Jesus Christ Himself, who is the Son of God, and our everlasting High Priest, build you up in faith and truth, . . . and may He bestow on you a lot and portion among His saints, and on us with you, and on

---

[1] Ep. to Phil., ch. III.   [2] Ibid., ch. XI.   [3] Ibid., ch. IV.

all that are under heaven, who shall believe on our Lord Jesus Christ.'[1]

We therefore learn from Polycarp that early in the second century through the Priesthood of Christ all Christians were given a part and lot in the life and work of the Church, that women were already included in this priesthood of all believers, and that all members were called upon to exercise this priesthood in questions of discipline. Their lives were dedicated to one continual priesthood.

And sometimes this obligation could not be discharged without sacrifice, and the Christian was called upon to seal his witness with his blood. Priestly service demands priestly sacrifice. Polycarp did not shrink even from this demand. When his opponents wanted to secure him to the stake he said: 'Let me be as I am. He that granted me to endure the fire will grant me also to remain at the pyre unmoved, without being secured with nails.'[2]

So Polycarp's teaching on priestly sacrifice could only be truly fulfilled when the sacrifice was made complete.

The High-priestly race of God

JUSTIN MARTYR (100–65)

(a) *The Sacrifice of Thanksgiving*

Justin draws attention to the twofold sacrifice which takes place at the Eucharist—first, there is the sacrifice of thanksgiving, then there is the sacrifice of service. He says: 'Then we arise *all together* and offer prayers; ... when we have concluded our prayer, bread is brought and wine and water, and the president in like manner offers up prayer and thanksgiving with all his might; and the people assent with "Amen": and there is the distribution and partaking *by all* of the Eucharistic elements.'[3]

Now although Justin three times refers to the 'president of the brethren', he finds nothing contradictory in going on to speak of all who are present as 'the genuine high-priestly race of God'. He says:

> Just as Joshua who is called by the prophet (Zech. iii. 1) a priest, was seen wearing filthy garments ... and was called a brand plucked out of the burning because he received remission of sins, the devil

[1] Ibid., ch. XII. [2] The Martyrdom of Polycarp, ch. XIII.
[3] Apologia I. 67.

E

also, his adversary, receiving rebuke, so we, who through the name of Jesus have believed as one man in God, the Maker of all, have been stripped though the name of the First-begotten Son of the 'filthy garments' of our sin; and being set on fire with the word of His calling are the genuine high-priestly race of God, as God beareth witness Himself, saying that, 'in every place among the Gentiles men are offering sacrifices acceptable to Him and pure', and God receives from no man sacrifices, except through His priests. So then, of all the sacrifices through this name, which Jesus the Christ delivered to be made, that is (the sacrifices or thanksgivings) at the Eucharist of the bread and of the cup, which in every place of the earth are made by the Christians, God by anticipation beareth witness that they are acceptable to Him.[1]

(b) *The Sacrifice of Service*

The sacrifice of Thanksgiving thus described is inseparable from the sacrifice of Service which immediately follows. The high-priestly race of God offers a sacrifice whose culmination is service.

And they that are prosperous and wish to do so, give what they will each after his choice. What is collected is deposited with the president, who gives aid to the orphans and widows and such as are in want by reason of sickness or other cause; and to those also who are in prison, and to strangers from abroad, in fact to all that are in need he is the protector.[2]

This then is the priesthood of all believers as it was understood in the second century in relation to the Eucharist. There is no reference to material sacrifices. A sacrifice of thanksgiving was offered in which all the people shared, and this corporate act culminated in the sacrifice of service on behalf of their brethren in need.

It is necessary, however, to elucidate one of the phrases which Justin used. In arguing with the Jews, it is evident that Justin regards the whole Christian community as 'a high-priestly race of God' who collectively take the place of the Aaronic priesthood and that of the eternal Melchizedek. In what sense can such a phrase be used? Christians are a high-priestly race by their unique election, their unique worship, and their unique mission.

1. *A high-priestly race by their unique election*

There is strong Scriptural support for this idea. 'Thou art an holy people unto the Lord thy God: the Lord thy God hath chosen thee to be a special people unto Himself, above all people that are upon

---

[1] Dialogue with Trypho, ch. 116.   [2] Apologia I. 67.

the face of the earth' (Deut. vii. 6). St Peter transfers this unique privilege to the whole Christian community: 'But you are a chosen race, a royal priesthood, a dedicated nation, and a people claimed by God for His own, to proclaim the triumphs of Him who has called you out of darkness into His marvellous light' (1 Pet. ii. 9, *N E B*). Christians claimed this inheritance and maintained that all that God had done in the world was on their behalf:

> Thus, whatever has been spoken aright by any man belongs to us Christians; for we worship and love, next to God, the Word which is from the unbegotten and ineffable God; since it was on our behalf that He has been made man, that, becoming partaker of our sufferings, He may also bring us healing.[1]

Justin continues, 'We are not only a people, but a holy people.'[2] Again, he contrasts Israel and the Christian Church in respect of its relation to God; 'As from the one man Jacob, who was surnamed Israel, all your nation has been called Jacob and Israel; so we from Christ who begat us unto God, like Jacob and Judah and Joseph and David, are called and are the true sons of God.'[3] This idea of the pre-existent Church is also emphasized by 2 Clement. He affirms that Christians belong to 'the first Church':

> If we do the will of God our Father, we shall be of the first Church, which is spiritual, which was created before the sun and moon. And the Books and the Apostles plainly declare that the Church existeth not now for the first time, but hath been from the beginning: for she was spiritual as our Jesus also was spiritual, but was manifested in the last days that He might save us.[4]

The same idea is expressed in Hermas: 'She (the Church) was created before all things: therefore is she aged; and for her sake the world was framed.'[5]

Doubtless, it is on the basis of such patristic writings that Harnack declares certain definite convictions which were taken over by Christians:

1. Our people are older than the world.
2. The world was created for our sakes.

---

[1] Apologia II. 13.   [2] Dialogue with Trypho, ch. 119.
[3] Trypho, ch. 123.   [4] 2 Clem. ch. xiv. 'The Second Epistle of Clement' dates from the beginning of the third century and is in no way connected with Clement of Rome.
[5] Visions II, 4.

3. The world is carried on for our sakes; we retard the judgment of the world.
4. Everything in the world is subject to us and must serve us.
5. Everything in the world, the beginning and course and end of all history, is revealed to us and lies transparent to our eyes.
6. We shall take part in the judgment of the world and ourselves enjoy eternal bliss.[1]

Two peoples already existed—the Jews and Greeks, but with these astounding convictions it is little wonder that the Christians considered themselves to be a new kind of people, a new race, a new creation, embracing both Jews and Greeks and bringing them to a higher unity. If, as they firmly believed, they were chosen to the God's race, it is not surprising that Justin could think of no more appropriate title for them than 'the high-priestly race of God'.

2. *A high-priestly race by their unique worship*

Their worship was not like that of the Gentiles who worshipped idols and did not know the true God.

> We need not tell you—you know—what the craftsmen contrive of their material, carving and cutting and casting and hammering. Often a sordid pot—and they by their skill change its looks, give it a shape, and call it a god! That we count not just nonsense, but blasphemy. What madness, that dissolute men should be said to fashion gods for your worship![2]

But the Christians did not win an easy victory. Frequently they were accused of atheism. 'Thus we are called atheists. And we admit that in respect of such supposed gods we *are* atheists: but not in regard to the most true God, the Father of righteousness and moderation and the other virtues, the God who is without a trace of evil. Him we worship and adore, and His Son.'[3]

It was this sublime conception of the God they worshipped which determined the nature of their worship. When asked where they assembled, Justin replied, 'Wherever we can. You don't think we all meet in the same place. Our God fills heaven and earth, and is worshipped and glorified by the faithful everywhere.'[4] Such ideas are far removed from the idolatrous customs of the Greeks and Romans, and the Christians felt themselves to be heralds of a new

---

[1] A. Harnack, *The Mission and Expansion of Christianity*, I, p. 240.
[2] Apologia I. 9.   [3] Apologia I. 6.   [4] *Acts of Justin*, II.

type of spiritual worship which was clearly linked up with their priestly destiny.

But if the Christians were not atheists or idolators, neither were the Jews. In what sense did their worship differ from that of the Jews? It differed in that they worshipped God through His Son. There were those who believed that Jesus was only a man and not the Son of God but Justin would not countenance such false notions:

> There are some of our race who confess that He is Christ, while holding that He is man of men; with whom I do not agree, nor would the majority of those who hold the same opinions as myself, say so; since we have been bidden by Christ Himself to put no faith in human doctrines, but in those proclaimed by the blessed prophets and taught by Himself.[1]

It was for this reason that the Christian Church had to separate itself from Judaism. In commenting on Psalm 45 Justin suggests that the king's daughter who is bidden to leave her father's house, is the Church.

> To those who believe in Him as being one soul and one synagogue and one church, the word of God speaks as to a daughter; that it thus addresses the church, which has sprung up from His name and partakes of His name (for we are all called Christians), is distinctly proclaimed in the following words which teach us to forget even our old ancestral customs, when they speak thus: Hearken, O daughter, and consider, and incline thine ear; forget also thine own people and thy father's house: so shall the king desire thy beauty: for He is thy Lord; and worship thou Him.[2]

The truth is that with the Christian religion there had appeared a new kind of worship which differed from that of both Pagan and Jew. They shall worship not in this mountain (like the Samaritans), nor in Jerusalem (like the Jews), 'But the hour cometh, and now is, when the true worshippers shall worship the Father in spirit and truth; for such doth the Father seek to be His worshippers.' (John iv. 23). The priests of God are to bring all mankind to a knowledge of the true God and to an understanding of true, spiritual worship; this is the paramount task of the high-priestly race.

3. *A high-priestly race by their unique mission*

The unique mission of the Church is stated simply and beautifully by Justin: 'By the will of God He became man, and gave us this

[1] Trypho, ch. 48.   [2] Trypho, ch. 63.

teaching for the conversion and restoration of mankind'.[1] The people of God received their universal commission from Christ Himself:

> In these Books of the Prophets we find announced as coming, one born of a Virgin, and growing to manhood—Jesus our Christ, and dying and rising again, and ascending into heaven, both being, and being called, Son of God; and certain sent by Him to every race of men to preach these things, and its being the men from the Gentiles rather, who believe in Him.[2]

Justin believes that the Universal Priesthood *is* the fulfilment of the destiny which the old Israel refused:

> When as prophesying those things which are to happen the prophetic Spirit says this, 'Out of Zion shall go forth a law, and a word of the Lord from Jerusalem'—even so it has come to pass, as you can be persuaded. For from Jerusalem there did go out men, twelve in number, into the world, and these unlearned, and with no ability in speech. And in the power of God they proclaimed to every race of men that they were sent by the Christ to teach to all the word of God. And we who formerly used to kill one another, not only do not make war on our enemies, but, rather than lie and deceive our inquisitors, willingly die confessing the Christ.[3]

If, in the fulfilment of their unique mission, the Christians were called upon to make the offering of their lives, they faced this with faith and courage, being assured that this also was part of their priestly calling and destiny. Truly, they were a priestly race, as Justin says; priestly in their unique election, in their unique worship and in their unique mission.

The Priestly Nature of the Church

IRENAEUS 125–202

(a) The Church is priestly because of the priestly character of all her members

The sacerdotal views of Irenaeus embraced the whole Church and were not confined to the Episcopacy alone. He ascribes to the Church a priestly character, transferring to the Christian dispensation the priestly terms which are used in the Old Testament of

---

[1] Apologia I. 23.   [2] Apologia I. 31.   [3] Apologia I. 39.

Judaism. He does not envisage any notion of a mechanical succession but proclaims a priesthood of all just men. Commenting on his view Lightfoot says:

> He recognizes only the priesthood of moral holiness, the priesthood of apostolic self-denial. Thus commenting on the reference made by our Lord to the incident in David's life where the king and his followers eat the shew-bread, 'which it is not lawful to eat save for the priests alone,' Irenaeus remarks, 'He excuseth His disciples by the words of the law, and signifieth that it is lawful for priests to act freely. For David had been called to be a priest in the sight of God, although Saul carried on a persecution against him; for all just men belong to the sacerdotal order.'[1]

Ignatius (martyred c. 110) had already emphasized the same truth, and in one sentence refers to the members of the Church as stewards, sons and servants. 'Labour together with one another. As stewards of God, and as sons of His household, and His servants, please Him and serve Him, that ye may receive from Him the wages promised.'[2] On the strength of the evidence from Irenaeus and Ignatius, the following comment is justified: 'It is important to notice that this sacerdotal character belongs to the entire Church. All members of the Church, as such, stand in a direct relation to God and exercise a priesthood.'[3] If, as these Early Fathers declare, all Christians are stewards of God's grace, servants of the divine will, and sons of God's household, we may indeed confirm their verdict that 'all just men belong to the sacerdotal order'.

(b) *The Church is priestly because God bestows spiritual gifts upon all members*

Those who are truly His disciples receive grace from Him and put this grace into action for the benefit of other men, as each has received gifts from Him. Some drive out devils . . . some have foreknowledge of the future . . . others heal the sick through the laying on of hands . . . and even the dead have been raised up before now and have remained with us for many years. Why, there is no numbering of the gifts which all over the world the Church has received from the Lord, and put into action day by day in the name of Christ Jesus. For as the Church has received freely from the Lord, so it freely serves mankind.[4]

[1] R. H. Lightfoot, *Epistle to the Philippians*, p. 252. (He quotes 'Against Heresies' IV. 8.) [2] The Epistle to Polycarp, VI.
[3] J. C. V. Durell, *The Historic Church*, pp. 41–2.
[4] Against Heresies II. 32.

These spiritual gifts are bestowed upon Christians so that they may effectively serve mankind. It is clear that the salvation of the world partly depends upon the continued exercise of such gifts. In this consists the priesthood of all Christians. This view is exemplified in the epistle to Diognetus which refers to the 'high rank' to which God has appointed His people and from which there is no exemption.

> In general, we may say that Christians are in the world what the soul is to the body. The soul inhabits the body but does not belong to the body. Christians inhabit the world but do not belong to the world. The soul is locked up in the body, but it sustains the body. Christians are detained as it were in the custody of the world: but they sustain the world. This is the high rank to which God has appointed them; and it is not permitted to seek exemption.[1]

There is no higher rank as there is no greater responsibility, and to it all the people of God are called.

(c) *The Church is priestly because spiritual sacrifices are offered by all*

It is important to notice that in the teaching of Irenaeus the priesthood of the Church is always closely connected with the priesthood of the glorified Lord. In referring to the vision of St John he regards the seven-branched candlestick as figuring the Church, 'which carries the light of Christ'.[2] Christ stands in the midst of the Church as its great High Priest. Yet even here the Church is seen as the light bearer, with Christ as the unifying Centre and directing Authority.

Yet the Church can reveal and proclaim the High Priesthood of Christ only if she is identified with His central sacrificial action. Irenaeus made this his favourite theme. Of our Lord he says, 'When He was incarnate and made man, He recapitulated (or summed up) in Himself the long line of the human race, procuring for us salvation thus summarily, so that what we had lost in Adam, that is, the being in the image and likeness of God, that we should regain in Christ Jesus'.[3] The restoration of all mankind is made possible by His sufferings and death. It is because He has freed us from our sins by His life-blood that we are made a royal house, to serve as priests to God His Father.

The sacrifices of the Church have meaning only in the light of

---

[1] Epistle to Diognetus VI.   [2] Against Heresies V. 20.
[3] Ibid. III. 18.

His Sacrifice. In her priestly capacity the Church offers the sacrifice of prayer, of thanksgiving, and the sacrifice of the bread and wine. Irenaeus exhorts men to offer their prayers at the altar frequently and without intermission. But he usually reserves the word 'altar' for the spiritual altar in heaven. 'In every place incense is offered unto me and a pure sacrifice. But the incense, saith John in the Apocalypse, means "the prayers of the saints".'[1]

This sacrifice of prayer has nothing to do with the magical pretensions of the Gnostics: 'Nor does the Church do anything by angelic invocations, nor incantations, nor other perverse meddling. It directs prayer in a manner clean, pure and open, to the Lord who made all things, and calls upon the name of our Lord Jesus Christ.'[2]

It is the duty of Christians to offer a sacrifice of thanksgiving. Jews may not offer this sacrifice because they have not received the Word through Whom it is offered to God. Heretics may not offer it for they do not recognize that all blessings proceed from the Father. Christians offer the sacrifice of thanksgiving to God through Christ, and as they have received the blessings of freedom, they owe a greater debt of gratitude to God. 'We are bound to make our oblation to God and thus to show ourselves in all things grateful to Him as our Creator. . . . And it is only the Church which offers a pure oblation to the Creator, presenting an offering from His creation, with thanksgiving.'[3]

The sacrifice of the bread and wine is offered by the whole Church, and Irenaeus does not make any mention, in this connexion, of the Christian ministry. The priestly action of the whole Church is emphasized throughout.

> From all this (i.e. the prophetic denunciation of sacrificial cults) it is clear that what God required of them for their salvation was not sacrifices and holocausts, but faith, obedience and righteousness. . . . And our Lord also counselled His disciples to offer to God the firstfruits of His creatures, not because He needed these gifts, but so that they should not be unfruitful nor unthankful. This He did, when He took bread, of the natural creation, and gave thanks and said, 'This is My body.'[4]

In such ways Irenaeus expounds the meaning of the priestly nature of the Church. His strong emphasis upon episcopal succession

[1] Ibid. IV. 17. [2] Ibid. II. 32.
[3] Ibid. IV. 18. [4] Ibid. IV. 17.

did not prevent him from holding the views here stated. His basic concept is that of the priestly nature of the Church, for without this assumption no particular form of priesthood is possible. If the whole Church is priestly, it is necessary to attach a priestly character to the Apostles. Thus Irenaeus says, 'All the Apostles of the Lord are priests. They inherit neither fields nor houses, but ever serve the altar and God.'[1]

At the same time it is essential to draw attention to two modifications in the teaching of Irenaeus so as to see his teaching on succession in its true perspective. First, the divine charismata are bestowed upon all members of the Church and are not confined to the Apostles. On this point Irenaeus is explicit, 'There is no numbering of the gifts which all over the world the Church has received from the Lord.' Second, according to Irenaeus episcopal succession is a means whereby the transmission of apostolic tradition is guaranteed. The purity of doctrine is preserved by succession. This was the simple interpretation of succession; the elaborate theory of lineal succession came later. It is significant that scripture does not say that the faith was committed to the apostles only, but refers to 'the faith which was once for all delivered unto *the saints*' (Jude ver. 3), and this clearly means 'believers'. Whatever interpretation we give to Irenaeus' theory of succession, we must certainly place it against the background of his teaching on the universal priesthood. The Church never lost sight of this fundamental emphasis. Even two hundred years after Irenaeus, and in spite of the strength of Cyprianic teaching, the doctrine emerges again in the teaching of Narsai[2] in unambiguous terms: 'In another order it is the type of that kingdom which our Lord entered and into which He will bring with Him all His friends. The adorable altar thereof is a symbol of watchers and men in the clear day of His judgment.'[3] At the consummation of all things our Lord is envisaged as the Priest standing in the midst of His friends before the adorable altar. From this sublime conception it is a short step to Narsai's plain and bold declaration: 'Instead of the People He called all people to be His . . To this end He gave the priesthood to the new priests.'[4]

[1] Against Heresies IV. 8.
[2] Narsai was the Nestorian head of the Syrian School at Edessa (437–57.)
[3] R. H. Connolly, ed., 'The Liturgical Homilies', *Texts and Studies*, VIII, No. 1, p. 45.
[4] Ibid., p. 63.

The Priestly Succession of all True Believers

CLEMENT OF ALEXANDRIA 150–216

In the sphere of theology Clement of Alexandria was a pioneer. He it was who first realized that Christianity must face and answer the questions raised by the secular philosophies of his age. He read the signs of the times and saw the absolute necessity of applying the Christian message to the world of philosophy. He first grasped the fact that the *hope* of the conversion of the Gentiles was not enough, it was necessary to convince them of the truth of the Christian Faith. Clement's distinction is that he opened the door of Christianity to the cultured Greek, and this he was well-equipped to do, for as Hort says, 'There is no one whose vision of what the faith of Jesus Christ was intended to do for mankind was so full or so true.'[1] The introduction of the cultured Greek to Christianity had far-reaching consequences: it led to the expansion of Christian thought throughout the pagan world. Clement was always on the look-out to further this cause, and his liberal approach to his task is revealed by the fact that his pupils were drawn from both the pagan and Christian communities. His aims as well as his teaching were original. These aims were as follows:

(*a*) To train all his pupils for Christian living.
(*b*) To show them that the secret of Christian living lay in the possession of true knowledge.
(*c*) To teach them that in the life of the ideal Christian perfect love and true knowledge are combined.

Certain fundamental truths stand out clearly in his teaching, and as these have a direct bearing on our theme, we must consider them here.

1. Writing on the downward and upward movement of salvation Clement pictures the love of God reaching out to man, and man in turn returning to God through the great High Priest.

> I suppose that from the supreme power comes that careful examination which is applied to all the parts, down to the very smallest; to all the parts till we reach the supreme controller of the whole universe who governs all things according to the Father's will; while all beings,

[1] F. J. A. Hort, *Six lectures on the Ante-Nicene Fathers*, p. 93.

rank on rank in order, behold the universal salvation; until we arrive at the great High Priest.[1]

It is noteworthy that Clement parts company with the non-Christian gnostics when he insists upon the sole mediatorship of Christ, the High Priest, through whom is brought not only salvation to men but universal cosmic redemption.

2. Clement often drew a parallel between the celestial and ecclesiastical hierarchy and refers to clerics as God's ministering angels. The presbyters were said to render 'meliorative' services which included healing for the body and guidance for the soul, while the deacons rendered 'ministrative' services on behalf of society at large. This leads to a surprising development in his teaching, for while holding to the conception of a hierarchical clericalism he does not hesitate to place the true spiritual gnostic on the same level as the cleric. 'As both these services (meliorative and ministrative) are performed by the ministering angels for God in their ministration of earthly things, so they are also performed by the gnostic himself.'[2] From this he moves on to the idea of a spiritual Israel in which holiness of character qualifies for office. These spiritual qualifications give the Christian gnostic clerical honour, if not all the clerical functions.

> He, then, who has first moderated his passions and trained himself for impassibility, and developed to the beneficence of gnostic perfection, is here equal to the angels. Those who have exercised themselves in the Lord's commandments and lived perfectly and gnostically according to the Gospel may be enrolled in the chosen body of the apostles. Such a one is in reality a presbyter of the Church and a true deacon of the will of God, if he do and teach what is the Lord's, not as being ordained, nor regarded as righteous because a presbyter, but enrolled in the presbyterate because righteous. And although here upon earth he be not honoured with the chief seat, he will sit down on the four-and-twenty thrones, judging the people, as John says in the Apocalypse.[3]

3. Those who have received the gnosis direct from the Master and are obedient to His commands are the 'true priests'. Such men are enrolled in the chosen body of the apostles in every age. This is far from the Cyprianic idea which envisages a succession *from* the

---

[1] Strom. VII. 2. [2] Strom. VII. 1.
[3] Strom. VI. 13.

apostles. Clement is obviously thinking of a succession *of* apostolic men in every age. No wonder Professor Lindsay says:

> The great Alexandrian conceives the continuity of the Church to exist in the succession of Christian generations, and to be made evident by the appearance among them from time to time of saintly men of apostolic character who are known to God, and whose supreme importance in preserving the true character of Christianity will be revealed in the future. This he deems to be a much better guarantee than a succession of office-bearers, chosen and ordained by fallible men.[1]

This gives rise to a richer conception of the Church for the One Body is present not only in every age but in every Christian society, and all the spiritual actions of the smallest community—Prayer, Preaching, Baptism, the Holy Supper—are actions of the whole Church. The whole Church of the redeemed, with Christ and His angels, is present in the public worship of the individual congregation.

4. This spiritual priesthood offers a sacrifice of prayer, for Old Testament sacrifices are spiritualized by Clement as follows:

> And that compounded incense which is sanctioned by the Law, is that which consists of many tongues and voices in prayer ... brought together in praises with a pure mind, and just the right conduct, from holy works and righteous prayer. For the sacrifice of the Church is the word breathing as incense from holy souls, the sacrifice and the whole mind at the same time unveiled to God.[2]

By his emphasis upon the universal appeal of the Gospel; upon the spiritual priesthood of those who possessed the gnosis; upon the succession of men of apostolic character; as well as upon the spiritual sacrifices which are offered by the Church, Clement undoubtedly gives an impression of the priesthood of all believers as it was then understood. In this respect, as in the case of other doctrines, Origen developed the work of Clement. But before considering Origen's work we must turn to an examination of the writings of Tertullian.

Universal Priesthood and the Responsibilities of the Laity
TERTULLIAN (155-222)
1. *A Community of Spiritual Men*

The words of Jesus to Peter: 'I will build my Church,' were, according to Tertullian, spoken to Peter because he was a man

[1] Lindsay, op. cit., p. 283.   [2] Strom. VII. 6.

devoted to Christ. This fact furnishes Tertullian with his Montanist view that the Church is composed of spiritual men. 'For,' he says, 'in accordance with the person of Peter, it is to spiritual men that this power will correspondingly appertain, either to an apostle or to a prophet.'
This view had important consequences for Tertullian's theology.

> Thus he is led to state his view that the Church itself is really the Spirit Himself, 'in whom is the Trinity of the one divinity', Father, Son and Holy Spirit. Wherever a number of persons have combined together in this faith they constitute a Church. This Church will forgive sins, but it will not be the Church which consists of a number of bishops, but that which consists of spiritual men.[1]

It follows that ordination and succession from the apostles could not be regarded as the authority of the true priest. The direct visitation of the Holy Spirit alone qualified a Christian to be a prophet or teacher or minister. The growing distinction bteween the clergy and laity was rejected by Tertullian on the ground that the priesthood was as universal as the Holy Spirit.

Tertullian avers that the true priests are those who, being spiritual, offer to God the spiritual sacrifice of prayer.

> What, then, God has required the Gospel teaches, 'An hour will come,' saith He, 'when the true adorers shall adore the Father in Spirit and truth. For God is a Spirit, and accordingly requires his adorers to be such.' We are the true adorers and the true priests, praying in spirit, sacrifice, in spirit, prayer—a victim proper and acceptable to God, which assuredly He has required, which He has looked forward to for Himself. This victim, devoted from the whole heart, fed on faith, tended by truth, entire in innocence, pure in chastity, garlanded with love, we ought to escort with the pomp of good works, amid psalms and hymns, unto God's altar, to obtain for us all things from God.[2]

2. *Universal Priesthood and Discipline*

If the true Church is composed of spiritual men, and if their sacrifice is the spiritual sacrifice of prayer, if, in fact, they exercise a spiritual priesthood, they should also be content to abide by those rules of discipline which apply to priests. In short, priestly privilege involves

---
[1] R. E. Roberts, *The Theology of Tertullian*, p. 186.
[2] An Exhortation on Prayer, 28.

priestly discipline. 'We should be wrong,' he writes, when arguing against second marriages, 'to suppose that a latitude is allowed to laymen which is denied to priests. Are not we laymen also priests?'[1]

Tertullian affirms that it is seemly that Baptism, for instance, should be performed by the 'president of the brethren' or by the deacons, but in cases of necessity the layman may perform it, 'for what has been equally received may be equally given'. But whilst recognizing the position of 'the Order', Tertullian does not equate it with the Church, for laymen alone, without the Order, may consitutute the Church.

> The difference between the Order and the people is due to the authority of the Church and the consecration of their rank by the reservation of a special bench of clergy for the order. Thus where there is no bench of clergy you offer and baptize and are your own sole priest. For where there are three, there is the Church, though they be laymen. Therefore, if you have the *rights* of a priest in your own person when necessity arises, you ought likewise to have the *discipline* of a priest, when it is necessary to exercise his rights.[2]

On the other hand, there is no doubt that some of the laity in Tertullian's day had claimed the privilege of priesthood only when it was convenient to them and rejected it as soon as the accompanying discipline became irksome. These he addresses with considerable irony, 'When we begin to exalt and inflame ourselves against the clergy, then we are all one; then we are all priests; but when we are required to submit ourselves equally to the priestly discipline, we throw off our fillets and are no longer equal.'

It will not do to disregard the testimony of Tertullian on the ground that he became a Montanist. It should always be remembered that the Montanists were not driven out but separated themselves from the main body of the Church. They were condemned as heretics *after* they had seceded, not before. It was not likely that the orthodox party would appreciate some of Tertullian's statements such as 'The Holy Spirit is the only prelate, because He alone succeeds Christ.' The truth is that the doctrine of the universal priesthood was not a Montanist monopoly, it was deeply rooted in the teaching of many of the Early Fathers.

[1] An Exhortation on Chastity, 7.
[2] Ibid., 7.

The Meaning of Spiritual Priesthood
ORIGEN (185-254)

In order to understand Origen's views on priesthood it is necessary to examine the general trend of his teaching.[1] The first thing to notice is that in Origen's view the redemptive work of Christ is not confined to any stereotyped form: sometimes it means 'redemption from evil', and sometimes 'enlightenment'. It is generally when Origen is thinking of redemption in the latter sense that he links it with the idea of spiritual priesthood.

1. *The Restoration of Man to God*

There is one sublime truth which dominates the thought of Origen: it is that in some way or other man *must* be brought back to God. Salvation equals the restoration of fallen spirits to their original oneness with God. There is a need for direct communion with God and this is possible only when man appears before Christ. In Origen's teaching the ideal is to live in God, and he delights in Jesus as the One who reveals the splendours that are hid in God. Jesus is 'the Uniter with the Father', and Origen assumes that all men must enter into the presence of God. Yet not all can do this in the same way or in the same period of time. Nor can it be done apart from Jesus. The cosmos and mankind cannot exist apart from the presence and influence of Jesus. How does our Lord do His work?

(*a*) To every living soul He transmits life.
(*b*) To every believer He is the up-flowing spring of immortality.
(*c*) To the chosen few He imparts the supreme knowledge (the transcendent Gnosis).

In this sense Jesus is the efficacious instrument for the return to God.

Origen's doctrine was determined by the principle that the end should resemble the beginning—i.e. it should be a restoration. One of the purposes of the mission of Jesus is to be the Instructor of men. The outstanding characteristic of a serious education is that it will succeed even in the most difficult cases. Origen believed that Jesus

---

[1] See McGiffert, *History of Christian Thought*, ch. XI, 'Origen'; Fairweather, *Origen and Greek Patristic Theology*, ch. VIII; Eugene de Faye, *Origen and his Work*, ch. V.

would surely succeed in bringing men back to God. Indeed there was no other way in which this could be done. The fundamental *truth* underlying Origen's theology is that man alone is incapable of approaching God. As he says: 'Although man could not rise, God could stoop. By this He taught man the art of free obedience. The Word has brought redemption and eternal blessedness according to the measure of acceptance. It is much more Christ's blood than our faith which justifies.'[1]

There were three classes of Christians:—

(a) Those who were σάρξ (carnal)
(b) Those who possessed the σοφία (wisdom)
(c) Those who possessed the γνῶσις. (These were spiritually advanced.)

It is only those who have reached this advanced stage and possess the gnosis who may go 'straight to the Father'. The others have no such privilege. In the light of this it will be noted that Origen regarded spiritual enlightenment and not sacerdotal office as the Christian counterpart to the Aaronic priesthood. Those who have received this spiritual enlightenment are priests unto God.

2. *The privileges of the Universal Priesthood*

> You have heard of the two sanctuaries: one as it were visible and open to the priests; the other invisible, to which the High Priest alone had access, while the rest remained outside. ... And pray do not marvel that this sanctuary is open only for priests. For all who have been anointed with the unction of the sacred chrism have been made priests.[2]

And because of this priesthood the members of the congregation have a share in ordination.

> For in the ordination of a priest the presence of the people is also required that all may know for certain that the man elected to the priesthood is of the whole people the most eminent, the most learned, the holiest, the most outstanding in every kind of virtue. And this must be done in the presence of the people to avoid any subsequent change of mind or lingering doubt.[3]

Also because of this priesthood they are committed to a worldwide task. Origen was the first to envisage a Christ-ruled world.

[1] Fairweather, op. cit., ch. VIII. [2] *Hom. in Leviticum* IX. 9.
[3] Ibid. VI. 3.

'Every religion will be overthrown except the religion of Christ which alone will prevail. And indeed it will one day triumph as its principles take possession of the minds of men more and more every day'.[1]

This task demands that they live and die like true priests of the Lord. In Origen's thought their sacrifices are closely related with the Sacrifice of our Lord: 'And at the same time we rejoice that as the high priest Jesus the Christ has offered the sacrifice of himself, the priests of whom he is high priest offer the sacrifice of themselves.'[2]

Those who have reached the third stage in Origen's classification and are in possession of the gnosis are even named 'high priests'. But there are often subtle dangers in high privileges and Origen warns his hearers: 'The Apostles and those who are like the Apostles, being priests after the fashion of the great high priest, who have gained knowledge of the service of God; all these know, through the instruction of the Spirit, what are the sins for which one should offer sacrifice . . . and what sins admit of no sacrifice.'[3] And Origen does not hesitate to rebuke those who arrogate to themselves priestly rights without taking the trouble to attain priestly knowledge.

Although the possession of the gnosis was the final stage in spiritual development, Origen was quite sure that this experience could be attained by all. Yet this could only be effected if the Church fulfilled her true function. The function of the Church as the universal priesthood was 'ministering to the salvation of men everywhere', and he sums up the world-wide mission of the Church in the following words:

> If anyone desires to see many bodies filled with a divine Spirit, ministering to the salvation of men everywhere, in a spirit like Christ's, let him take notice of those who preach the Gospel of Jesus in all lands. Christ is the Head of the Church, so that Christ and the Church form one Body. From the Head to the very hem of the garment there is something of Christ.[4]

We may therefore summarize Origen's teaching on the gnosis in the three great truths which he emphasized: Christians are priests insofar as they possess the gnosis—the means of spiritual enlightenment, insofar also as they offer spiritual sacrifices including the

[1] Contra Celsum VIII, 68.
[2] Exhortation to Martyrdom, 30.
[3] De Oratione, p. 28.
[4] Contra Celsum VI, 79.

sacrifice of self, and as they share the universal ministry of their Lord.

But even when he is not thinking specifically of the gnosis, Origen still emphasizes the doctrine of the universal priesthood:

(a) *The priestly character of the believer*

Those who are despised as ignorant fools and no better than slaves, no sooner commit themselves to God's direction by accepting the teaching of Jesus, than, forsaking their sins, many of them, like perfect priests for whom such pleasures have no charm, keep themselves pure in act and thought. The Athenians had one priest who, not having confidence in his own power to restrain his passions, resolved to smother them at the seat by hemlock, but amongst the Christians are men who have no need of hemlock to fit them for the pure service of God, and for whom the Word, instead of the hemlock, is able to drive all evil desires from their thoughts.[1]

(b) *The priestly sacrifice of the believer*

The close connexion between the priesthood of Christ and that of all believers is clearly enunciated by Origen in the following passage:

Just as the High Priest, Jesus Christ, offered Himself in sacrifice, so the priests, whose high priest He is, offer themselves in sacrifice and therefore appear by the altar in their proper place. Those priests who are blameless and offer blameless sacrifices used to serve the worship of God; but those who were at fault as Moses set out in Leviticus, were banished from the altar. Who then is the blameless priest who offers a blameless offering other than he who holds fast the confession and fulfils every requirement made by the doctrine of martyrdom.[2]

(c) *The priestly sacrifice of the Church*

He has given instructions so that we may know how we may approach God's altar. For it is an altar upon which we offer our prayers to God. That we may know, then, how we ought to offer them, He bids us put aside our soiled garments—the uncleanness of the flesh, the faults of character, the defilements of lust. Or do you not recognize that the priesthood has been given to you also, that is to the whole Church of God and the nation of believers? (1 Pet. ii. 9). You have therefore a priesthood being a priestly nation. Therefore you ought to offer God a sacrifice of praise, of prayers, of pity, of purity, of righteousness, of holiness. To offer this aright you have need of clean garments, of

[1] Contra Celsum VII. 48. [2] Exhortation to Martyrdom, 30.

vestments kept apart from the common clothing of the rest of mankind; and you must have the divine fire, God's own fire which He gives to men, of which the Son of God says, 'I have come to send fire on earth.'[1]

According to Origen, then, Christians reveal their true priesthood in holiness of character, in the sacrifices which they offer in worship, and in their readiness to hold fast the confession even in the face of martyrdom.

CYPRIAN (195–258)
A New Interpretation of the Priesthood

This consideration of the views of the Early Fathers will show that the doctrine of the Universal Priesthood was by no means a fringe topic in theology but that it held an important place in their teaching. While no individual among the Early Fathers deals with the subject exhaustively, the cumulative evidence is very strong. We have noticed that the doctrine was related by the Fathers to a great variety of subjects, ten of which we have specified. The result of our investigation is that the doctrine of the Priesthood of all Believers is directly connected with the High Priesthood of Christ, the layman's ordinances, the authority of the whole congregation, the Eucharist, the offering of spiritual sacrifices, the conception of the Church as a High Priestly Race or the Priesthood of all Just Men, the unity of the Church, questions of discipline, the believer's access to the Father, and the Church's missionary task.

Two of these ten subjects are mentioned much more frequently than the others, and these are—the conception of the whole Church as a High Priestly Race, and the offering of spiritual sacrifices to God. The significance of this lies in the fact that the transition which took place under Cyprian was directly connected with these two ideas. As a difference in the idea of priesthood emerged, so also a different conception of sacrifice followed. Cyprian's view may be summed up in one sentence—he conceived that the bishops were a *special priesthood* and had a *special sacrifice to offer*. So the High Priestly Race gave place to a High Priestly Class, and the spiritual sacrifices gave place to an actual sacrifice offered to God in the Eucharist. That the latter was conceived of as something other than a purely spiritual sacrifice is beyond dispute. This transition can-

[1] Hom. in Leviticum IX. 1.

not be regarded as a slight deviation in the Church's teaching on priesthood, it is rather the antithesis of the interpretation which was prevalent in the first two centuries. Certain factors in the religious and political situation at that time made the transition relatively easy. It proved a far more difficult task to re-establish the original doctrine of priesthood.

(A) Reasons for the Transition under Cyprian

Since the earliest Christians were Jews, it was natural that they should interpret the New Testament in terms of the law and priesthood of the old covenant, and this is, in fact, what happened. It should be noted, however, that it was possible for New Testament writers to refer to law and priesthood without any sacrificial connotation, a practice which tended to disappear in the third century. Moreover, a priestless religion would be almost unintelligible to the Gentiles, for the Greek temples possessed their own hierarchy. Roman political organization also facilitated the transition. In a Roman province power was exercised by an imperator, and as Church and State became more closely identified, imperial rule became the pattern upon which ecclesiastical supervision was based. Indeed, it is asserted that every city which had a 'flamen' (a priest of some particular deity), to superintend the old State religion—the worship of Rome and Augustus—became the seat of a Christian bishop in the new State Church. So there is some evidence for Mommsen's contention that: 'the conquering Roman Church took its hierarchic weapons from the arsenal of the enemy.'[1]

The study of theology cannot be separated from a study of history, and if we take historical circumstances into consideration, as indeed we must, there is little room for doubt that the Cyprianic ideas of the Church were powerfully influenced by Greek and Jewish religious ideas on the one hand, and by Roman political organization on the other. That there was something providential in this development may also be admitted, for a firm and effective Church organization was demanded in order to withstand the pagan onslaughts of the Middle Ages. Effective Church organization has contributed not a little to the progress of the Christian religion. All the same, the whole system was fraught with grave dangers. It is easy to see in retrospect dangers which may not have been perceptible at the time.

[1] T. Mommsen, *Provinces of the Roman Empire*, Vol. I, p. 349.

The principal danger was the deification of unity in the religio-secular organization. Constantine, for instance, found nothing inconsistent in affirming that those who would not or could not conform to a particular Church organisation were excommunicate. Unity became the sole guarantee of continuity, so unity had to be defended at all costs. It became the avowed policy of the Church to destroy all movements which were outside the religio-secular organization, and the resultant intolerance and persecution is too well-known to require repetition. The Church had not only borrowed the ideas of the Roman State but had also used its methods.

In vain was it argued that the independent sects and movements might have been inspired by the Spirit, for the Spirit was conceived as operating only in accordance with a particular 'form'. This fallacy raises a further and more serious problem. Form now took precedence over content, and the result was that the message was forced into the strait-jacket of organization. It is surely Faith that must be decisive in matters of Order, and not Order which must determine Faith. It is in this context that the well-known formula of St Vincent of Lerins (450) is frequently misunderstood. He says: 'True orthodox teaching is that which is *believed* always, everywhere, and by all,' and the operative word is 'believed'. True doctrine does not exist independently of faith, for doctrine is something that is believed. Cyprian's claim, however, that the Church possessed *the* tradition meant that univerality of content as well as universality of form must be maintained. So there emerged an exclusive standard of doctrine as well as an exclusive form. Hence, an exclusive doctrine encased in an unalterable form emerged as the sole Catholic pattern, a pattern which, since Cyprian's day, has been known as 'Catholic Unity' and which has come to be regarded as the one thing needful.

(B) Cyprian and Church Government

If Catholic Unity was the one thing needful, it was necessary to make adequate provision for its preservation. In his teaching Cyprian entrusted this task to the bishop and to him alone. The bishop was the custodian of doctrine and the guardian of unity, and indeed the fulfilment of this twofold task was guaranteed because embodied in the person and office of the bishop.

(*a*) The bishop was appointed to ensure peace and unity in the life of the Church and to guard against schism. From the time of

Cyprian the bishop ruled the Christian community, controlled its finances, and presided at its worship. Originally the first and third of these functions were open to all Christians who had special gifts of 'charismata', but as Cyprian's ideas developed, power came to be invested in one officer—the bishop. Once the bishop's special functions were allowed, his possession of special powers inevitably followed. It was the bishop who introduced the people to the Church in Baptism; it was the bishop also who confirmed their Baptism by the laying on of hands; again, it was the bishop who brought the people into actual communion with Christ in the Eucharist, so that entrance into the Church as well as continuance in it were virtually dependent upon the bishop. The position is summed up by Cyprian himself, 'They are the Church who are a people united to the priest and the flock which adheres to their pastor . . . the bishop is in the Church, and the Church is in the bishop.'[1] It will be noticed that a new note has now been sounded, it is the *authority* of the priest. This note was to be sounded incessantly by Cyprian and those who succeeded him, and he never ceased to emphasize the fact that Israel's greatest sin consisted in refusing obedience to the Priest Samuel.

There was, however, another reason why the bishop assumed an important position. It was his responsibility to guard against heresy. We have noticed from our study of Clement of Rome that during the first century these matters were submitted to the whole congregation which was the supreme authority. The Corinthians were asked 'to do what is ordered by the people.' But this was now changed and the living centre of authoritative teaching became the bishop. The bishops were the guardians of orthodoxy because they were the successors of the apostles. Such ideas are not to be found in the works of any of the Apostolic Fathers we have mentioned, with the exception of Tertullian who did refer to the question of succession in his pre-Montanist days. Even so, for Tertullian, such ideas existed side by side with clear enunciations of the doctrine of an essential priesthood inherent in all Christians. Cyprian's view is different. By virtue of his authority the bishop alone possessed the credentials to define the truth of Christian teaching. This teaching had been handed down from the apostles, and the bishop was regarded as the sole guarantor of its validity. This is probably why

[1] Ep. lxvii. 8.

the early persecuting edicts were directed, not against the people in general, but against the bishop who had become the visible centre of the Christian Church.

(b) While it was the duty of the bishop to ensure the unity of the Church, and preserve the purity of her doctrine, it was also his duty to control her worship at its most vital point. With the idea of apostolic succession came the notion of the Ministry as a sacrificial order. Now one thing stands out very clearly in our study of the first two centuries, and that is that the idea of a sacrificial order was quite alien to the Church's teaching. But now the bishop had become the representative of Christ and the priest of God. This meant that he possessed the authority over his own congregation which our Lord possessed over the universal Church. It throws an interesting if disturbing light upon the problem when it is realized that the *nature* of the authority was the same, it was only the extent of it that differed. The bishop's authority was local, and Christ's universal.

We have already noticed that no less than six of the Early Fathers refer to Christians as the High Priestly Race, but Cyprian's interpretation of the Eucharist effectively obscured this idea of the universal priesthood. The bishop, being *the* priest, emerges with independent, exclusive and dominical powers, and it is in the service of the Eucharist that these powers are exercised. Three statements made by Cyprian were quite revolutionary even though they are unwarranted in Scripture. Even so, they are still regarded as authoritative by those who advocate the doctrine of a mediating priesthood.

1. Cyprian calls the Holy Supper the sacrament of the *sacrifice of the Lord*.
2. The power to offer this sacrifice resides in the bishop. 'The bishop does that which Jesus Christ our Lord and God, the founder and teacher of this sacrifice, did and taught' (Ep. lxiii. 62).
3. What is this sacrifice? Cyprian says, 'The Lord's passion is the sacrifice we offer.'

The revolutionary nature of these three propositions is self-evident. The first makes the unprecedented statement that the Holy Supper *is* a sacrifice; the second affirms that only the bishop has the power to offer it, and the third stipulates the *nature* of the sacrifice—it is no less than the Passion of our Lord. It is not surprising that these ideas, so ably expounded by Cyprian, persisted in the teaching of the Church; what is surprising is that they should persist until the time of Luther without any serious and forceful opposition. The advocates of a mediating priesthood have always appealed to Cyprian for support, and this is not to be wondered at, for his ideas inaugurated such a change in Christian thought as became significant for the whole of Christendom. Lindsay has noted its significance:

> If the whole people were priests, and if the main thought in priesthood was authority and supremacy in judging in all matters of rule and discipline, then the people, the congregation, were the rulers in the last resort. But this primitive conception did not suit the ideas which Cyprian, the Roman lawyer, had about the special omnipotence of the bishop ... His thought was that the bishop was *the* priest, and that the people were not priests but those whom the priest introduced into the presence of God. The whole conception of Christian thought began to change, and the change dates from Cyprian and his influence.[1]

We must now show how Cyprian came to the same conclusion but by a different route.

(C) *Cyprian and the Reclamation of Christians who had failed*

(a) *Reinstatement*

The unity of the Church, the purity of doctrine, and the regularity of worship, which were guaranteed and embodied in the office of the sacrificing priest were so important that it was unthinkable that anyone should be separated from them. Yet some had failed even after baptism. Here, then, was a dilemma which must be faced. What was to be done for those who had, by their sin, forfeited their privilege, and, by their penitence, sought to be reinstated. Novatian and his party pressed for the instant excommunication of the lapsed. A more lenient party desired to offer reinstatement on the strength of indulgence certificates received from the Confessors who had been afforded the right to issue such certificates on account of their suffering and imprisonment for the Faith. Actually, this party oversimplified the issue and made the question of re-admission altogether too easy. Cyprian adopted a middle course, maintaining that the Church should not deny reinstatement to those who were truly repentant. 'He can no longer have God for his Father, who has not the Church for his mother.'[2]

---

[1] T. M. Lindsay, *The Church and the Ministry in the Early Centuries*, p. 309.
[2] On the Unity of the Church, Treatise III. 6.

(b) Repentance

Cyprian held no shallow view of repentance and insisted that definite signs of sorrow for sin should be forthcoming from those who sought, a second time, the fellowship and blessing of the Church. The problem was a serious one and not easy of solution. It is one which is never out-dated, and has to be faced continually on the mission field:

> We are faced with the problem in several villages, of people who have been baptized for many years but who refuse to have anything to do with the Church. We are enforcing such discipline as we can against them but our Church discipline is naturally such that those who have little interest in the Church will feel it very little.[1]

On the other hand, there are those who recognize the enormity of their sin and are anxious to be reinstated. Richardson has shown how important was this matter to the early Christians: 'The idea, so familiar to us, that joining the Church is of little ultimate significance and a kindly God will receive all decent-living people into His care no matter how little they trouble about their faith, never entered the mind of the Early Church.'[2] If they adopted stringent conditions and heavy penances, we may assume that this was done in the best interests of the Church. But here we must make a distinction between the beginnings of this system and its ultimate developments. There was little that was harmful and much that was helpful in the intention behind the system of discipline as it was *originally* applied. There was, of course, the possibility of abuse in such a system, and, in fact, the subsequent abuses far outweighed the scheme's original usefulness. It led to the whole indulgence system of the Middle Ages, where the satisfaction of the Church's discipline became identified with the satisfaction rendered to God. But if it was possible to render satisfaction to God for sins already committed, what was there to prevent a believer storing up merit against the sins that he may conceivably commit in the future? Perhaps it would be possible for him to secure the eternal welfare of his own soul by the same system of penance and good works which had availed for his past sins. It seemed logical and reasonable enough, but in fact, when the Church adopted it, it was a fateful step. From

---
[1] *South India Report*, 1947, p. 126.
[2] C. C. Richardson, *The Church through the Centuries*, p. 43.

this notion it was a short step to the idea of a 'treasury of merit' which became the bane of medieval religion. The whole idea presupposes many difficult questions which Cyprian chose to answer far too easily. Who is to impose the satisfactions? Who is to say that the satisfactions rendered are commensurable with the sins committed? Who is to take the awful responsibility of pronouncing absolution? To these searching questions Cyprian gave but one answer and never deviated from it. He stated that this remarkable power belonged solely to the bishop, the priest of God. 'They only who are set over the Church... can remit sins.'

(D) *The eclipse of the doctrine of the universal priesthood*

To draw attention to a specific development in sacerdotal theory is not to say that such a development was envisaged or intended by the early exponents of it. Nevertheless, the soil had been very well prepared, and wittingly or unwittingly, this fact enabled the plant of sacerdotalism to thrive for a thousand years. There were two incipient factors in the Cyprianic doctrine; first, the eclipse of the idea of the universal priesthood, and second, the rise of the Roman doctrine of the Papacy. It is true that at first Cyprian[1] consulted the laity on questions of discipline, but when he doubted whether he would receive their support, he turned for support to the neighbouring bishops and never consulted the laity again. Thus the concept of the universal priesthood, whose privileges, responsibilities and duties were so highly treasured by the first two centuries, vanished at the first Council of Carthage and was not revived by the Church until the appearance of Martin Luther in the sixteenth century.

The second factor is equally important. The eclipse of the doctrine of the universal priesthood left the way open for a further significant development. The supreme authority of the bishop in the local Church presupposed the possibility of a supreme authority over the universal Church. So the passing of the universal priesthood, resulted ultimately, perhaps inevitably, in the sole priesthood of one man whose powers were immeasurable, whose position was unchallengeable, and whose words were infallible. History takes account not of the intention but of the result, and Lindsay's conclusion is justified: 'Men who insist on an episcopal gift of grace, "specific, exclusive, efficient", coming from a higher source than

[1] See Ep. x. 1.

the Holy Spirit working in and through the membership of the Church, may protest against the thought that their theories lead to a conception of a "bishop of bishops", but the unsparing logic of history sweeps their protests aside.'[1]

The transition in the meaning of priesthood is one of the important landmarks in the history of the Church. As Dr Workman puts it: 'No step more momentous for good or ill has ever been taken by the Christian Church than its adoption of the sacerdotal and hierarchical idea.'[2] Even those who claim for the views of Cyprian the primitive authority of Christ would not deny that the exemplification of his ideas in the indulgence system of the Middle Ages was not always helpful and sometimes definitely harmful to the witness of the Church.

Protestants have always regarded this subject as embodying the very heart of their protest. But the word 'protest' does not possess merely a negative meaning; it represents less a remonstrance than a declaration. It is a mistake to think of it simply as the setting forth of rival truths. Protestants view the Reformation as an affirmation of religious truth which involves a revolution in religious values. This is the idea which underlies Kenneth Hamilton's words:

> It is noteworthy that the Reformation began with a challenge to the values, both theoretical and practical, of the dominant party. Luther attacked the authority of Rome by his crusade against indulgences, but equally by his theological innovations; the two were opposite sides of the same coin. Once the institutional prestige of Rome had been proved vulnerable, the field was open for alternative values to be championed.[3]

The Reformers considered that religious values had been misplaced and misinterpreted, and they did not understand their task as instituting new values but as setting in their true focus the old. Nor did the Reformers consider their movement to be a disruption of continuity. On the contrary, they firmly believed that they were responsible for maintaining the faith and doctrine of the earliest times. This may be because their view of continuity is not in accordance with the Catholic pattern. Dr Visser'T Hooft puts the Protestant case as follows:

> If there is any continuity in the life of the Christian and in the life of the Church, it is not a continuity in time and space but a continuity

[1] T. M. Lindsay, op. cit., p. 319.
[2] H. B. Workman, *Christian Thought to the Reformation*, p. 107.
[3] K. Hamilton, *The Protestant Way*, p. 22.

of God's creative action. They (Protestants) cannot see the action of Luther as an arbitrary break-away from a sacred tradition, for to them it represents the restoration of a deeper and invisible continuity in faith.[1]

The doctrine of the Royal Priesthood of the Faithful had suffered eclipse not extinction, and it survived in spite of Cyprianic Teaching. Indeed it should be recorded that it was still a living issue in the fourth century. Even John Chrysostom (345–407) whose writings frequently emphasize the high calling and dignity of the ordained priesthood does not hesitate to recognize the evangelistic obligation which is placed upon all members of the royal priesthood.

Ought not every Christian landowner to build a church, and to make it his aim before all things else that his people should be Christian? ... Nothing can be more chilling than the sight of a Christian who makes no effort to save others. Neither poverty, nor humble station, nor bodily infirmity, can exempt men and women from this great duty. To hide our Christian light under pretence of weakness is as great an insult to God as we were to say that He could not make His sun to shine. Every house should be a church, and every father of a family a priest over his household, responsible for the welfare of all its members, even of the slaves, whom indeed the Gospel places in their relation to God on the same level with their owners.[2]

It was, however, the theory of the special priesthood which developed until it had become so firmly established in the Middle Ages that it became a part, perhaps the principal part, of the whole structure of life—social, political, as well as religious. The powerful instrument which was wielded by the priesthood was the granting and withholding of Indulgences, the purchase of which was supposed to impart peace of mind, but in fact, they left the believer in a state of perpetual uncertainty concerning his eternal salvation. If inward assurance had been possible, Indulgences would have become redundant. Even the possibility of salvation was a speculative affair, and the offer of temporal forgiveness was human-controlled. It is just this idea which Protestants have always felt impelled to resist. But even so stout a defender of Roman Catholic doctrine as Karl Adam admits that: 'the historical form of the Indulgence has undergone some change,' and 'the theology of Indulgences has only been gradually elaborated'.[3] It is doubtful however whether Roman theologians have ever faced the full implications of a theology of

[1] V. 'T Hooft, *Anglo-Catholicism and Orthodoxy*, p. 172.
[2] Homily on the Acts of the Apostles, XVIII.
[3] Karl Adam, *The Spirit of Catholicism*, p. 121.

Indulgences. What exactly is the underlying truth? Richardson's observation may help here:

> What was deplorable about the Inquisition was not its cruelty, in which it was the child of its age, so much as its presumptuous identification of the Roman hierarchy and decrees with the perfect expression of God's will upon earth. It gives us in the most vivid and dramatic form the dreadful consequences of elevating that which is human to the sphere of the divine, and confusing the judgment of man with the judgment of God.[1]

It was the arrogant assumption that the Roman hierarchy equalled the Divine Will, that hierarchical authority was to be identified with dominical authority, that the hierarchy had the power to control and dispense the favour of God; it was these assumptions which have always been unacceptable to Protestants. From time to time voices were raised within Catholicism against the ascription of such powers to the hierarchy: there were the Waldenses, the Cathari, the Lollards, the 'Friends of God' and others, but their protests were sporadic and localized, although by no means ineffectual. The circumstances demanded a theologian, an orator, and a dynamic leader, and the Church waited until the sixteenth century before the appearance of a man in whom these three qualities were combined. The faint notes of protest of the previous centuries now sounded forth like a trumpet at dawn. Martin Luther challenged the position of the hierarchy on the basis of Biblical theology. God had chosen a fearless instrument to put forward an invincible argument.

History is an impartial witness; and the witness of history is that as the idea of the universal priesthood receded, the indulgence system, the absolute priestly authority, the frenzied resort to 'good works', the soul-destroying Interdicts, and the perils of the Inquisition, unquestionably increased. It is little wonder, then, that the foundation theme of Luther's theology was the doctrine of Justification by Faith alone, and its inevitable corollary—the Priesthood of all Believers. These doctrines which are firmly based in the Scriptures, and which were emphasized in the first and second centuries, Luther rediscovered. He was the reactionary: it was Cyprian who was the innovator. And although the doctrine of the universal priesthood suffered a serious setback, it was never entirely obscured, as we shall see.

[1] C. C. Richardson, op. cit., p. 127.

CHAPTER FOUR

SAINT AUGUSTINE (354-430)

BAPTISM: INITIATION TO THE SPIRITUAL PRIESTHOOD

A TREATISE written in the fifth century and attributed to 'Dionysius the Areopagite' affirms that men are brought into Fellowship with God in three ways, namely, by means of cleansing, illuminating and perfecting. These three ways were symbolized by various ceremonies which took place at Baptism which, at that time, was known as a 'Priestly Consecration'. There were three Sacraments generally applicable to mankind: Baptism, Communion, and the consecration and use of Chrism. It appears that these Sacraments formed part of one ceremony as far as adults were concerned, Communion following immediately the Sacraments of Baptism and Confirmation. If we explain them separately, we must not overlook the fact that originally they were closely connected.

In considering the theology of St Augustine we must first take notice of his teaching on Baptism. Baptism conveys three blessings: forgiveness of sins, incorporation as members of Christ, and the communication of the Holy Ghost. Augustine recognized that Baptism had no magical power of instantaneously creating a well-instructed, fully developed Christian, but he also recognized that forgiveness of sins was the distinctive beginning as well as the inalienable requirement of the Christian life. Forgiveness produces a real deliverance and not an imaginary one. Sin is an infirmity, and deliverance comes when the cause of the infirmity as well as the infirmity itself are removed.

> Certainly this renewal does not take place in a single moment of itself, as that renewal in Baptism takes place by the remission of sins; for not one, be it ever so small, remains unremitted. But as it is one thing to be freed from a fever and another to grow strong again from the infirmity which the fever produced, and again one thing to pluck out of the body a weapon thrust into it and another to heal the wound thereby made by a prosperous cure, so the first care is to remove the

cause of the infirmity, and that is wrought by the forgiving of all sins: but the second care is to heal the infirmity itself, and this takes place gradually by making progress in the renewal of the image, which two things are plainly shown in the Psalm where we read, 'Who forgiveth thine iniquities', which takes place in Baptism, and then follows, 'and healeth all thine infirmities', and this takes place by daily additions, while this image is being renewed.[1]

In this passage Augustine explains the negative and positive aspects of Baptism. It includes cleansing and healing, forgiveness and the consequent renewal of the divine image in man. To this action of divine grace the believer made his faith-response by the following symbolism. Turning his face towards the west, the candidate renounced Satan and all his pomp and service; then, facing the east, he vowed fidelity to Christ and confessed his faith in the Triune God by rehearsing the Creed. There followed the threefold immersion in the name of the Triune God symbolizing, on the one hand, the activity in Baptism of Father, Son and Holy Ghost, and on the other, our Lord's three days and nights in the tomb.

In the light of these views on Baptism it is easy to understand why Augustine was greatly perturbed in mind because he had not been baptized in childhood. 'Thou sawest, O my God, because Thou wast even then my keeper, with what inclination of mind and with what faith I desired the baptism of Thy Christ, my Lord, at the pious hands of my mother and the mother of us all, Thy Church.'[2] But his own mother, adhering to the customs of the age, deferred his Baptism, believing that the consequences of sins committed after Baptism were both greater and more dangerous than those committed before. Augustine was puzzled and sorrowful about this and leaves us in no doubt as to his own opinion about it.

> Yet I would fain know, O my God, if it were pleasing to Thee, to what effect was my baptism then deferred, and whether it was for my good that the reins of sin should be laid loose upon me, or were they not laid loose? ... How much better, therefore, had it been if I had been quickly cured; and by the diligence of myself and my friends so good effect might have followed as that my soul, its health assured, might have been safe in Thy custody who didst create it. Yea, this had been much better.[3]

Baptism has a twofold significance: on the one hand, it signifies the priestly action of Christ, and on the other, the priestly action of

[1] *De Trin.*, XIV, 23.   [2] *Confessions*, I, xi.   [3] Ibid.

the whole Church. Augustine clearly states that it is Christ Himself Who is active in Baptism and this conclusion was reached as the outcome of a long struggle with the Donatists who affirmed that the efficacy of Baptism depended upon the personal virtue of the priest who administered it.

> Christ, therefore, is properly the functionary, and the priest is simply His organ ... The seed, of which I was born, is the Word of God, which I must obey even though the preacher himself practise not what he preaches. I believe not in the minister by whom I am baptized, but in Christ, who alone justifies the sinner and can forgive guilt.[1]

Further, those who are baptized, infants or adults, are made members of Christ, parts of His Body the Church. It is this fact of being incorporated into the redeemed community which makes them new beings. The baptized child is no longer only an earthly child with needs that must be satisfied and ambitions to be fulfilled, he has a real part in a higher life and in a universal campaign. He is incorporated into a family and enrolled in an army. When it was argued that it was difficult to understand how a divine influence could take effect in the case of infants devoid of all conscious moral action of their own, Augustine's reply was based on a profound feeling of the essential nature of Christian fellowship. He says, 'The faith of the Church, which consecrated infants to God in the spirit of love, takes the place of their own faith; and albeit they possess as yet no faith of their own, yet there is nothing in their thoughts to hinder the divine efficacy.'[2] At an early age a child knows that he receives love and care and food from his parents and responds unquestioningly to the love that is offered. By the same token a child of God responds to the love that is offered and realizes that he has a place in the family of God.

> The conscious sense may come to a child in earliest years that God is a Father, that he himself is that Father's child; he may come to know that the Church is an army, and that he himself is a soldier who marches with the rest; he may come to have the hope of a Blessed Life which shall be his when death shall have laid him cold and still.[3]

The Sign of the Cross which was made on the forehead and breast was the mark of the soldier of Christ. Augustine often compares

[1] Against the letters of Petilian, I, i. 7.
[2] Ep. 23, ad Bonifacium.
[3] W. Cunningham, St Austin, pp. 125-6.

this to the 'nota militaris' which marked the soldier once for all, for it was branded on his body by his captain, binding him forever to his captain's service and exposing him to punishment for disobedience. The early use of the metaphors of the family and the army shows that the corporate aspect of Baptism was clearly understood. Its importance is recognized by the words of the Baptismal rite: 'We receive this child into the congregation of Christ's flock... and trust that he may be Christ's faithful soldier and servant unto his life's end.' This corporate faith-response is the priestly action of the whole Church.

We must not underestimate this corporate act of faith. In the last resort only two things matter: the Word of God and faith. In the Sacrament of Baptism the Word of God is proclaimed and the Word of God is always the Word of Grace. But if faith cometh by hearing, what is the position of the helpless waiting child? The first fact we must notice is that the Word of Grace is offered. Nothing can alter or minimize this great fact. The second truth is that the congregation is present and hears the Word of Grace. Hearing the Word of God is much more than merely listening, it means receiving and understanding the Word as well as decision and action. But it means even more than this, for when the people hear and accept the Word of Grace they recognize themselves as members of the Church, i.e., the people of God, the Royal Priesthood. The faith of the whole Church is operative for the child that is brought to the Font, indeed it is in this way that the Church's priestly office is exercised. In the Sacrament of Baptism Christians cannot but bring about a new kind of society—the fellowship of believers.

CHRISM; CONSECRATION FOR SERVICE

It is when we come to the third aspect of Baptism, however, that we realize how closely it is connected with the ceremony of Confirmation. One thing is clear: this single ceremony, combining Baptism, Confirmation and Chrism, signifies initiation into the Royal Priesthood. The work of the Holy Spirit in Confirmation is threefold: the insufflation, the 'sealing', and the equipping of the candidate for the general service of the Church.

The breathing upon the candidate was the sign of the communication of the Holy Ghost. It is significant that by this symbolism

SAINT AUGUSTINE 95

the early Christians perpetuated the insufflation of John xx. 22 which concerned only the disciples. But if, as Hort says, 'It is but natural to suppose that it was likewise as representatives of the whole Ecclesia of the future, whether associated with other disciples or not, that they had given to them these two assurances and charges of our Lord',[1] it is equally natural that the Church should apply this symbolism not only with reference to the Apostles but also to every follower of Christ. It also signifies that the universal authority of Christ is transmitted to individual Christians as well as to the Church in its totality. As Hort says, 'The whole Ecclesia shares alike in that transmitted Mission'.[2]

After the feet-washing, reminding Christians of the necessity of humility and service, there followed the completion of Confirmation in the 'sealing'—the Laying on of Hands, in which the prayer for the sevenfold gift of the Holy Ghost was offered. The Apostle says, 'And grieve not the Holy Spirit of God in whom ye were sealed unto the day of redemption' (Eph. iv. 30), and Dollinger, commenting on this, observes, 'It is, therefore, a common ordinance designed for all believers, having a divine promise and meant always to endure, for else it could not belong to the first and elementary principles of Christian doctrine and life.'[3]

The Chrism, the anointing with oil, is given in order that Christians may be equipped for service in Christ's kingdom. Commenting on the verse, 'But they shall be priests of God and of Christ' (Rev. xx. 6), St Augustine says, 'Now this is not meant only of those whom the Church peculiarly calls bishops and priests, but as we are all called Christians, because of our mystical Chrism, "our unction", so are we all priests in being members of one Priest.'[4] In Christ all priesthood inheres, and Augustine returns to this theme in order to emphasize that the universal priesthood is inseparable from the High Priesthood of Christ. 'I would fain be a doorkeeper, or anything in thy service and amongst thy people, for priesthood is put here for the people, to whom Christ the Mediator is the High Priest; which people the Apostle called an holy nation and a royal priesthood.'[5]

Within this royal priesthood there are several offices and callings,

---
[1] *The Christian Ecclesia*, p. 33. [2] Ibid., p. 32.
[3] J. J. I. Dollinger, *The First Age of Christianity*, p. 237.
[4] *De civ. Dei*, XX. 10. [5] Ibid., p. 5.

and loyalty to Christ is revealed by each man's readiness to fulfil his particular calling.

> He hath said as of universal application: 'If any man will follow Me, let him deny himself' (Mk. viii. 34). For it is not that the virgins should give ear to this and the married women not; or that the widows ought and those who still have husbands ought not; or that monks ought, and married men ought not; or that the clergy ought, and the laity ought not; but let the whole Church, the whole body, all the members distinguished and distributed throughout their several offices, follow Christ. But let these several members which have their place there, in their kind and place and measure, follow Christ.[1]

The implication is that within the universal priesthood different members have their specific functions, and those follow Christ most faithfully who fulfil their particular calling within the whole body. Indeed the whole Church only functions corporately when each member fulfils his calling. The New Testament suggests a new Dispensation (Eph. iii. 2), a new creation (2 Cor. v. 17), and a new man (Eph. iv. 24), but these receive their significance from the new Priesthood which is brought to light in Christ (Heb. x. 19-25). Commenting on the new Priesthood in Christ, Augustine says, 'Christ therefore shall exalt the horn of His anointed, that is, of every faithful servant of His, . . . for all that have received the unction of His grace may well be called His anointed, all which, with their Head, make one Anointed.'[2]

The Chrism is an unrepeatable consecration. It is derived from the Old Testament practice whereby kings and priests were anointed with oil to denote the power to reign on the one hand, and the power to offer sacrifices on the other. All the same, it referred only to consecration to a temporal office. 'But *this* Chrism, that is, the unction which has been put on you, has conferred the dignity of that priesthood, which, when once it has been conferred, is never to be closed. What we have said is marvellous, no doubt, that you, by that Chrism, have obtained the kingdom and priesthood of the future glory.'[3]

Chrism, therefore, is the unrepeatable consecration to the spiritual priesthood. Schaff gives clear expression to this idea:

> Baptism, according to the doctrine of the ancient Church, admits the man into the ranks of the soldiers of Christ; Confirmation endows him

---

[1] Serm. (de script N.T.), XCVI, vii. 9.   [2] Ibid., xvii, 4.
[3] A. J. Mason, *The Relation of Confirmation to Baptism*, p. 159.

with strength and courage for the spiritual warfare. The outward form of Confirmation consists in the anointing of the forehead, which symbolizes the consecration of the whole man to the spiritual priesthood; and in the laying on of hands, which signifies and effects the communication of the Holy Ghost for the general Christian calling.[1]

Just as Ordination was the solemn consecration to the special priesthood, so Confirmation is the introduction to the universal priesthood. This idea has never been entirely absent from the teaching of the Church. 'What then does Confirmation mean to us, especially? It means being consecrated and ordained to the lay-priesthood, or rather, to put it still more broadly, to share in the three messianic offices of our Saviour, those of Prophet, Priest and King.'[2]

PRIESTLY SACRIFICES

(a) *Threefold sacrifice of Martyrdom, Humility and Praise*

If a Christian is consecrated to the universal priesthood, what are the sacrifices which he may offer? According to Augustine's teaching he may offer a threefold sacrifice of martyrdom, humility and praise.

> To Him we owe that Greek *latria*, or service, both in ourselves and sacrifices, for we are all His temple, and each one His temples, He vouchsafing to inhabit us all in some and each in particular, being no more in all than in one: for He is neither multiplied nor diminished; our hearts elevated to Him are His altars: His only Son is the Priest by whom we please Him: we offer Him bloody sacrifices when we shed our blood for His truth: and incense when we burn in zeal to Him: the gifts He giveth us, we do in vows return Him: ... we offer Him sacrifices of humility and praises on the altar of our heart in the fire of fervent love.[3]

(b) *The sacrifice of Christian Unity*

When Augustine turns to a consideration of the Eucharist he envisages the whole Church as identified with the Sacrifice of the great Priest.

> Wherefore seeing the works of mercy being referred unto God (be they done to ourselves or our neighbours) are true sacrifices: and that their end is nothing but to free us from misery and make us happy, by that God, (and none other) of whom it is said: It is good for me to

---

[1] P. Schaff, *History of the Christian Church A.D. 311–600*, Vol I, p. 488.
[2] E. W. Watson, *Life of Bishop John Wordsworth*, p. 276.
[3] *De civ. Dei*, X. 4.

adhere unto the Lord: truly it follows that all the whole and holy society of the redeemed and sanctified city, be offered unto God by that great Priest Who gave up His life for us to become members of so great a head in so mean a form: this form He offered, and herein was He offered, in this is He our Priest or Mediator and our sacrifice, all in this.[1]

Underlying all this is the unity of all Christians with Christ, the Head. Augustine saw the striking significance of the question to Saul on the Damascus Road, 'Why persecutest thou *Me* ?' Saul had relentlessly persecuted Christians, yet the question that is asked is, Why persecutest thou *Me* ? The whole Christ is not the Head alone but the Head and the members—in this sense the two are One Man. Indeed the sacrifice that is offered in the Eucharist is the unity of all Christians in Christ. 'If ye are the Body of Christ and His members, it is the sacrifice of yourselves that is set upon the Lord's table, the sacrament of yourselves that you receive. Be what you receive, and receive what you are.'[2]

(c) *Self-sacrifice*

Yet there is a sense in which every man is his own priest in the Eucharistic action as the following passage shows:

> The sacrifice of the priest, therefore, as he is as it were the mouth of the assembly, is merely external and vocal: and those who are the good members of the congregation, whether the priest or any of the people, joining their true inward and properly spiritual sacrifice to the public ministration of the priest, do their whole duty. But in this affair every man is his own priest, because, as I hinted above, he alone can visibly offer such a sacrifice.[3]

In all these passages there is the underlying assumption that the whole body—the universal priesthood—is offered in Christ.

In his doctrine of the Universal Way Augustine is seeking an answer to a vital question, namely, is there a way to an immediate experience of the reality of God, and will this way bring purification of soul as well as spiritual freedom ?

PRIESTLY PRIVILEGES

In Augustine's teaching there are three such privileges: knowledge of God, purification of soul, and participation in a universal mission.

---

[1] *De civ. Dei*, X. 6.   [2] Sermon CCLXXII.
[3] *De Baptismo*, I. 18.

SAINT AUGUSTINE

(a) The Universal Way to the knowledge of God

Personal knowledge of God was the first essential. This is made clear in the Confessions:

> Thou hast created us for Thyself, and our heart knows no rest, until it may repose in Thee. Grant then, O God, that I may understand whether of these two things be first, to call upon Thee or to praise Thee, and whether it be first to know Thee or to call upon Thee? But yet, who callest upon Thee if he know Thee not? For he that doth not know Thee may call upon somewhat else instead of Thee. Or art Thou rather to be called upon to the end that Thou mayest be known?[1]

Augustine was seeking an immediacy of communion with the Divine and not a mediated contact. This immediacy had brought him a sense of certainty and therefore he commended this way to others. In a moving passage he explains this experience: 'With the eye of my soul I discerned, even beyond my soul and mind itself, the unchangeable light of the Lord . . . This light, I say, was not the former light but another, and altogether different from all such . . . He that knoweth Truth knoweth the Light, and he that knoweth that Light knoweth Eternity.'[2] According to Augustine this is the one way which has a universal application and that is why he calls it the universal way. It is the way of access to God whereby He is known in an immediacy and intimacy of spiritual experience. 'That this strait way, leading to the knowledge and cohesion of God, lies plain in Holy Scripture, upon whose truth it is grounded; they that believe not, and therefore know not, may oppose this, but they can never overthrow it.'[3]

That this sense of immediacy of communion with God had also brought him a sense of certainty is made clear in the Confessions. 'Thy words did cling even to the very roots of my heart, and I was entrenched by Thee on every side. . . . All the doubts which I was wont to have were now taken away . . . and I desired not to be made more certain concerning Thee, but only to be more established in Thee.'[4] Having discovered this secret, Augustine was now ready to communicate it to others. Writing of the spiritual experience of Augustine, St Francis, Luther and Wesley, J. Arundel Chapman observes, 'Their greatness lies in this—that the solution they found

[1] *Confessions*, Bk. I, i.   [2] Ibid., Bk. VII, 10.
[3] *De civ. Dei*, X. 32.   [4] *Confessions*, Bk. VIII, i.

of their own problem was a representative one; it availed for others. Their experience was communicable. As has been well said, a spiritual experience is in its ultimate nature something universal; it comes first to one, but it is only that it may be passed on to all.'[1]

(b) *The Universal Way of the soul's purification*

There is no purification of soul apart from immediate contact with God. Sin is a universal fact and every soul stands in need of the divine mercy. If this mercy is offered, the soul finds cleansing and peace; if it does not find cleansing and peace, it is not in contact with God. Divine Mercy is God's unique and supreme offer to man; others cannot offer it because they have not got it. Where divine mercy is not known, sin reigns. No one grasped this truth more clearly than Augustine. Dr Tennant's view that Augustine emphasized the universality of sin but failed to allow adequately for the responsibility of the individual, fails to take into account the whole theme of the Confessions.[2] Augustine's long struggle for forgiveness and peace is the story of an individual seeking deliverance from sin and guilt. Almost every page of the Confessions is the cry of a man seeking salvation. 'The way, the Saviour of the World, did please me well, but I could not find it in my heart to follow it through the strait gate.'[3] But it was not only the cry of one man, it was the cry of the whole race. Only the Saviour of the *World* was sufficient to deal with one man's sin. But just because the sin of one man is also the sin of Man, God has provided the Way, the Universal Way of salvation. Hence Augustine's words, 'This then is the universal way of the soul's freedom which the saints and prophets did both adumbrate in their temple, sacrifice and priesthood, and foretold also in their prophecy, often mystically and sometimes plainly. . . . This way cleanses every soul, and prepares a mortal man for immortality.'[4]

(c) *The Universal Way of World Redemption*

People of many nations had sought the way of the soul's freedom in their own doctrines and philosophies. By this standard all other faiths and philosophies are judged. According to Augustine, the Chaldaean, the Indian and the Greek had not found what they were

---

[1] E. J. Ives (ed.), *Eleven Christians*, p. 51.
[2] Cf. *Origin and Propagation of Sin*, p. 15.
[3] *Confessions*, Bk. VIII, i.   [4] *De civ. Dei*, X. 32.

looking for. It was not that these other doctrines had nothing to offer to man, or that they could not accomplish anything, but that they had no power to do the one thing needful. Christianity offers a way of spiritual freedom for people of all nations. What, then, is this way that is common to all the world and given to it by the power of God? Augustine replies: 'This therefore is that universal way of the soul's freedom, that is granted to all nations out of God's mercy, the knowledge whereof comes, and is to come unto all men. This, I say, is the way that will free all believers . . .'[1]

In another passage Augustine puts the matter much more plainly, 'The days are come. Aaron's seed has now no priest: and his whole offspring behold, with failing eyes and fainting hearts, the sacrifice of the Christians gloriously offered all the world through.'[2] The matter could not be put more succinctly: the Judaic way has now become the universal way, the Aaronic priesthood has now become the universal priesthood, the national cult has now become a universal Faith. When men have been conquered by the grace of Christ they must needs go forth to conquer the whole world in the name of Christ. 'The Church grew, the nations believed, the princes of the earth have been conquered under the name of Christ, that they might be conquerors in the whole world.'[3]

From the teaching of Augustine, therefore, we infer that the universal priesthood is based on the catholicity of the Gospel. The Church is catholic in teaching the wholeness of the Faith, in bringing to all sorts and conditions of men healing for all sins, and in its worldwide extension. The Church's catholicity depends altogether on the catholicity of the Gospel and it is this Gospel which offers to all men everywhere and in all ages the universal way. It is the way to life's three greatest blessings—the way to God's presence, to holiness of life, and to the soul's freedom. Every man may sing with Charles Wesley:

> *To me, with Thy dear name, are given*
> *Pardon, and holiness, and heaven.*

---

[1] Ibid. [2] *De civ. Dei*, XVII. 5. [3] Serm. XLIV, 1.

CHAPTER FIVE

THE MIDDLE AGES

THE history of the Church from the fifth to the eleventh centuries is the story of four great conflicts, all of which are connected with the subject of our study. There was the struggle between East and West, between Islam and Christianity, between the Priesthood and the Laity, and between the Church and the State. The dominant figure in the first phase was Gregory the Great; in the second, Muhammad. The third phase concerns various controversies within the Church, the results of which are of great significance, while in the last phase which centres on the issue between Church and State, we shall be concerned primarily with the work of Hildebrand. In this undulating period of history, two important questions arise: what was the effect of those momentous events upon the doctrine of the priesthood of all believers, and in what specific ways has this affected the subsequent history of the Church?

A. EAST AND WEST

At the beginning of the fourth century Rome had no legal superiority over the other bishoprics. The Council of Nicaea (325) knew nothing of a sovereign Pontiff. Yet even at that stage Rome was emerging as a power to be reckoned with. Many factors contributed to the emergence of papal authority and jurisdiction.

Rome was the capital of an empire which virtually spanned the world. She then held a position of superiority which no city has acquired before or since. She was acknowledged to be the queen of land and sea. When, in the fourth century, the five Patriarchates were formed, Rome was named first followed by Constantinople, Antioch, Jerusalem and Alexandria. In 381 the argument was not about who was first, for apparently that was not in question, but about who was second, and it was declared, 'the Patriarch of Constantinople is second only to the Pope'. Although all the Patriarchates were held in cities of world-wide importance, Rome's place was supreme. But Rome's position at that stage was due to factors other than religious. It was due to Roman Law, Roman government and Rome's military strength. Rome gave her name to that ordered system of government and civilization which marked off imperial citizens from barbarians, and in the far-flung corners of empire men claimed with pardonable pride that they were citizens of Rome.

It was, however, the religious factor which consolidated Rome's unassailable position. Rome was regarded as the Apostolic See and the Pope as the successor of St Peter. Each Pope was deemed to inherit the plenitude of power promised by Christ to Peter, and in course of time this meant that all authority and divine blessings were mediated only through the papacy. The ecclesiastical absoluteness of the Roman See is the greatest single reason for the undisputed strength of the Roman Church in the Middle Ages. Whether Rome would have achieved this position apart from the Pseudo-Isidorian Decretals and the so-called Donation of Constantine, it is impossible to say, but it is conceivable that her primacy would have been achieved without them.

What is certain is that Augustine's City of God wielded a definite and decisive influence upon both Church and State in the Middle Ages. The inauguration of the Holy Roman Empire under Charlemagne by Pope Leo III on Christmas Day, 800, was regarded as the realization of Augustine's dream. Yet this notable event which was heralded as a great victory for the Church, turned out to be her greatest problem, and the story of the Middle Ages is the story of her attempt to solve it. The plain question was: which was the superior power, the Church or the State?

Augustine had been able to say with startling finality, 'Rome has spoken, the matter is ended,' and from that time to the coronation of Charlemagne no lay power had been near enough or great enough to present any serious challenge. It is true that before this time the Church had been subjected to strong external pressures, but these had come from barbarian forces and not from within the jurisdiction of the Church. There had been the hordes of Alaric and the invading armies of Attila and Agilulph, yet the resilience of Rome is the one outstanding memory of these events. The last two invaders were repelled by Leo I and Gregory the Great, and Innocent I found, on his return to Rome after the ravages of Alaric, that his authority had been strengthened rather than weakened by the onslaught. Rome under pressure from barbarian forces always showed astonishing resources, and the courage of these three Popes, no less than their administrative skill, helped to lay the foundations of papal power. In days of unparalleled calamity men began to speak of her as the Eternal City.

In addition to this, the growth of the Pope's territorial jurisdiction increased his power. This was brought about not only by military conquests in various parts of the empire but by the lavish gifts of the faithful. Consequently, in addition to ecclesiastical and political power the Papacy became an economic power of considerable importance.

Further, the influence of Rome spread by the remarkable labours of her greatest emissaries, the monks. These men were at once her most effective ambassadors and her strongest supporters. Their zeal spread the Faith and their doctrine defended it. Among them were philosophers and theologians, administrators, artists and poets, who have left their mark upon the whole of Western Christendom. Although the Pope did not always smile upon them and although some of their actions were countenanced rather than encouraged, there is no doubt that they established papal authority wherever they went in their unceasing missionary activity.

In 312 Constantine declared that he would build on the site of the ancient Byzantium a city which would surpass the grandeur of Rome. But he had first to defeat his chief rival Licinius and when this was accomplished in 323 Constantine became the sole head of the Roman Empire. This new city, Constantinople, became the residence of the Emperor and was known as the New Rome. According to legend, after Constantine had been healed of leprosy and baptized by Pope Sylvester, he withdrew from the seat and patrimony of St Peter, and, in gratitude to the Pope, donated to him and his successors the free and perpetual sovereignty of Rome, Italy, and the provinces of the West. Some of this is true but the 'donation' is a fabrication. Perhaps the elements of truth in it gave credance to the rest of it. What is important is that the Popes accepted it and for many centuries acted upon the assumption that they had been granted authority over the Western World. All the same, Constantine's most compelling reason for taking up his residence in Constantinople was his uncertainty about the continuing stability of Rome in his absence. During the time of

Rome's dire peril under Alaric and Atilla, some of the Patriarchs of Constantinople seem to have contemplated the transfer of spiritual primacy to their city but this was because they had not Augustine's faith in Rome nor had they reckoned with the energy and influence of one man—Gregory the Great.

'Blow out the candles, the sun is up,' said a discerning philosopher when the Emperor Yao mounted the throne of China. It might well have been said in 590. Gregory was one of the greatest men who have occupied the papal Chair. He was great in godliness, great in administrative ability, and great in missionary zeal. By birth he was a Roman noble and in 574 was appointed by the Greek Emperor, Justin, to the highest civil office in Rome, that of imperial Prefect. But he was conscious of deep longings which such an office could not satisfy, and soon he renounced the world and devoted himself to religion in his own monastery on the Coelian Hill. But his abilities were too great to allow him to remain in obscurity and in 579 he was sent as ambassador to the Court of Constantinople. There he gained experience of the government of the empire at headquarters and no doubt was impressed by the magnificent ecclesiastical life of the New Rome. On his return to Rome in 590 he was elected Pope. His main concerns were the unity, purity and expansion of the Church.

Gregory and the Universal Episcopate

One of his biographers, James Barmby, writes of Gregory: 'Of the loftiness of his aims, the earnestness of his purpose, the fervour of his devotion, his unwearied activity, and his personal purity, there can be no doubt. These qualities are conspicuous in his whole career.'[1]

These qualities tended powerfully to establish the authority of the papal Chair. Although he exercised jurisdiction over the whole of the West, he firmly rejected the idea of a universal episcopate. John IV, the Patriarch of Constantinople, frequently used in his letters the title 'universal bishop' and Gregory resented the use of such a title by his eastern rival. He urged John not to use this arrogant title but his pleading was of no avail. After John's death Gregory wrote to the new Patriarch, Cyriacus, demanding that the wicked title be renounced, and he even addressed himself to the

[1] *Gregory the Great*, p. 191.

Emperor Maurice himself, saying, 'Whosoever calls himself universal priest, or desires to be called so, is the forerunner of Antichrist.'[1] Certainly Gregory had no wish to claim the title for himself and called himself—'the servant of the servants of God'. When Eulogius of Alexandria addressed him as 'universal Pope' he answered,

> I have said that neither to me or to anyone else ought you to write anything of the kind. And lo! in the preface of your letter you apply to me, who prohibited it, the proud title of universal Pope; which thing I beg your most sweet Holiness to do so no more, because what is given to others beyond what reason requires is subtracted from you. I do not esteem that an honour by which my brethren lose their honour. My honour is that of the universal Church. My honour is the solid strength of my brethren. I am truly honoured when all and each one are allowed the honour that is due to them.[2]

This is a noble statement and worthy of its author. It is unjust and altogether too glib to say that Gregory disclaimed the name but claimed the thing itself. Such a subtle interpretation would be quite inconsistent with what we know of Gregory's character. It is important to notice that in rejecting the title 'universal Pope' Gregory emphasizes the universal Church and the honour that is due to every member of it. There is here a hint of his conception of the Church as a universal priesthood, which as we shall see, he states more explicitly in his teaching.

The Universal Priesthood

The duty of Christian witness applies to priest and layman alike.

> The world is full of priests, yet there are few real labourers for God's harvest, since although we have undertaken the priestly calling, we do not fulfil its duties. He who is unable to occupy the congregation with a connected discourse may instruct individuals and edify them by private conversation. Let us ask ourselves, who have been converted by our tongue? We have received our talents to trade with; what profit have we brought to Him who said 'Occupy till I come'? Behold He is already come; He is looking for the profit from our traffic. What gain of souls can we show? The priest's lips should teach knowledge, for he is a messenger of the Lord; but all may attain the same high dignity if they will. Whosoever calls his neighbour from wicked ways to a

---

[1] Schaff, *History of the Church* 590–1073, Vol. I, p. 220.
[2] Ibid., pp. 223–4.

right course of life, he too, certainly is a messenger of the Lord. Hast thou no bread to give to the needy? Thou hast a tongue; thou hast something of more value than bread ... To the poorest, even the little that he has received will be reckoned as a talent.[1]

The duty of studying the Scriptures applies to priest and layman alike. In this respect Gregory was ahead of his time. The Church would have been saved from infinite loss if she had heeded the counsel of Gregory on this particular point. Two disastrous theories were abroad in his time; The first was that the possession of the Scriptures by barbarian hordes was a perilous thing and should not be tolerated. Doubtless it was thought that the Pauline doctrine of justification by faith without works was too precarious a word to commit to these undisciplined hordes. It is to Gregory's credit that he was prepared to take the risk. He has sometimes been criticized for condemning secular learning but the criticism is due to a single incident and has been overworked. He discouraged secular learning when it was undertaken to the exclusion of the study of the Scriptures. It was the primary duty of all Christians to study the Word of God. The Scriptures, he maintained, were a letter from Almighty God, and just as we should lose no time in reading the contents if we received a letter from an earthly sovereign, so must we reflect daily on the Creator's words. It was sound advice and it was not given for the benefit of the priesthood only. Dudden sums it up as follows:

> Gregory is never tired of urging his clergy to study the Bible, and he is not less eager to impress this duty upon laymen. The following words taken from a letter to a physician at Constantinople, prove that Gregory was far from regarding the Bible as the exclusive property of the clergy: 'The Emperor of Heaven, the Lord of men and angels, has sent you His epistles for your life's behoof—and yet you neglect to read them eagerly. Study them, I beg you, and meditate daily on the words of your Creator. Learn the heart of God from the words of God, that you may sigh more eagerly for the things eternal, that your soul may be kindled with greater longings for heavenly joys.'[2]

This letter was addressed to a layman and it serves to show how Gregory sought to remove the second erroneous theory, namely, that the Scriptures were the peculiar possession of the clergy.

Now there was a special reason why Gregory stressed the need

[1] Ep. to Dominicus XLVII.
[2] F. H. Dudden, *Gregory the Great*, Vol. II, p. 300.

for the study of the Scriptures: it was because of his doctrine that Christ is the subject of all Scripture so that every part of it must be understood as referring to Him. This doctrine brought forth some of Gregory's most penetrating and illuminating insights. Christ was foreshadowed in the Old Testament not only in its prophetical utterances but also in the individual lives of those who lived before the Incarnation. 'All the elect, being His forerunners in holiness of life, gave a prophetic promise of His coming by their actions and by their words. Every just man was in figure a herald of Christ.'[1] Is there here an echo of the doctrine of Irenaeus that 'all just men belong to the sacerdotal order'? At any rate there is the clear implication that the universal priesthood before the Incarnation consists in preparing the way for the coming of Christ, whereas in the New Testament it consists in an intimate union with Christ. Gregory asserts that whether it is stated obscurely in the Old Testament or clearly in the New, the central theme is Christ. It was this reasoning which brought forth from Gregory the great declaration that Christianity is as old as the world. But Gregory did not overlook the difference between believers in the Old and New Testaments. If men were heralds of the Kingdom in the Old, they were participants of it in the New.

Union with Christ is one of his favourite themes.

> Since the Body and the Head are One Person, the virtues of the Head are appropriated by the members ... They find acceptance with God, in whose righteousness they, through their Head, participate. Thus they are freed from slavery to sin, because they are one with Him who is truly free; and they have sure hope of heaven, for where the Head is there shall also the members be. The redemptive principle is found in union with Christ.[2]

The fruit of union with Christ is the unity of the whole Church. 'For as in the pomegranate many seeds within are protected by one outer rind, so unity in faith comprehends numberless people of Holy Church.'[3] So close is this unity that individual believers are called the Robe of Christ. Within this unity each member may have a different function yet each works for all and appropriates the work of all, and just because faith operates in the heart of the believer wherever it is awakened by the Spirit, the unity of the

---

[1] *The Morals*, Pref. 14.   [2] Dudden, op. cit., Vol. II, p. 344.
[3] Henry Davis, *Gregory's Pastoral Care*, p. 54.

Church comprehends all true believers of the past, the present and the future. United with Christ through faith, the believer also shares His power. Indeed it is by this means that he realizes his true inheritance which is a heavenly kingdom and a kingly priesthood.

He should, as it were, reject vice, ever setting his gaze on his interior regeneration and safeguarding by his way of living his right to the heavenly kingdom. It is this nobility of spirit that Peter mentions: But you are a chosen generation, a kingly priesthood. In regard to the power with which we subdue vices, we are fortified by the words of John: But as many as have received Him, He gave them power to be made sons of God . . . for indeed, the mind of the Saints is exalted to princely eminence, when in the eyes of the world they suffer abasement.[1]

Sufficient has been said to show that in Gregory's teaching the priesthood of all believers is expressed in the duty of daily witness to the Faith, the study of the Word of God by priest and layman alike, in the unity of all believers with Christ, and in the inheritance which is common to all Christians, namely, a heavenly kingdom and a kingly priesthood. That this Royal Priesthood was committed to a universal mission is evidenced by Gregory's untiring and effective efforts in the cause of world evangelization. And while all this was going on in the West, as far as the Eastern Church was concerned, the writing was on the wall. Within seven years of Gregory's death an unknown Arabian nomad began to speak of his divine visions and to proclaim a mission to the world.

B. ISLAM AND CHRISTIANITY

Outside Islam Muhammad has rarely been accorded the honour which by any standards is due to him. It will not do to regard him as no more than a fanatical revolutionary. The rapid triumphs of Islam are not accountable to force alone. Christianity was not ready for the kind of opposition Islam provided. The Church had faced many problems already, some of them theological, some ecclesiological and others political. But most of these had been within her own jurisdiction, and she had not hitherto been required to face a struggle on several fronts at the same time. The phenomenon of Islam was something quite novel. Here we find a new

[1] Ibid., p. 50.

doctrine, a united people, an expansionist policy, guided and directed by an outstanding leader of men. It is possible that a leader like Muhammad might have brought inspiration and hope both to a petrified Judaism and to a dormant Christianity, but as at other strategic points in history, the Church has lacked those qualities which might have saved the day—penitence, imagination and vision. Instead of viewing the rise of Muhammad as a judgment upon her laxity, and harnessing all her energies to shake off her lethargy, she simply stirred a little in her sleep and hardly noticed, until it was too late, the tremendous impact of a more resolute, vigorous and purposeful religious movement.

Muhammad's success must have surprised even himself, but the Church was weak and could find no answer to this man of clear-cut opinions and extraordinary drive. It is surely one of the great ironies of history that a man who trod firmly in the steps of Abraham—the father and pioneer of Judaism and Christianity—could not find congenial company among the disciples of these faiths. The following observation is entirely justifiable: 'To Christians it must ever be to their shame (till we know even as we are known) that the Muhammadan religion in its beginnings went behind Jesus Christ, even as it went behind the Moses of the Jews, to Abraham, the Father of the Faithful and the Friend of God.'[1] Abraham was the father of the nation, the custodian of the Covenant and the pioneer of faith, and yet in Muhammad's time the holy nation, the royal priesthood and the people of the Covenant, had not the spiritual perception to see in this staunch devotee of Abraham a champion of their cause. But it was no better in the Christian Church. For the new Israel, the elect race, the people of the New Covenant, failed to see in Muhammad a divine judgment upon their apathy and a stirring challenge to their waning faith. The new Community was already suffering from the malady of the Old. The elect race had forgotten the purpose of its election and the Royal Priesthood had neglected its priestly responsibility and consequently had lost sight of its unique mission to the world. The single condition whereby they were to win the world had already been forfeited. Bound to God by heritage, election, the Redeemer's Sacrifice and their own faith

[1] E. E. Bishop, *International Review of Missions*, Vol. XI, No. 159, p. 287.

in the Covenant, they had become weak and inept because of internal divisions. The Church, representing as it did, the Body of Christ, was already fractured. As a result the Church was guilty of two fatal errors: she was too blind to see in Muhammad an instrument of divine judgment, and too weak to summon all her latent powers and *be* the Church. To this extent A. C. Bouquet[1] is not mistaken when he compares Muhammad with the Prophet Amos, and Foster's verdict, though sad, rings true:

> There is no doubt that in stretching out his hands to something, some One, higher, he was feeling after, almost finding, the God and Father of our Lord Jesus Christ. The reason why he (Muhammad) did not, in the wholeheartedness of his early search, go all the way, was the weakness of the Church's witness in this its earliest outreaching. Here are all the possibilities of a mass movement . . . It did not happen. It remains one of the might-have-beens of Christian history.[2]

Yet the reason for the Church's failure lies deeper still. It was not simply that she lacked spiritual perception and failed to accept a unique challenge, it was that her sense of values had imperceptibly changed and her standards were almost indistinguishable from those of the world. The Church is weak when she is spiritually weak. Her apparent vigour in temporal affairs cannot hide her true condition. The Church is strong only when she is strong in faith. Her failure is worldly success. This is the crux of the problem. Measured in terms of worldly success Christianity must always fail. Its scale of values belongs to another category. But this is not always remembered and in the course of history Christians as well as Muslims have appealed to worldly success as a test of the truth of their religion, and it was in fact on these grounds that the Mongol Khans decided for Islam and against Christianity. But this is not surprising, for Christianity puts herself on false ground when she holds out the promise of worldly success. It is noteworthy that the marks of the Nestorian Church were worldliness, imperialism, division and enforced orthodoxy. But these have never been the true marks of the Church. The Mongols decided for Islam because they were asked to judge Christianity by a false criterion, and it has been aptly observed, 'It does not appear that any Christians protested that Christ's

---
[1] A. C. Bouquet, *The Christian Faith and Non-Christian Religions*, p. 169.
[2] John Foster, *World Church*, pp. 112–13.

kingdom was not of this world, and was not to be established by the sword'.[1]

The Christian religion had something to learn from Islam, especially along the lines of the three major emphases of Islamic religion. These are: one God, one Book, one Priesthood. The basic truth of Islam is, in Kraemer's phase, its 'radical theocentricity'. He summarizes it in these words, 'Muhammad was possessed by two great religious aims—to proclaim God as the sole, almighty God, the Creator and the King in the Day of Judgment; to found a community, in Arabia called *umma*, ruled by the Law of God and His Apostle.'[2] This uncompromising monotheism is expressed in the formula: God is great and he has no associate. The Quran leaves no ambiguity on this point:

> *To God belongeth the Earth and the World,*
> *Whithersoever ye turn yourselves to pray,*
> *There is the grace of God,*
> *For God is omnipotent and omniscient,*[3]

and again:

> *Say, He is God alone:*
> *God the Eternal,*
> *He begetteth not, and is not begotten,*
> *And there is none like unto Him.*[4]

It may seem strange that the Jews refused to accept a message which rang with genuine monotheism, but there were other reasons why the Jews rejected Muhammad's message and we must now consider them. First, Muhammad was a Gentile prophet, and it is unthinkable that a Jew should accept as divine and authentic the message of a Gentile prophet. Undoubtedly, this was the principal reason for the intransigent attitude of the Jews. Whatever claim Muhammad might make, he remained a Gentile. Secondly, all Jews had been schooled in the theory of dynamic revelation, and in their view, Muhammad's teaching failed at this crucial point. Kraemer tries to prove that 'in the most emphatic

---

[1] A Member of the Church of India, *The Heritage of an Indian Christian*, p. 78.
[2] H. Kraemer, *The Christian Message*, p. 220.
[3] *The Quran* (trans. George Sale), Surah 15.
[4] *The Quran* (trans. J. M. Rodwell), Surah 74.

sense of the word, Islam is a religion of revelation'.[1] He has a hard task. Islam is essentially an assertion of impersonal divine power; it calls for surrender to power rather than response to a Person. Apart from this repeated assertion of power and the need for unquestioning submission, little is known of the nature of Allah. The purpose of surrender is not disclosed and this excludes any idea of relationship. In fact, any approach from God to man is ruled out since, in Muhammad's doctrine, the terms 'divine' and 'human' are mutually exclusive. What happens to the idea of divine revelation and the possibility of human response if 'everything in Allah is different from the similarly named thing in men'?[2]

The third reason why the Jews rejected Muhammad's message was because there were many discrepancies between the Quran and the Old Testament. Muhammad felt that the strength of his case lay in the fact that he had not read the Bible and that the truths made known to him were revealed independently of the Bible. But that which he always regarded as the peculiar strength of his case was an inherent weakness in the eyes of the Jews. If Muhammad's message had been true, it would have corresponded more accurately with the Old Testament. In fact there is only one verse which agrees entirely with the Bible and that is a quotation from Psalm xxxvii. 29. For the rest there are many discrepancies. The statement, for instance, that Joseph's parents went down to Egypt could not be true for Rachel was already dead, and throughout the Quran the Virgin Mary is confused with Miriam. These are typical of many false representations which were unacceptable to the Jews. The fourth reason why they rejected Muhammad's message was because of his firm injunction that, when praying, all men should turn towards Mecca and not Jerusalem. Muhammad must have known what would be the outcome of such a command, but whether he realized it or not, it caused the final break with Judaism. The cumulative effect of Muhammad's teaching amounted to a complete denial of truths which had become inalienably associated with Judaism, namely, that they were God's elect people, custodians of a unique revelation, and committed to a universal task.

[1] H. Kraemer, op. cit., p. 217.
[2] D. B. MacDonald, *Encyclopedia of Islam*, Vol. I, p. 306.

But when all has been said, Muhammad's monotheistic emphasis was both necessary and timely. The Meccans themselves were worshipping three goddesses—Al-lat, Al-Uzza and Al-Manat and these were called daughters of Allah. In addition they worshipped the spirits of springs, wells, rocks, trees and mountains, and offered blood sacrifices at sacred stones. All this means that the Arabs themselves had fallen into a crude polytheism and animism. It is also significant that Islam made rapid progress in parts of northern India where polytheism was rampant and among the tribes of North Africa where fetish-worship was accompanied by the most brutal superstitions. Further, in some areas the Christian religion had degenerated into Mariolatry, image worship and superstition, and if Muhammad has become known as the great iconoclast, it will now be apparent that there is ample justification for the claim. Certainly the times demanded a radical reassertion of the sole creatorship and sovereignty of God, and in this respect, Muhammad was a worthy champion.

It is axiomatic that the spread of Christianity depends upon knowledge of the Bible, yet so completely did the Christian religion disappear before Islam in Arabia and North Africa that it is not easy to tell whether the Scriptures were ever translated into the vernacular. At any rate, knowledge of the Christian message was of so fragmentary a nature that the Christians were unable to withstand the sudden impact of Muhammad's message. Stephen Neill considers this to be the principal reason for the eclipse of Christianity in North Africa. For 'it does not appear that any part of the Scriptures had been translated. Even Punic words would have reached only a section of the people. The inland folk of Berber stock had their own dialects in which there was neither Christian preaching nor written Scripture.'[1] It did not take the Muslims very long to realize that they had in their possession an instrument of tremendous power—an infallible Book. In no religion in the world has the authority of the written Word been stressed so much and used more successfully. Muhammad was not only a man of supreme confidence but also a shrewd observer of events, and perhaps he knew that there would be no point in approaching Jews and Christians without an infallible Book. At any rate, he was convinced that a much greater use could

[1] S. Neill, *The Christian Society*, p. 77.

be made of his Book than the Jews and Christians had so far made of theirs. So while the Church was concerned to establish great centres of Christian learning at Constantinople, Hippo and Alexandria, Muslim soldiers, travellers and traders were penetrating into the African hinterland and teaching savage tribes the message of the Book.

The appeal of Muhammad was considerably strengthened by his claim that the revelation which he had received from heaven was the last in point of time. He never tired of saying that there was no prophet between himself and Jesus, and as the custodian of the latest significant revelation, he claimed the greater authority. This brings us to one of the fallacious but convenient principles of Islam; it is applied both to the discrepancies in the Quran and to the questions raised by the study of comparative religions. It is the principle that the later revelation or command supersedes the earlier. But this is based upon such an erroneous view of time and progress and revelation that it cannot now be taken seriously.

Two further factors made the path of Muhammad easier than it might have been: first, authority was imperceptibly but certainly passing into the hands of the papacy and this meant that the authority of the Bible was correspondingly minimized. The authentic Word of God was relegated to a place of secondary importance, and this was in striking contrast to the unrelenting emphasis which Muhammad placed upon the Quran as the Book. More serious still was the attitude of lethargy and hopelessness which was brought about partly by the waning influence of the Bible. Many questions were asked: who speaks for the Church and where is the authentic Christian Gospel to be found? Was it to be found with the Church in the East or the West? Was it to be found with the Emperor or the Pope? Or was the matter as yet undecided? If this was the case, there can be little wonder that Christians were no longer aware of their privilege as a redeemed community or of participating at least to some extent in the sufferings of their Redeemer. Being ignorant of the message of the Gospel and therefore unaware of the greatness of their calling, there was an absence of those qualities which are essential for an effective Christian witness: a sense of infinite indebtedness to Christ, an entire trust in Him, a strong desire to share in His sacrificial service for mankind, and an absolute loyalty to Christ in all circumstances. It is hardly surprising that a Church which lacked these qualities had no power to stem the triumphant march of Islam.

Nor is this all. Islam is built on three impregnable rocks—one God, one Book, one Priesthood. The Church, therefore, had another important lesson to learn from Islam, namely, that a religious movement can make astonishing progress even without the organization which is implicit in an hierarchical system. Islam was a brotherhood of believing men, and its members were bound to one another by a deep bond of fellowship; they were, above everything else, a witnessing community inspired with a missionary task. In his final speech Muhammad reminded them of the meaning of fellowship:

> Ye people, hearken to my words; for I know not whether, after this year, I shall ever be amongst you here again. Your lives and your property are sacred and inviolable amongst one another till the end of time. The Lord hath ordained every man the share of his inheritance ... Know that every Muslim is the brother of every other Muslim. All of you are the same equality.[1]

Is not the secret of expansion in Islam due in part to the fact that they are a fellowship where faith both binds them together and gives them power to witness?

> To be just we must acknowledge that the brotherhood of believers has always been accepted as Muhammad's doctrine. In the Arab clan the tie is that of blood, and Muhammad organized his community as a clan, only changing the tie to one of faith. Here we discover the attractive power of Islam. To say that the new religion was propagated only by the sword gives a wrong impression. The Muslim believer is a preacher, all the more influential because he receives no official status. Islam recognizes no priesthood, although men learned in the law are looked up to by the common people.[2]

This brings us to the all-important question: is there a particular reason which may account for the rapid expansion of Islam, one reason, perhaps, which overshadows all others? The following statement will help us to see the problem in its true perspective.

---

[1] The complete farewell utterance of Muhammad is given in A. C. Bouquet's *The Christian Faith and Non-Christian Religions*, pp. 170-1.
[2] A. S. Peake and R. G. Parsons (eds.), *Outline of Christianity*, Vol. II, p. 153.

In the recent healthy awakening to the responsibilities of the layman we have come to see that the doctrine of the priesthood of all believers means not only that every mature Christian has a part to play in the building up of the Church, but that he has a share in the function of the Church as an ambassador, proclaiming the message of the King of kings to those whose loyalty is given to other lords.[1]

It is easy for the Church to forget or overlook the fact that every Christian has a function to fulfil as an ambassador of the Gospel, and the inescapable lesson of the seventh and eighth centuries is that when this truth is neglected there is a high price to pay. But while the Church was neglecting this aspect of her message, Islam was showing to all the world what can happen when every believer is a dedicated ambassador. For Islam succeeded at least in this: she was able to harness all her resources to achieve a single end, and to this end all her people were committed in a kind of fierce dedication. In the task of spreading the faith every believer was inescapably involved. 'Though there is no priesthood in Islam, and though there have been few missionaries set apart for the sole purpose of propagating the faith, the Muslim is never shy of confessing his religion, or even of actively proclaiming it. The frequent statement that every Muslim trader is a missionary is on the whole a true one.'[2] It may be more true to say that although Islam has no priesthood, she *is* a priesthood. In practice each Muslim fulfils a priestly function. Even the Imam, the leader of prayers, has no official status, but is elected by the people to be their representative.

> Each mosque, however small, has its Imam ... The office is not in any sense a sacred one, the Imam not being set apart with any ceremony, as in the case of a Christian presbyter, nor the office being hereditary, as in the case of the Hindu Brahmins. The position of the Imam in this sense is not unlike that of the sheliach or legatus of the Jewish synagogue, who acted as the delegate of the congregation, and was the chief reader of prayers in their name.[3]

It must ever remain a rebuke to Christians that a religion which lacked the theological basis of true priesthood should have made such astonishing progress at the expense of those who possessed it.

[1] A. M. Ward, *Our Theological Task*, pp. 186–7.
[2] C. R. North, *An Outline of Islam*, p. 55.
[3] T. P. Hughes, *A Dictionary of Islam*, p. 204.

For it must be confessed that Islam had the letter but not the spirit of priesthood, the shell of an idea but not the kernel of it. It is surely impossible to estimate what might have happened in both Arabia and North Africa if the Christian doctrine of the priesthood of all believers had been grasped as firmly by Christians as the Muslims grasped an external and attenuated version of it. Yet Islam could never express the true meaning of priesthood because she did not know it. The Church knew it but did not express it—why?

The answer to this question is difficult and complex. We must first banish the idea that only the Eastern Church felt the impact of Islamic pressures. Certainly the main blow fell upon the ancient civilization of Byzantium, but it is also true that Rome and the Western Church suffered serious set-backs as Islam won its way in Western Europe. The truth is that in both the Eastern and Western Churches the Christian community was too sure of itself, too confident of its supposedly impregnable position. The Church's belief that she was impregnable proved that she was vulnerable. She claimed protection from God without learning the lesson of obedience to God. But her principal error was to take refuge in the mighty institution, forgetting that the real strength of the Church in any age is the faith, witness, and suffering service of individual believers. Personal faith in Christ is always essential; faith in an abstraction is not a substitute.

The idea, too often put forward, that failure in faith will always take place in the Church because of the historical character of our religion, is naive and inaccurate. The set-backs are inevitable but not the consequences. It is necessary to distinguish between the two. Set in the context of this world the Church will always be subjected to external pressures, her standards will be challenged and her message opposed. The Church is always in conflict, always under the Cross. But submission to those pressures, unprotesting acquiescence, and failure in faith are not inevitable corollaries of such a conflict. An easy surrender of faith in the face of an oppressor is always a severe temptation, but the question is: will the faithful remnant, the elect race, the royal priesthood succumb to it? The sword has no power to banish truth even though there are times when truth is on the scaffold. The answer to the Roman sword was the open sepulchre. Christian truth shines by its own light and the Church is most true to herself when she finds victory through sacrifice. The Cross penetrates Christian truth and action at every point and brings recovery and renewal through apparent defeat. When the impression of the Cross is clearly seen on the life of the Church, the expression of her priesthood will be clearly seen also. It will then be known that she is God's priestly community. Her dying is the sign of her life, her suffering the only means of victory. But she must hold the Faith at any cost. When the spirit of the Cross pervades her whole life, and when comfort, security, and the hope of success are placed on the altar of personal faith in Christ, the Church will become the believing priesthood she was always intended to be.

Islam is not short of an aim, she lacks a Saviour. This is why her interpretation of priesthood was defective, for it was based on a formula instead of arising out of a spiritual experience. This experience is nothing less than a participation in and continuation of the priesthood of Christ. Even as the great High Priest on the Cross was priest and victim, so will those who abide in Him offer the sacrifice of dedication, intercession and service, and thereby will themselves be the offering that is made. United to Christ they present themselves as 'a living sacrifice, holy, acceptable unto God', that they may be used for the fulfilment of the divine purpose in the lives of those for whom the sacrifice is made. Their absolute loyalty is to the High Priest Himself, and just because obedience to a Person is more difficult to achieve than obedience to a formula, the demands of Christianity in terms of witness, service and sacrifice, are more exacting than those of Islam. Yet in one sense the advantage lay with Islam, for from the beginning it was the religion of the conqueror. It was able to combine a demanding practical commitment with an unbending, rigid acceptance of given norms, thanks to the fact that, unlike Christianity, it began as the religion of the conqueror and not of the conquered. Hence unlike its monotheistic rivals, it had no cause to devise a rich armoury of devices for accommodating Caesar, it *was* Caesar. This is the crux of the issue: Islam is Caesar, Christianity is Servant. The one is represented by a Conqueror, the other by a Saviour. The Church is the redeemed community, united to Christ in the fellowship of His sufferings, living by the power of His Resurrection, interceding for the salvation of the world, serving and suffering, living and dying in the firm belief that the only symbol of true priesthood is the Cross. Ultimately it is Christ Himself who must determine the course the Church must take in any age, and as Pascal observes: 'Muhammad chose the way of human success, Jesus Christ that of human defeat.' The Church needs the constant reminder that in the Christian religion crucifixion is inevitable but it is not the end.

C. PRIESTHOOD AND LAITY

The conflict with Islam was not the only one, however, which troubled the Church in the seventh and eighth centuries. It was a period of the most vigorous, and sometimes bitter, controversy. Three of these controversies or discussions we must now consider, not necessarily because they are the most important, but because they are symptomatic of a strong tendency which was taking place in the life of the Church. We turn, therefore, to a consideration of the worship of icons, the Penitential System, and the doctrine of the Eucharist.

1. *The worship of icons*

In this prolonged controversy (725–847) the methods of Emperor Leo III are questionable, not his aims. There is little doubt that in the eighth century the Eastern Churches were full of statues and pictures even of the Persons of the Trinity, and especially of the Blessed Virgin. The orthodox case for the use of images has been stated as follows:

> The icons are likenesses engraved or painted in oil on wood or stone or any sort of metal, of our Saviour Christ, of the Mother of God, and of the holy men who from Adam have been well-pleasing to God. From earliest times the icons have been used not only to give internal dignity and beauty to every Christian house, but, which is much more essential, for the instruction and moral education of Christians. For when any Christian looks at the icons, he at once recalls the life and deeds of those who are represented upon them, and desires to conform himself to their example. On this account also the Church decreed in early times that due reverence should always be paid by Christians to the holy icons, which honour of course is not rendered to the picture before our eyes, but to the original of the picture.[1]

[1] W. H. Hutton, *The Church and the Barbarians*, pp. 156–7.

This statement is moderate enough and an impartial observer might be excused for wondering what all the fuss was about. But this statement gives a somewhat romantic and idealized view of image worship, and that there was a pronounced deterioration of the practice in the eighth century is now commonly accepted.

There were four reasons why Leo became the leader of the iconoclasts: his genuine zeal for the extension of the Church and the banishing of superstition, his monophysite background, his struggle against Islam, and, a less creditable reason, his concern to demonstrate his superiority over Germanus, the Patriarch of Constantinople, and the Popes of Rome. The impression, too often given, that Leo was no more than an over-zealous and misguided fanatic, is very wide of the mark. His aim was to preserve the purity and simplicity of the Christian Church which he maintained was assailed by idolatrous superstitions. Again, he was of Monophysite stock, and Monophysites, denying the continuance of humanity in the glorified Christ, had no room for images in their churches. Moreover, his native Isauria was in close proximity to the Mohammadan Empire and he was familiar with the Muslim taunts against Christians. Stung by the continual charges of idolatry, and convinced of the truth of them, he determined to stamp out the practices on which such accusations were placed. Germanus, the patriarch, was a staunch defender of image worship, and wrote many discourses in praise of the Virgin Mary, in connexion with whom many superstitions had arisen. But when Leo became aware that the Pope had joined hands with Germanus, the Emperor became more resolute than ever in the radical pursuit of his aims.

In the last analysis image-worship is the resort of a people deprived of grace. The trenchant arguments of Germanus and John of Damascus do nothing to minimize the force of this conclusion. Germanus writes:

> Nor did men worship the image of Christ, which is of earthly materials, but the worship was addressed to that which is represented by the image to the devotional mind, the incarnate Son of God. But to the Mother of God, and to the saints, no devotion of any sort was paid, not even to their persons; no religious homage ($\lambda\alpha\tau\rho\epsilon\iota\alpha$) such as belongs to God alone ... In the image we do not invoke the saints but the God of the saint.[1]

[1] Germanus, *Letter to Thomas, Bp. of Claudiopolis.*

The repetition of this defensive argument indicates both the diffidence of those who held it and the assurance of those who opposed. John of Damascus adopted a similar position to that of Germanus. Commenting on his writings, Hutton says: 'The practical bearing of John's writings was in direct relation to the great controversy of his age, to which he devoted three addresses in particular. He defined the "worship" of icons as all based upon the worship of Christ, and attacked iconoclasm as involving ultimately an assault upon the doctrine of the Incarnation.'[1] Moreover, John does not hesitate to call an icon 'a channel of divine grace', a curious phrase for one who held such a high conception of the Incarnation. Some clarification is called for. John assumed that icons represented, in some way, the humanity of our Lord. Hence those who sought to remove them were guilty of assaulting the doctrine of the Incarnation. His opponents argued that the Incarnation, by which our Lord's humanity was revealed, rendered all icons unnecessary. The question arises as to whether the orthodox party were really safeguarding the Incarnation or making a concession to human weakness. Not only the Incarnation, but the sufficiency of Christ and His unique place in relation to God, as well as the believer's access to God, are placed in jeopardy if the use of icons is permitted.

Few will question that there is a place for art in Christian worship. It serves as an aid to devotion, as a means of inspiration, and as an expression of man's aspirations towards Truth, Beauty and Goodness. But that was not the crucial issue in the eighth century. The real issue was between those who believed that pictures and images possessed intrinsic value and supernatural power and those who did not. Underneath all this was the deeper question as to whether or not such icons were indispensable in Christian worship. Do they, in fact, possess value in themselves? It is a fundamental belief of those who worship images that an image is invested with the power of deity only when it is being worshipped. Sarma writes with considerable authority on this point: 'One may ask: How can God be made to come and go? Is He not always present? The answer is—He is always present, but what comes and goes is the modification in the mind of the worshipper. The worshipper informs or reminds himself that the Lord is present. Similarly, bidding the Lord depart means that

[1] W. H. Hutton, op. cit., p. 160.

the mind of the worshipper has ceased to worship the image.'[1] Again, Radhakrishnan maintains that image worship is permissible only for those who have not attained spiritual maturity, yet he does not hesitate to say that the power of the image is solely dependent upon the devotional attitude of the worshipper. The Hindu admits that nothing can be known except in the mode of the knower. Canakyaniti says: 'Neither in wood nor in stone nor in clay is the deity. The deity is there by virtue of mystic feeling. Therefore the mystic feeling is the cause'.[2] The plain implication is that supernatural power indwells the image at the behest of the worshipper. If this is true, the presence of deity is determined by the mind of the worshipper. But is this any more than a projection of the human mind, and does it not imply that at best the image possesses a relative rather than an absolute value? However well-intended, such an interpretation, whether found in Hindu or Christian worship, implies such a diminished view of divine revelation as to reduce it to absurdity. Such a view would turn the deity into no more than a puppet of the human mind. To be sure, faith may respond to the divine revelation, but faith does not produce it.

There is a further objection: an image is a work of art, and art is indifferent to religious truth and moral value. Hence Streeter's observation: 'Religion differs from Art in that it is concerned with quality or "value" in its moral as well as in its aesthetic aspect.'[3] The conclusion is that an image possesses no intrinsic value. There remains the alternative that a process of transvaluation may take place which is produced by the mind of the worshipper. In either case an image is not and cannot be a medium of divine revelation and should not be worshipped.

The ultimate verdict, however, of the Eastern Church was that images were indispensable to Christian worship. It was a Pyrrhic victory. Untouched by the penetrating insights of the Protestant Reformation, the Eastern Church has not realized that such a position is a negation of the doctrine of justification by faith, of the believer's direct access to God, and of the spiritual nature of Christian worship. The Archimandrite, Theodore, might argue

---

[1] D. S. Sarma, *What is Hinduism?*, p. 32.
[2] S. Radhakrishnan, *Religion and Society*, p. 124.
[3] B. H. Streeter, *Reality*, p. 39.

that his aim was to resist the imperial attempt to dragoon the Church but he was surely on dangerous ground when he said: 'The worship of the image is the worship of Christ, because the image is what it is in virtue of likeness to Christ.'[1]

Although the dramatic presentation or representation of religion may be justified on aesthetic grounds, there remains the danger that it may lead either to a religion dependent on sensory experience rather than on faith, or to a religion in which an image becomes an intermediary rather than an aid to devotion. The Christian 'endures as seeing Him who is invisible' (Heb. xi. 27) and 'we walk by faith, not by sight' (2 Cor. v. 7). These are words which enshrine profound truths for the Christian and they would seem to leave no room for icon worship. It is not only that religion is turned into a purely sensory experience and that the worshipper becomes a passive onlooker instead of an active participant in what Christ has accomplished, it is also that the second commandment is broken and Paul's impressive declaration: 'Faith cometh by hearing and hearing by the word of Christ' (Rom. x. 17) rendered meaningless.

The danger in image worship does not end there. Because virtue was believed to reside in the image there emerged another and a more serious development—the veneration of an image as a meritorious act. On the other hand, the withholding of such veneration was regarded as blasphemy and invoked the cruellest punishments. The images now assumed a far greater importance, for profane hands touching them, were withered, and such as endeavoured to remove them were struck dead. That all this strengthened the prestige, position and power of the priest, cannot be doubted. What is not certain is that the common people understood what was taking place. Fear turned into uncertainty and uncertainty into superstition. The grip of the priest on the minds of the people was never more pronounced than in the eighth century. The doctrine of the priesthood of all believers receded into the background, and although it was not entirely obscured, the gulf between the priesthood and the laity widened to an alarming extent. Yet the situation was not entirely without hope. The unbroken succession of believers continued, as Stephen Neill has indicated:

[1] W. H. Hutton, op. cit., p. 164.

The Byzantine Church has always laid great stress on the hierarchy and the unbroken succession. Patriarchs might come and go; but always, far and near, there would be the holy man, in whom the power of the Christian life would be manifestly present. . . . The importance of the saint as against the hierarch has been a continuing feature of the life of the Christian society in the east until the present day.[1]

Leo failed because he tried to inaugurate a puritan reformation without first securing the support of the majority of his Christian subjects. Perhaps he tried to do too much too soon. Although he lost the struggle, more through faulty methods than misguided aims, the truths for which he contended—the sufficiency of Christ, the free access to God without any intermediary, the spiritual nature of worship, and the protest against materialistic tendencies in the Church—were commendable enough. The succession of saints continued, and although their worship was sometimes mixed up with the strangest superstitions, the fault lay in the neglect of the shepherds rather than in the wilfulness of the sheep.

2. *The Penitential System*

If the result of the iconoclastic controversy militated against a true understanding of the priesthood of all believers, the penitential system struck a mortal blow. The fear and ignorance of the Christian community were exploited to such an extent that the hope of salvation, let alone its certainty, was placed in the hands of the priesthood.

For six centuries the accepted manner in which a Christian was readmitted into Christian fellowship after he had committed grave sin was by public confession and the performing of certain prescribed satisfactions such as fasting or almsgiving. During the seventh century two significant changes took place: Public confession gave place to private confession to a Priest, and satisfactions imposed by the whole congregation gave place to satisfactions imposed by the Priest. This eventually resulted in a complete change in the system of satisfactions which is marked by three innovations:

(i) The introduction of a 'treasury of merits'.
(ii) The Institution of Penance became the Sacrament of Penance.
(iii) The introduction of the idea of attrition.

[1] S. Neill, *The Christian Society*, p. 92.

(i) Treasury of merits

Upon this only one comment is necessary: it meant that the control of divine grace had passed from God to man, for the custodian of the 'treasury' was the Bishop of Rome. Payment out of the 'treasury' was the equivalent for any satisfaction due by the penitent.

(ii) Institution of penance

Originally the order of sequence was as follows:
(*a*) Sorrow for sins.
(*b*) Confession of sins to a Priest.
(*c*) Satisfaction for sins.
(*d*) Pardon for sins.

When the Institution became the Sacrament of Penance the order was changed. Pardon followed Confession and came before Satisfaction. This Pardon (or Absolution pronounced by the Priest) removed the guilt of all sins confessed as well as the eternal punishment due. *But* there remained temporal penalties which had to be endured, some of which could be endured in this life and others only after death. It was the priest who had to prescribe the temporal punishments. But who could be sure that he had calculated rightly? Since no one could be sure about this, the pain of temporal punishments after death threatened every man. All this assumes that absolute pardon is impossible in this life, for if it were possible, the system of satisfactions would no longer be necessary.

(iii) The idea of attrition

Contrition (godly sorrow) was acceptable to God, and upon this basis the penitent was forgiven. Attrition (servile fear) derived from a low motive, and could not of itself bring pardon to the penitent. Attrition strengthened by confession to a priest could win absolution, but it could not win freedom from temporal penalties. So temporal penalties had to be endured, and again forgiveness became a matter of uncertainty.

From these three changes in the system of satisfactions one important result followed: the power of God was limited, and the power of the priest exalted. Even when the Church's scheme of salvation had been most scrupulously observed by a penitent (Attrition, Confession, Indulgence), his salvation remained a matter of doubt and uncertainty. Even if there was a possibility of absolute pardon, the believer did not know it.

As long as forgiveness in this life is regarded as a matter of uncertainty, and as long as the believer's sanctification is a matter of doubt, the Catholic conception of priesthood will be maintained. It will be seen, therefore, that the priesthood is not simply to be regarded as a convenient form of Church government, it is a necessity of Catholic theology. The problem is not one of ecclesiology but of doctrine; it is not a question of 'form' but of 'content'; it is a question of Faith rather than Order. Strictly speaking, the Catholic doctrine of priesthood arises out of and is necessitated by Catholic soteriology. The crux of the matter lies in questions such as the following: How can man please God? How can man commune with God? These simple but strategic questions of the believer's relationship with God cannot be answered by Catholicism without the inclusion of the word 'Priest'. It was Luther who first realized that the problem was theological and doctrinal, and so he set himself the task of expounding the doctrine of Justification by Faith alone, for he had concluded that everything revolved around this great issue. Justification by Faith does not need to be buttressed by innumerable subsidiary aids. As long as redemption requires human mediation and as long as human satisfactions must be added to divine justification, so long will indulgences, meritorious acts, the prayers of the saints, the aid of the celestial hierarchy, and the sacrificial powers of the priesthood, be necessary. If, on the other hand, man's justification may be regarded as a certainty, and if sanctification is a fact and not a dream, and if these incomparable blessings are bestowed on men on the basis of faith and not on the basis of the external conditions already mentioned, then the case for the Protestant doctrine of the universal priesthood of believers is not in doubt.

3. *Developments in the doctrine and practice of the Eucharist*

It is a characteristic of medieval philosophy that ideas cannot exist alone, they require a concrete form. Christ and the saints were often represented by visible images, and, as we have seen, where the image was, there was Christ. From this concept it was but a short step to the belief that where the symbols were, there was Christ. The material was a veil of the spiritual reality. It was already widely believed that Christ was present in the bread and wine and that His presence was revealed to faith. The significance of the teaching of Radbert (800–865) lies in the fact that faith was no longer essential since the bread and wine changed their substance (not their appearance) through the power of the priest. Radbert gave a literal interpretation of John vi. 54, and claimed that there was an identity between the Eucharistic and historic body of Christ. All that has followed in Roman theology on this theme has been more or less a commentary on the position of Radbert. Although the notion of transubstantiation is stated by him only in germinal form, the Roman Church has not deviated to any great extent from the essence of his teaching.

It is fair to say, however, that the first comment on his teaching is easily the most impressive. Ratramnus denied the basis of Radbert's case, the identity of the Eucharistic and historic body, and maintained that the bread and wine were the body and blood of Christ only in a spiritual sense, and even then, only to the faith of believers. Unbelievers could not receive Christ because they lacked the gift of faith. Ratramnus excluded any miraculous change in the elements on the ground of the ubiquity of Christ's presence. All the same, the part of the priest is not underestimated, for by the consecration of the priest, the regenerating power of the Holy Spirit is added to the elements which bring, albeit in a mystery, healing virtue to the soul.

Although Radbert's opinions have been assailed, they have never been dislodged from Roman theology, and there is no doubt that his teaching marks a vital stage in the development of Christian doctrine. The priest was the instrument of the miracle by which the elements were changed, and consequently the sense of awe and fear on the part of believers was intensified. But this was not the only consequence:

> For adults the great sacrament was the Mass. It was conducted in Latin, and the people did not understand the lines. In any case, much of the liturgy was inaudible. The congregation was encouraged to occupy itself with private devotions so that two parallel services were taking place coincidently. At the same time, the dramatic acts of the liturgy, such as the elevation of the host, were readily intelligible, and besides, the church was richly endowed with symbolism that it might

be 'a book to the ignorant people that they may read in the imagery and painture that clerks read in the book'.[1]

As far as the Roman Church is concerned Radbert built better than he knew, and the theory of transubstantiation, (though the word is not used till three hundred years later), became the norm for all future interpretations as well as the sanction for all the sacerdotal tendencies of the past. It also served to underline the strong tendency which had developed in the Church since the days of Cyprian.

Before referring to this tendency in detail, let it be noted that the Eucharist is a sacrament of unity. The idea of sacrifice in the Old Testament is based on communion with God. The Covenant of promise, which postulates the unity between God and His people, is fulfilled in the New Covenant of grace. 'The Blood of our Lord Jesus Christ'—the true Vine—implies the unity of Christ and His people. The drinking of the cup is the present participation in the fellowship of the kingdom both as it is and as it will be. The eating of *the same loaf* bears a similar significance, for Paul says: 'Because there is one loaf, we who are many are one body, for we all partake of the same loaf' (1 Cor. x. 17). The conclusion is inescapable: the words and phrases used in the Communion Service as well as the thought-forms which are associated with it, emphatically illustrate the unity of believers with Christ and with one another. The experience of this unity brings ecstatic joy to the believer:

> *My feet touch earth no longer: it is as I were eating*
> *At the high God's own table, of heaven's ambrosia.*

This is the earnest of that perfect union which will one day exist between all God's people. As Charles Wesley sings:

> *It gives my ravished soul a taste,*
> *And makes me for some moments feast*
> *With Jesu's priests and kings.*

Now it is against this background of the aim and purpose of the Eucharist that the developments in the Middle Ages must be considered. First there was the screen between the laity in the nave and the priests in the chancel, so that the laity could not even see

[1] H. R. Niebuhr and D. D. Williams, *The Ministry in Historical Perspectives*, p. 96.

what was taking place. Then there was the strange custom of encouraging the laity to engage in private devotions as if all hope of their understanding the Service had been surrendered. There was also the use of the Latin tongue which excluded the laity from any real participation. Then the notion developed that the wine could be withheld from the laity, partly because the whole Christ was present in every particle of the consecrated wafer and partly because the laity were deemed to be too ignorant to understand the awfulness of the occasion. And soon we have the strange spectacle of the observance of the Sacrament of union with Christ in which the laity have no part whatever. The question arises as to whether such a Service can be regarded as a true Eucharist when one of its chief purposes is obscured. If the unique opportunity of union with Christ and His followers is lost, what, we may ask, remains? This curious sequence of events has led to the virtual exclusion of the laity from the central act of the Church's worship. All attention came to be focused on the words of consecration which became a sort of magical formula, and, as the priest became the mediator between heaven and earth, whose words had the power to effect a repetition of the Incarnation as well as a re-enactment of the Sacrifice of the Cross, the laity became entirely dependent upon him. This resulted in an abject subservience which is alien to any true interpretation of the Eucharist.

The great feast of Christian fellowship gave place to unintelligible priestly incantations. The separation between priest and people was accomplished, and if this was not the aim of the Roman Church, it will be difficult to explain and still more difficult to deny, the unambiguous nature of the result. Indeed Church architecture, Church worship and Church government indicate all too clearly how completely the idea of the royal priesthood of the faithful was eclipsed. The doctrine might have been accepted in theory but it was denied in practice.

The victory of the orthodox party in the iconoclastic controversy, the penitential system, and the developments in the doctrine and practice of the Eucharist, in their cumulative effect, had one unmistakable outcome—a denial of the priesthood of all believers. This vital principle of the New Testament was not only obscured but obliterated, and as far as official Roman doctrine was concerned, so it remained for nearly seven hundred years.

That these developments should have repercussions far beyond the bounds of the Church was, perhaps, inevitable, and in the eleventh century there appeared a man who possessed both the power and the ability to work out their implications in relation to the State.

D. CHURCH AND STATE

*Hildebrand** (1020–1085)

Every time Christians pray 'thy Kingdom come' they join hands with Hildebrand in his noble and meritorious aspiration. While there is no doubt about the value of his aim, there is doubt about the means whereby he sought its fulfilment. Ever since the days of Augustine, and perhaps because of his work, Christians had been inspired by the theocratic ideal. This ideal implies that God must rule and be seen to rule in all the affairs of men. It also implies that the law of God must take precedence over all other laws and that all secular powers must be subservient to the divine authority. We must now consider how Hildebrand proposed to turn this dream into a reality. He set out to establish beyond all doubt the authority, independence and purity of the Church.

The Authority of the Church

Not only were Hildebrand's ideas clear in his own mind but he had the facility to state them with tremendous power. These ideas produced a definite policy which has influenced the Roman Church ever since. He believed that the survival of the Church could only be ensured if her authority was centralized, comprehensive and final. If the world was to be unified under one law, it must be the law of God. But the law had to be pronounced if it was to be known. It could be effectively pronounced only if all spiritual authority was invested in a single unassailable office. This spiritual authority was represented by and focalized in the holder of that office. Although the idea of infallibility is implicit in the teaching of Hildebrand, it is the infallibility of the office and not of its holder. His simple but far-reaching plan was to establish once for all an unassailable centre of authority. The overt claim to infallibility on the part of the holder of the office came eight hundred years later but even then it did not mean 'the Pope can do no

* Gregory VII.

wrong' but that in matters of doctrine and morals, by the mercy of God, he is protected from error.

> The Pope in himself is subject to error like other men; his infallibility comes from the Spirit of God, which on certain occasions protects him from error in faith and morals. He has no infallibility in merely historical or scientific questions. Even in matters of faith and morals he has no inspiration, and must use the same means of theological enquiry as other men. Even when he speaks with Apostolic authority he may err. The Vatican Council only requires us to believe that God protects him from error in definitions on faith or morals when he imposes a belief on the Universal Church.[1]

The idea of authority centralized in the office was first envisaged by Hildebrand. To him also is due another development of equal importance, the idea that this authority must be of a comprehensive nature. It was to embrace secular as well as spiritual matters. Kings and princes might question and challenge it but they were subject to it. But this claim brought conflicts for which even Hildebrand was not wholly prepared. To William of Orange he wrote: 'As I have to answer for you at the awful judgment, in the interests of your own salvation, ought you, can you avoid immediate obedience to me?' The fact that William bluntly rejected the argument meant that in the eyes of Rome, he forfeited the right to rule. Henry IV of Germany was less effective in his resistance, and, after a long controversy with the Pope, he was compelled to make an abject submission at Canossa. Although Henry's penance was short lived the fact remained that the Pope had daringly pointed a way whereby papal authority might be exercised, a way which his successors were not slow to follow. Yet the last word in the conflict was not Rome's, for Germany did not easily forget Henry's humiliation, and it would be a misreading of history to say that this event was wholly unconnected with the Reformation. Hildebrand, however, had so relentlessly insisted on the comprehensive nature of papal authority that it could not lightly be challenged by the most powerful prince.

This centralized and comprehensive authority was vulnerable if its finality was in doubt. No one knew this better than Hildebrand. How was its final and irrevocable nature to be established and safeguarded? It could only be achieved by the impenetrable shield of Canon Law. By this time it was clearly perceived that

[1] Addis and Arnold, *A Catholic Dictionary*, p. 736.

intermittent modifications of Roman Law could no longer be regarded as sufficient to deal with the doctrinal, political and legal problems which the Church had to face in many lands. The very expansion of the Western Church brought to light many questions to which Rome had no answer. Hitherto the Church had been dependent upon whatever light might be shed by various papal rescripts, conciliar canons and civil enactments, and although such light had been useful in the past it was now seen to be altogether too sporadic and uncertain to guarantee the defence of the Church's position in the future. Something much more enduring, more doctrinal and authoritative was demanded. Although the final codification of the laws of the Church did not take place until fifty-seven years after Hildebrand's death, with the appearance of Gratian's Decretum (1142), it will be readily acknowledged that much of the preparatory work had been done by Hildebrand himself, and it is certain that the necessity of such a codification was the direct result of his reforms.

What is meant by Canon Law? It is comprised of four parts: precepts of the natural law, positive divine precepts, directives left by the Apostles, and ecclesiastical constitutions. Its sources are:

1. Holy Scripture:
2. Ecclesiastical Traditions:
3. The decrees of Councils:
4. Papal constitutions and rescripts:
5. The writings of the Fathers:
6. The Civil Law.

Gratian's work is a detailed statement concerning the application of these precepts in relation to the ranks and duties of the clergy, to the procedure in ecclesiastical courts, and to the rites and ceremonies employed in the service of religion. To be sure certain corrections were made by later popes, but the substance of the Decretum still stands as a *corpus juris* and is applicable to the whole Catholic world. If there is any doubt about the success of Canon Law in preserving Catholic dogma, there is no doubt that it has protected and enhanced papal authority. With its formation Hildebrand's emphasis upon the need for a centralized, comprehensive and final authority in the Roman Church reached its fulfilment.

The Independence of the Church

It will be noticed that by these developments the Church had already moved away from the patristic idea of the universal priesthood which, as we have seen, was characterized by participation in the priesthood of Christ, by suffering which sometimes involved martyrdom, by sacrificial service, by mutual dependence in matters of material possessions, and by the exercise of various charismatic ministries. If the laity had overlooked the essential value of this doctrine, it was not least because the clergy had overlooked it also. It is not always recognized how much the medieval Church sacrificed by losing sight of this patristic ideal. A fuller understanding of the relation of the Royal Priesthood to the government of the Church as well as its mission, would have obviated many of the difficulties which now faced the Church. The clergy had lost sight of the concept of servanthood and had become concerned primarily with the acquisition of secular power. In this deviation from New Testament principles the laity had learned some lessons from the clergy. The transition in the meaning of priesthood which had become apparent during the ascendancy of Cyprianic ideas was now seen to be fraught with great perils for the Church. No vital doctrine can be neglected with impunity, and the hierarchy is by no means blameless for the anomalous position in which the Church found herself in the eleventh century. The laity became dominant and pressed home their advantage with almost unholy zeal. This attitude was not due to an abuse of the doctrine of the priesthood of all believers but to ignorance of it. The defect was doctrinal although it was not treated as such at the time. So the Church set herself to face a problem which, had she remained true to Biblical and Patristic teaching, need not have arisen.

First there was the problem of lay investiture. In the eleventh century society was patterned on the Feudal System by which a vassal was bound to his lord by obligations of service and defence, and in return for the service rendered he was granted the protection of his lord. The clergy, however, were exempt from this requirement and in many countries the Church possessed half the land. In these circumstances it was inevitable that the lords and nobles would rebel, which is exactly what happened. The Feudal System was applied to the Church, and the rulers of Europe treated religious benefices like other feudal ones, demanding large sums of money before bestowing them. Consequently the clergy became a sort of feudal community owing personal service to a ruler. They were invested with the symbols of their dignity only after they had done homage to a temporal ruler and become pledged to his service. Hildebrand opposed this with great vigour on the ground that it undermined the spiritual character of the Church which received its power and commission from God and not from any man. He issued a decree in 1075 forbidding any clergyman to accept a benefice by lay investiture. A bitter conflict followed and the matter was eventually resolved at the Concordat of Worms in 1122 when the Church surrendered little and the State a great deal. But it was an uneasy truce and proved to be unsatisfactory because it was based on two fallacies, namely, that the Church can fulfil her true function without the voluntary goodwill and free co-operation of the State, and that the rulers of the Church will always be more righteous than others in both aim and conduct. The result is of the utmost importance for our study since the ultimate outcome was to drive a wedge between the clergy and the laity which was destined to remain until the Reformation.

Closely allied to this was another move which further separated the clergy from the laity. Justice for churchmen was to be administered solely by the Church and the clergy were no longer subject to the civil courts. We shall see later how vigorously Marsiglio of Padua dealt with this problem but for the moment it is necessary to note the discontent among the laity that a clergyman guilty of rape, theft, or even murder, was able to claim the benefit of clergy. The question of justice was also imperilled and clerical immunities were all the more conspicuous in a society where the ratio of the clergy to the laity was estimated at 1 in 35. In these circumstances clerical emancipation easily became clerical licence.

In worship also the line between the clergy and the laity was heightened. At Communion the priest was at the altar and the people before the altar rail. The priest stood and the people kneeled. The clergy partook of both elements and the people partook only of the bread. These developments may not appear significant in themselves but they became crucial issues at the

Reformation where Luther, pleading the words of our Lord: 'All ye, drink of this,' and the priesthood of all believers, restored to the People of God their true place in the worship of the Church.

At this time also there was introduced a distinctive dress for the clergy which emphasized that they were in a class apart. This would not have been very important if it had indicated only the distinctive calling to a holy life, but when it also meant special privileges and immunity from the law it became very serious indeed and was strongly resisted.

The clergy were further separated from the laity by the new rule about celibacy. Hildebrand had three reasons for the imposition of this rule. He demanded an exclusive obedience to the Pope and he rightly reasoned that married clergy in different countries might tend to be more obedient to the ruler of their own nation than to any one outside it. Since a priest's first obedience must be to the Papal See, Hildebrand made his hierarchical system nonnational. Again, there was always the danger that the Clergy might develop into an hereditary caste, the office being handed down from father to son by a family arrangement; this also was to be deplored. Therefore his system became non-hereditary also. The third reason is concerned with discipline and asceticism, for it had long been believed that the state of virginity was higher than the married state. There is much in the first two arguments that is worthy of commendation, while the last reason is based on the false notion that celebate asceticism is in some way a higher form of Christian life than any other. But we are mainly concerned with the final result of this development. It meant that another sharp line of demarcation had been drawn between the clergy and the laity. Trench sums up the outcome as follows: 'Henceforth the Clergy became an exclusive body, not patterns to the flock, models on which other Christians should fashion the lives of themselves and their families, but a separate class, lifted above the rest of the faithful, and in this central fact of their lives divided from them.'[1]

In striving to secure the authority, independence and purity of the Church, Hildebrand had developed such a theory of hierarchical government as had never been known before. Against this high-powered conception of ecclesiastical rule, buttressed as it

[1] R. C. Trench, *Medieval Church History*, pp. 119–20.

was by Canon Law, Gratian's Decretum, clerical immunities, sacerdotal claims and rules of celibacy, there was no appeal. In the teaching of Hildebrand the power of the hierarchy received its fullest expression, and as the priesthood of the clergy increased, the priesthood of all believers decreased. Indeed the doctrine which had inspired many of the early Fathers, as well as St Augustine, and which Gregory I had not ignored, was now completely overshadowed. As far as the priesthood of believers was concerned these were dark ages indeed. With all his skill as an administrator, and this is not in doubt, it does not appear to have occurred to Hildebrand that he had secured benefits and privileges only for a part of the Church and not the whole. But to secure such privileges for a few at the expense of the whole body of the faithful was not in the highest interests of the Christian Church. The Church would have been better served by a considered and vigorous exposition of the doctrine of the priesthood of believers, so that a recalcitrant and ill-informed laity might have understood the spiritual meaning and implications of their priestly calling rather than be compelled to submit before the steam-roller tactics of a powerful organization. It was inevitable that voices of protest would be raised, voices in places as far apart as Padua, Lutterworth and Erfurt, but the time was not yet. But before we turn to the work of Marsiglio and Wyclif, we must consider how the 'Royal Priesthood of the Faithful' has taken shape in Roman Catholic theology.

CHAPTER SIX

THE IDEA OF PRIESTHOOD IN ROMAN CATHOLIC THEOLOGY

1. THE HIGH PRIESTHOOD OF CHRIST

OUR starting-point must be the priesthood of our Lord, for whatever views may be held about the priesthood implicit in Holy Orders or about the priesthood of the faithful, it is certain that their meaning may be properly understood only in the light of the essential priesthood of Christ. What is meant by this priesthood? 'As Priest He worships, praises and thanks the divine majesty in His own name and that of all people; He intercedes before the throne of the Father for us; He sends down therefrom the blessings of heaven. This priesthood of our Lord is the one and only fundamental priesthood in the Church.'[1]

It is true that this priesthood manifests itself visibly in the priesthood of the whole Church and in a special manner in the priesthood of Holy Orders, yet there are aspects of our Lord's priesthood which are unique and incommunicable. No man can do for our race what He has done. St Thomas reminds us of the nature of this priesthood:

> A priest's office is to be mediator between God and the people. Appropriately, then, is Christ a priest: for through Him gifts are bestowed on men, by whom He hath given us exceeding great and precious promises, that by these you may be made partakers of the divine nature. Furthermore, He reconciles the human race to God, for in Him it hath well pleased the Father that all fullness should dwell, and through Him to reconcile all things unto Himself.[2]

Here are clearly stated those functions of our Lord's priesthood which are peculiar to Himself. He is the mediator by the offering of His own life, He is the Giver of all gifts of divine grace, and He reconciles all men to God. The distinctive nature of His priesthood is at once apparent. But there is also a cosmic dimension

[1] *Cath. Enc. Dict.* (ed. D. Attwater), p. 400.
[2] *Summa Theologica*, 3a, xxiii. 1.

to His priestly work, for through Him the Father reconciles all things unto Himself. In its nature and functions, in its universal scope and its finality, our Lord's priesthood is unique.

In order to understand this more fully it is necessary to examine St Thomas's teaching on the motive and fact of the Incarnation as well as his interpretation of the Atonement. He takes the view that if there had been no Fall, there would have been no Incarnation:

> The son of Man is come to seek and to save that which was lost. Therefore, Augustine concludes, if man had not sinned, the Son of Man would not have come. ... Theologians think differently on this point. Some hold that even if man had not fallen the Son of God would have become incarnate. Others hold the contrary. Personally I think their opinion is to be preferred.[1]

But does not such a view deny the *eternal* nature of Christ's priesthood? It was the love of God, not the sin of man, which brought the long-sought Saviour down. The Incarnation is first and foremost the revelation of divine love, and although the remedy for human sin is the outcome of it, it is still the outcome and not the primary cause. It cannot be too strongly affirmed that the love of God is the governing principle of the Incarnation. God is love, and it is the nature of love to communicate itself. The Incarnation is the completion and crown of the spiritual process in the history of mankind dating from creation, and not merely a remedy for the catastrophe by which mankind has been severed from its relationship with God. The essential Christ has always existed and He became man in order that He might manifest the fulness of the Godhead bodily. The incarnate Word is the eternal Word, for 'in the beginning was the Word'. The priesthood of Christ is without beginning and without end—'Thou art a priest forever after the order of Melchizedek' (Heb. vii. 17).

The close relation of Creation and Incarnation in the work of Athanasius marks off his Christology from that of Aquinas. He maintained that the Son came to show the loving-kindness of God. It is true that a cure was needed for 'things that come to be', but a cure had always existed in the eternal purpose of God in Christ. If, however, the Incarnation was implicit in Creation, man's sin must be considered as confirming the necessity of the Incarnation

[1] S.T., 3a, 1, 3.

but not as initiating it. Again, the idea of restoration is most prominent in the teaching of Athanasius. Even though God might have wiped out man's guilt with a word, He did not do so because human nature required to be healed, restored and recreated.[1]

In preferring the teaching of Athanasius to that of Aquinas, we are preserving the eternal nature of our Lord's priesthood, for, quite apart from the question of the Fall, our Lord was predestined to be the eternal Priest.

If the teaching of Aquinas undermines the eternal nature of Christ's priesthood, it also casts doubts on the *completeness* of it. He writes exultantly and convincingly of our Lord as Head of the Church and as the representative of humanity. Then he considers our Lord's all-embracing knowledge and divine perfection. 'He beheld God's essence and all things in God. For the master-principle of a movement should be high above the process of movement.... We are the subjects of the process; He is the origin. From the beginning of His life He saw God; unlike the blessed, He did not arrive at the vision of God.'[2] There follows the statement that Jesus knew God, not with His human mind but by virtue of an uncreated wisdom. 'He is the person of the Word, uncreated and single in two natures: it is for this reason that we do not say that Christ was a creature simply speaking, for His proper name indicates His personality.... His uncreated wisdom, not his human mind, comprehends God.'[3] Does this imply that in our Lord's earthly existence there was no seeking or striving or development? 'Christ's soul was raised to the highest level of knowledge possible to any created mind, first, as regards seeing God's essence and all things in God, secondly, by knowing the mysteries of grace, and thirdly, all objects of human knowledge. Here no advance was possible.'[4]

In such statements Aquinas vitiated much of what he has previously said about our Lord as Head of the Church and the representative of humanity. One who is far above all process of movement, who knows God by virtue of uncreated wisdom, and in whose knowledge no advance is possible, is so far removed from the struggles and strivings of our human condition that the gulf seems so wide as to be impassable. For, on this showing, Christ is

---
[1] See *De Incarnatione*, xx and xliv.
[2] Aquinas, *Comp. Theol.*, p. 216.   [3] Ibid.   [4] Ibid.

PRIESTHOOD IN ROMAN CATHOLIC THEOLOGY

altogether too distant from any real experience of the feelings of our human nature, and for Him faith and hope seem unnecessary on account of his transcendent perfection in grace and knowledge. We look in vain for *our* High Priest. In the Scripture the completeness of our Lord's priesthood and his identification with our human conditions are not in doubt: 'For we have not a High Priest that cannot be touched with the feeling of our infirmities, but one that hath been tempted like as we are, yet without sin' (Heb. iv. 15). His wisdom did not exempt Him from temptation, and His knowledge did not preclude all development in thought and obedience. 'Though He was a Son, yet *learned* He obedience by the things which He suffered' (Heb. v. 8). It really must not be overlooked that by voluntary limitations our Saviour subjected Himself to an experience of human weakness, human emotions and physical suffering. In relation to His people, this is the essence of our Lord's priesthood: long before we had any hope of being identified with Him, He became identified with us.

> *He became our Fellow*
> *In the morning of our days;*
> *Us He chose for housemates,*
> *And this way went.*

Our Lord's priesthood culminates in His Death on the Cross. Aquinas sums it up thus:

> Strict satisfaction is rendered when the person offended is given as much as, or more than, he hated the offence. By suffering from charity, Christ offered to God more than what was demanded as recompense for the sin of the entire human race.... Head and members make up, as it were, one mystical body. Therefore the amends made by Christ are made also by all His members. Satisfaction, however, is an external deed, for which we adopt auxiliaries, among which are reckoned our friends.[1]

This reference to external satisfaction and the adoption of auxiliaries was at least unfortunate, and at most, harmful. For there is no doubt that it opened a door to error and abuse which the Roman Church has found very difficult to shut. It is to be expected, however, that Aquinas would be in general agreement with Anselm who taught that the sufferings of Christ were the voluntary

[1] *S.T.*, 3a, xlviii. 2.

payment of a penalty not otherwise due from Him to the Divine Justice. As long as Aquinas stayed close to Anselm, he was safe, but when he moved away from the teaching of Anselm on this point, he led the Church into the gravest error.

From the particular angle of our study it is important to notice that this error in doctrine was due to a misinterpretation of the priestly office of Christ. Aquinas developed a new theory of satisfactions which later became the most elaborate system of punishments and rewards that the Church had ever known. It resulted in a reduced conception of sin as well as an external and legalized doctrine of forgiveness. Aquinas urged that the compensation offered by our Lord far exceeded the heinousness of the offence, and that the overplus of merit redounded to the remission of offences in others. Thus he introduced into Church teaching an element of error which was abundantly mischievous in its future application.

This was even more dangerous because, according to the theology of the day, the premiss was true. The corollary, however, was false. Certainly Christ's Death is a full, perfect and sufficient sacrifice, oblation and satisfaction for the sins of the whole world, but this is something very different from the belief that the merits of Christ freely won and freely given, should come under the command and control of the hierarchy. The treasury of merits means the end of free grace. It is useless to argue that if this 'treasury' is controlled with care and restraint, it will have a salutary effect on the life of the Church. The error is in thinking that it can be controlled at all. Ultimately it led to that heretical situation against which Luther raised his voice—a situation in which the arrogant assumption was made that the Church had achieved power over God. The overt claim was not made, but the conclusion is inescapable.

The Roman system of satisfactions is false on two main grounds: if the Sacrifice of Christ is a divine, voluntary act, it cannot be subjected to the imposition of rigid human conditions. Further, if Christ is really Priest, and if He fulfils His priestly functions not only adequately but perfectly, then there is no need for us to adopt auxiliaries. If we are thinking of the sufficiency of the Death of Christ, then other satisfactions are unnecessary. If, on the other hand, other satisfactions are necessary, what becomes of the sufficient Sacrifice of our Lord? We are driven to the conclusion that all accompanying satisfactions are as obnoxious to God as they are unnecessary to man.

In the Church which is the Mystical Body of Christ, His priesthood is revealed. The spiritual unity of the members of the Mystical Body is a very real one, and even so staunch an advocate of the Papacy as St Peter Damian is quoted as saying:

> The whole Church forms, in some part, one single person. As she is the same in all, so in each one is she whole and entire; and just as a man is called a microcosm, so each one of the faithful is, so to say, the Church in miniature. We individuals are the Church, he proclaimed in the name of all, priests and layfolk, in one of his sermons.[1]

The Schoolmen rely upon the mystical interpretation of the Church to answer a difficult question. They admit that Christ possesses the 'Grace of Head' because He is Head of the Church and because He communicates supernatural life to the whole Church which is His body. But the very pertinent question arises as to whether the Headship is proper to Christ alone, or whether and in what manner He shares it with ecclesiastical persons. The answer of the Schoolmen is emphatic even though somewhat unexpected:

> So intimate is the union of Head and body that when they treat of the Head and discuss His most personal gifts, that is, the grace whereby his human nature is sanctified, the Schoolmen are naturally led to speak of the organism to which the grace is communicated for the sanctification of all Christians.[2]

It follows that the Headship of Christ is shared in a mystical sense with all Christians and not only with those who hold clerical office.

It is important to notice that the priesthood of Christ relates to the Church Triumphant as well as the Church Militant. In Catholic thought the doctrine of the Communion of Saints is characterized by three great vital movements: first, the stream of love which flows from the Church Triumphant to the members of Christ on earth; second, the traffic of love which takes place between the members of the Church Suffering and the Church Militant; and third, the communion which operates between the several members of the Church Militant. These three movements

---

[1] Quoted in H. de Lubac, *Catholicism*, p. 167.
[2] E. Mersch, *The Whole Christ*, pp. 457-8.

of loving fellowship may be understood in the light of the invisible priesthood of Christ. The communion of the members of Christ with the priesthood of their Head is of fundamental importance for their mutual commerce of love. There is but one priesthood in the Church, the priesthood of the God-man, who redeemed us by His whole life, but especially by the sacrifice of His death.[1] In this threefold traffic of love Christ the priest does three things: He suffers with the Church, He unites in mystic love the members of the Church, and He unites the Church on earth with the Church in heaven.

The invisible priesthood of Christ is continued in heaven. It is this continuous priestly activity of Christ which gives meaning to the phrase 'The Communion of Saints'. Jesus is the one High Priest in the hierarchy of creation. He is our kinsman, the One who took to heaven a human brow. He was anointed to fulfil that priestly work which was decreed in the eternal councils of God. He is the Lamb slain from the foundation of the world. His eternal oblation constitutes His eternal priesthood. 'Our Lord then inaugurated on earth a priesthood which, having its source in the heavenly sphere, is there continued by Him who is a priest forever. Now, as ascended and glorified, He is ever active in His unchanging priesthood as the one mediator between God and man.'[2]

II. THE PRIESTHOOD OF THE CLERGY

From Aquinas onwards Roman Catholic theology has made a distinction between an inward priesthood which applies to all and an outward priesthood which belongs only to the ordained. The former is described as follows: 'Layfolk are united spiritually to Christ through faith and charity, but not by active sacramental power. Theirs is a spiritual priesthood. The sacrifice God loves is a contrite spirit'.[3] On the other hand, the outward priesthood is seen most clearly in the outward functions of the bishop. 'He is bound to dispense spiritual blessing, for he represents the man Christ Jesus. ... He impersonates the people when he offers prayers and petitions to God. ... He acts in God's person when

---

[1] K. Adam, *Spirit of Catholicism*, p. 124.
[2] E. Scyzinger, *The Glory of God*, p. 25.   [3] *S.T.*, 3a, lxxxii. 1.

he turns towards the people, by our Lord's power ministering to them doctrine, example and sacraments.'[1]

In fact, however, this distinction between the outward or visible priesthood of the ordained and the inward or spiritual priesthood of all Christians is not as clear-cut or as convincing as at first appears. Firstly, to ascribe to the ordained priest alone the term outward priesthood is to give the mistaken impression that he alone may show his priesthood in outward functions. But what about the priesthood exercised in confessions, praises, prayers, material gifts, the sacrifice of self, missionary service, daily witness and secular vocation? All these are related to the Royal priesthood in the New Testament, and surely these are outward acts.

Secondly, the distinction between outward and inward priesthood is artificial when it is used in relation to clergy and laity. The real distinction between outward and inward priesthood is between priesthood in the Old Testament and the New. Indeed, the error of the Hebrews was that they clamoured for priests and that as the Aaronic priesthood developed, the meaning of the spiritual priesthood was lost. In the New Testament, however, only the inward and spiritual priesthood remains, and, while it is true that within this universal priesthood there are varied ministries, it is certainly not in accordance with New Testament teaching to draw a distinction between a priesthood of sacramental power and a spiritual priesthood.

At the same time we must examine the importance of the sacramental power of the ordained priesthood as it has come to be understood in Catholic thought. The priesthood of Christ implies the derivative priesthood of those who have received the dominical authority. Catholicism regards this priesthood as not only desirable but as indispensable. Its divine origin is clearly affirmed:

> All Catholics would agree that it is an inversion of right thinking to conceive of the hierarchy as a structure built up from below. Christ is the Head of the Church, and all authority is derived from Him. Its ministry is the divinely appointed channel of communication. ... Through the Church, as a whole and acting in unity, Christ makes known His will for the Church, and the hierarchy and the councils are the means whereby unity of faith and action can be secured.[2]

[1] Aquinas, *de Perfectione Vitae Spiritualis*, p. 16.
[2] K. L. Carrick Smith, *The Church and the Churches*, p. 37.

There is the further assumption that Christ lives in all Christians only through the priesthood and the teaching Church.

> While it is true that Christ lives in all Christians, He does so only through the priesthood and the teaching Church, the magisterium; and the priesthood and the magisterium are not complete unless they include the entire episcopate and the Pope. The progress will only be accomplished by the Christians: by the saints, the faithful, the theologians etc. But it will be accomplished by all these only through union with and submission to the magisterium; and it will not be final until the magisterium shall have spoken, or rather, until Christ shall have spoken through the magisterium.[1]

In view of the foregoing we must ask in what sense Christ may be said to rule the Church? The Catholic answer is that while He rules every soul immediately He does so mediately too.

> Thus Pius XII, after proclaiming that Christ is the one Head of the Church—ruling indeed each and every soul immediately, but also mediately through His Vicar on earth, continues: 'It is then a dangerous error to think that one can adhere to Christ, the Head of the Church, and refuse allegiance to His Vicar on earth. For to remove this visible head and break asunder the visible bonds of unity, is to blur and mutilate the Saviour's Mystical Body, in such a way that it can no longer be seen by those who are looking for the harbour of eternal salvation.'[2]

If this means that the Pope is a convenient human head of the Christian Church, Protestants would understand its meaning even if they could not accept it. But if it means, as it seems to mean, that Christ cannot rule His Church apart from the institution of the Papacy, then Protestants would have to register an emphatic denial. The weakness of Catholic theology at this point is that it does not leave sufficient room for God's justifying grace. The limiting and conditioning of the divine action is a denial of the doctrine of justification by faith.

Even the action of the priest in the Mass preconditions and predetermines the action of divine grace. 'The priests of the Church ascend upon the Son of Man that is, by the ladder of the Cross of Christ, to heaven, bearing with them "the gifts and sacrifices" for the sins of the people, and descend from heaven by

---
[1] E. Mersch, op. cit., p. 212.
[2] R. N. Flew (ed.), *The Nature of the Church*, p. 40.

the same means, bringing as the gift of God for the people the sacramental and other graces of which they stand in need.'¹

In spite of the unique position of the Pope, the sacramental powers of the priests, the co-operation of the saints, and the aid of the celestial hierarchy, the Church is unable to say with certainty that during a man's earthly life, all his sins are forgiven. Perhaps this is due to an inadequate conception of the nature of grace, or to the assumption that failure and imperfection are permanent and ineradicable marks even of the redeemed Church, but it is more likely due to that Pelagianism and works-righteousness which linger in Catholic thought.

Dr Adam's comment on Luther is of more than passing interest. He says: 'When Luther narrowed the Scriptural idea of God's all-efficiency into the doctrine of His sole-efficiency, he cut the native strength of the creature free from its moorings in God, and delivered it over to total unfruitfulness.'² It must be admitted that Luther had not a very high respect for the 'native strength of the creature', but this fact did not separate him from God, it rather drove him back to God. In his early days Luther had tried every way except reliance upon the sole-efficiency of God. All these ways having failed to meet his need, Luther was compelled to find *all* in God. This is a very different thing from the view mentioned above that 'Luther cut the native strength of the creature from its moorings in God'. Catholicism could not, however, accept Luther's doctrine of God's sole-efficiency because this would have undermined the whole structure of the hierarchical system upon which Catholic religion rests. A thorough-going belief in the sole-efficiency of God would also involve the belief that God was able to redeem the Church entirely and deliver it from failure and imperfection. Believers are not mistaken when they sing: 'And the great Church victorious shall be the Church at rest.' But they must surely believe that a victorious Church is a possibility and not simply a fleeting dream. Ironically enough, it is this inherent weakness even of the redeemed soul which gives to the Catholic priesthood its peculiar power. It is dangerous to dwell upon the idea that redeemed nature is weak and unreliable, yet the Church of Rome forbids free thought on just this ground. Thought would

¹ See *Scottish Journal of Theology*, Vol. IX, No. 2, p. 165.
² K. Adam, op. cit., p. 108.

go wrong if it were free, it needs to be guided by tradition and authority. These, however, are enshrined only in the official priesthood. This emphasis upon the weakness and unreliability even of the 'New Man' is at the root of the Catholic penitential system.

III. THE ROYAL PRIESTHOOD OF THE FAITHFUL

1. *Participation in the Priesthood of Christ*

In the words of St Thomas:

> The faithful are deputed to a twofold end. First and principally to the enjoyment of glory; for this purpose they are sealed with grace. 'Hurt not the earth, nor the sea, nor the trees, till we sign the servants of our God on their foreheads' (Rev. vii. 3). But secondly, each of the faithful is commissioned to receive, and to bestow on others, activities appropriate to God's worship. This, properly speaking, is where sacramental character plays its role. All Christian ritual derives from Christ's priesthood. Consequently the sacramental character manifests Christ's character, and configures the faithful to His priesthood.[1]

2. *Priests by Baptism*

The sign and seal of this configuration is baptism. There is, of course, an identification of our Lord with all men, whether they are Christians or not, by virtue of the Incarnation, but this universal identification is something different from participation in the life, death and victory of our Saviour. Such participation is effected only by baptism. Identification with the whole race is due to an action of our Lord—to His gracious condescension, but participation in the benefits of His grace is due partly to His action and partly to human action—to that faith, hope and love which are expressed in the baptismal rite. Baptism means human response to the divine offer. The essential element in Catholic theology is the sacramental character of human response.

> By the Incarnation God the Son becomes united not only with a particular human body but with all mankind. Every Christian becomes by baptism a participator in the priesthood of Jesus Christ, a participation strengthened and extended by the holy Eucharist and Confirmation, an objective relationship distinct from the personal relationship that subsists between each soul and her Lord, the sacramental characters are nothing else than certain sharings of the priesthood of Christ, derived from Christ Himself.[2]

[1] *S.T.*, 3a, lxiii. 3.   [2] *Cath. Enc. Dict.*, p. 400.

It is not always appreciated that in Catholic teaching priesthood is the rightful heritage of the Christian, and this heritage of grace must always precede the idea of priesthood as an office. The office of priesthood involves gifts, powers and duties which are not the heritage of all Christians, nevertheless the office is impossible apart from the prior heritage. The centrality of this idea is borne out by the following statement:

> And in case any reader should think that all this is a kind of fancy doctrine dug out by speculative theologians, let me end this section by quoting the confirming words of Pope Pius XII in the encyclical Mediator Dei: 'By reason of their baptism Christians are in the Mystical Body and become by a special title members of Christ the Priest: by the "character" that is graven upon their souls they are appointed to the worship of God, and, therefore, according to their condition, they share in the priesthood of Christ Himself.' [1]

It is, therefore, a mistake to imagine that this priesthood is metaphorical or that it does not involve certain obligations as well as privileges. Of course, the fulness of the Christian's heritage cannot be grasped initially. There is a growing awareness of the meaning of priesthood, but even this awareness is conditioned by baptism. The 'armour of God' is unmistakably bestowed in baptism but the Christian soldier will not then understand the necessity of it, and still less will he know how to make use of it. But eventually this spiritual armour will be seen to be not only desirable but indispensable. Faith will be awakened but it will be an awakening to what God has done and not only to what He promises to do. It is important to stress this truth because the consciousness of the Christian's priesthood is inseparable from baptism.

> That baptism cannot reveal all its powers at the temporal moment of the outward act, is not its weakness but its wealth, by which the whole life must be adorned, which Luther meant when he said, 'The whole life of the Christian is meant to be a continuous baptism.' From this it follows that the genesis of conscious faith and regeneration is brought about in the most normal and happy manner under the influence of the baptismal blessing, and therefore under the consciousness of having been received preveniently by Christ's love. [2]

[1] M. De La Bedoyère, *The Layman in the Church*, p. 15.
[2] J. A. Dorner, *System of Christian Doctrine*, Vol. IV, p. 292.

Dorner is right when he refers to the blessing of baptism 'by which the whole life must be adorned', for this heritage of which baptism is the seal, must always be characterized by a priestly life. The glory of the martyrs is not that by a sudden impulse they made the supreme offering of life itself, but that their martyrdom was the final expression of a life that was already offered to God, and therefore already priestly. The mark of perpetual priesthood is upon every Christian life.

> Every Christian has thus been made priest with Christ in every spiritual sacrifice which he makes right up to his own supreme self-sacrifice, should he be called upon to make it, the sacrifice of his life in witness of Christ in martyrdom. 'True sacrifice is to be found in every deed done with a view to union with God in a holy communion, that is, every act that is referred to the end that can make us truly blessed,' wrote St Augustine. In fact, the whole of our spiritual lives as Catholics are in an absolutely true sense *priestly* lives.[1]

3. *Worship as the function of the Royal Priesthood*

The priesthood of the Faithful is expressed in the corporate nature of worship. While it is true to say that the hierarchical principle has often been given undue prominence in Catholic thought, it is also true that there is now a growing tendency to emphasize the real part of the laity in the worship and service of the Church. There is the tacit admission that Christ is at work through His chosen instrument and that this instrument is the whole Church and not merely the hierarchical element in it.

> Thus it is not the individual bishop who baptizes, preaches, governs, but Christ through him; Christ and the Church sacrifice with the priests; the individual Christian prays not alone, but Christ and the Church pray in his person (and in liturgical prayer hardly ever in the singular number).[2]

It may be argued that the emphatic corporate element in worship implied in the above statement is not always borne out in practice. The answer is that in modern Catholicism there is a resolute attempt to apply this corporate principle in every aspect of worship. As far as Protestantism is concerned, this principle was applied at the Reformation. Catholics, however, are sometimes slow to understand that the first product of reformed doctrine

---

[1] M. De La Bedoyère, op. cit., p. 13.
[2] *Cath. Enc. Dict.*, p. 337.

was reformed worship. Father Congar declares that the glory of the Reformers was that

> they brought into lay life, into everyday life, the holiness which had formally been kept in the cloister; that they denounced the distinction between an ordinary goodness and morality just sufficient for salvation, and a higher morality available to churchmen; that they restored dignity and Christian value to the various activities of secular life, and particularly to men's trades and professions.[1]

This is the truth but it is not the whole truth. There is in the above statement a significant omission. It pays no regard to the real and active part which was afforded to the laity in the worshipping life of the Church. The important fact is that the reforms mentioned above were dependent upon reformed worship and could not have taken place without it. The liturgical revival in Catholicism is taking place under a different terminology but it cannot be too strongly emphasized that the *aim* is precisely the same as that of the reformers.

This revival is welcomed by all, and not least by the Catholic laity, for it restores to them their true place in the liturgical life of the Church. This revival is noticeable in certain specific directions. It is significant that the Mass, so often regarded as the monopoly of the priest, has become the focal expression of the religion of the people.

The participation of the people in the Mass means that they are no longer regarded as passive onlookers at a mysterious and unintelligible drama but are active participants in the Eucharistic action. The self-offering of each member is made on the grounds of sharing in the priesthood of Christ. This identification, which is effected through faith in our Lord's Sacrifice, enriches the meaning of the Mass. The idea is lucidly expressed by Pope Pius XII: 'They (the faithful) will consecrate themselves to the glory of God, desiring intensely to make themselves as like as possible to Jesus Christ who suffered so much, and offering themselves as a spiritual victim with and through the High Priest himself.'[2]

The basilicon position of the priest, already adopted by the Church of South India and widely approved, is becoming more and more common in the Catholic Church. When the priest does

[1] Y. Congar, *Lay People in the Church*, pp. 12–13.   [2] *Mediator Dei*.

not face the congregation the impression is given that he acts independently of his people. It should not be forgotten that in patristic times the church was often round in structure so that the eyes of the congregation were focussed on the Table in the centre. It is sometimes argued that in these circumstances the priest's back is inevitably turned on some section of the congregation. But this is to miss the point which is that in a round building the priest is, in any event, *with* the congregation and not apart from it. In this regard, the Catholic Church has shown initiative and courage in pioneering a form of church architecture which will restore the Table to the centre and thus give a deeper meaning to the liturgical action of the congregation.

One of the most striking features of the liturgical revival is the use of the vernacular in worship. This ensures the active participation of the laity in many lands, a privilege not hitherto afforded them. It is not to be denied that there have been historical and psychological advantages in using one language for Christian worship in any place. But the question arises as to whether these factors have not pushed out altogether the existential factor in worship. Worship must be intelligible if it is to have the maximum effect upon the life of the believer. But even apart from the question of worship, this new tendency will have a salutary effect upon the spiritual lives of the people and upon the Church's missionary endeavour.

The phrase 'the communion of the laity' is of the utmost significance even though it is not a happy one. It means that the cup should not be withheld from the laity. This implies that the Eucharist should no longer be considered as a communion of priests alone, but of priest and people together. But the phrase is unfortunate because there is no such thing as a communion of the laity only. The dilemma may be resolved if we think in terms of the communion of the royal priesthood which is what the Eucharist is and is intended to be. For in every Eucharist the Church offers her unity in Christ, and this includes priest and people, as well as symbolizing the oneness of the universal Church.

It is our contention that in these developments in catholic thought and practice—the participation of priest and people in the Mass, the adoption of the basilicon position, the use of the vernacular in worship, and the granting of the cup to the laity—

the priesthood of all believers is realized. It may be that for historical reasons there is a natural reticence on the part of Catholics to use the precise phrase, nevertheless the fact is self-evident. Catholic practice arises out of catholic theology, and the idea that priesthood characterizes the devotional, secular and sacramental life of the believer is aptly stated by De La Bedoyère:

> In our lives of sacrifice, prayer and devotion, we are priests with Christ the High Preist. In our active and secular lives as Catholics, we are teaching and authoritative witnesses with Christ the Prophet and Christ the King. This priestly, teaching and authoritative quality of the faithful is part and parcel of the Christian life, in itself in fellowship with Christ. But we are also priests in a sacramental sense, especially in partaking in the Sacrifice of the Mass . . . .[1]

4. Catholic and Protestant Interpretations

Perhaps the most significant contribution on this subject by a catholic writer is *Le Sacerdoce Royal Des Fidèles*, in which the author, Father Paul Dabin, considers very carefully what degree of authority the doctrine has and whether it is really an essential part of the Faith. He finds that the Royal Priesthood of the Faithful has the unanimous approval of the Fathers, of the theologians (thirteenth to eighteenth century), and of the faithful. So unanimous are they about it that it is rare for a Church writer of importance to keep silent about it (pp. 14-20), He also stresses the fact that even at the Reformation Catholic controversialists did not in general fall to the temptation to deny the Royal Priesthood of the Faithful (p. 61). In the light of this statement we must examine the difference between the Catholic and Protestant interpretations of the Royal Priesthood. But first we must take note of Father Dabin's definition:

> The Royal Priesthood is a functional participation, both individual and collective, largely passive but also active, in the triple office of Christ as King, Priest and Prophet: entered on by Baptismal incorporation into Christ: perfected in Confirmation and symbolized by the charismation: identifiable with the sacramental character of the Christian: admitting him to perform various acts of worship and cult: creating for him various moral and religious obligations: all without prejudice to the special priesthood of the hierarchy within the Body.

[1] M. De La Bedoyère, op. cit., p. 25.

This definition is important because of its positive and constructive character. Protestants also regard the Royal Priesthood as a functional participation in the triple office of Christ, and it is noteworthy that this particular truth was emphasized by Calvin. All the same, Father Dabin's definition reveals the sharp cleavage between the Catholic and Protestant approach to this subject. According to the Catholic view the functional participation is regarded as largely passive; secondly, it is entered on by a process of gradation, namely, by sacramental incorporation; and thirdly, it is conditioned and controlled by the special priesthood of the hierarchy. The Protestant case is almost entirely the opposite. This functional participation in the triple office of Christ is wholly active; it is a single existential relationship which is entered into by faith; and it is not conditioned by or subjected to any priesthood save that of Christ.

Protestants believe that spiritual participation in the Priesthood of Christ is the privilege and heritage of every Christian, and that it is independent of everything except justifying faith. The relegation of the Christian's participation in the work of Christ to a purely passive role is regarded by Protestants as a serious limitation. To impose upon Christians a passive attitude in the work, witness, worship, intercession, and service of the Church is to misunderstand the purpose of the Gospel which is to enlist all men into the full service of the kingdom and not in any sense to deprive tham of that privilege. Yet the Christian's role in Catholic theory is largely passive because of his dependence upon the various functions of the hierarchy. The question is whether all Christians may or may not participate in the threefold office of Christ. This subject is dealt with by Anglo-Catholic writers in *The Apostolic Ministry*. It is considered within the context of the work of the Ministry as a whole, of the Church, and of our Lord Himself.

> He is 'Priest' exhausting in Himself the whole meaning of the word, just as He manifests and indeed is the whole revelation of God as Prophet—'the Word'; just as He is the originating Head of the whole redeemed race as the Second Adam, in whom all His posterity are in some sort contained. . . . Thus He is Priest not only by office but by nature, right down to the substance of His being. . . . He is *the* Priest inevitably, because of what He is, Very God and Very Man, the Mediator. He at once glorifies and propitiates God and atones for

other men's sins by His own latreutic and sacrificial action. That, and nothing less than that, is Priesthood according to the New Testament.¹

Dom Gregory Dix goes on to say that by nature the Priesthood is Christ's alone, and asks whether by *office* He can clothe His Priesthood upon other men. He avers that 'the Reformers emphatically denied that He could or did bestow it upon other men even as an office.'² But is it possible to make a rigid distinction between an incommunicable nature and a communicable office? Is there not a deep truth enshrined in Wesley's lines:

> *Hear us, who Thy nature share,*
> *Who Thy mystic body are.*

Certainly the Reformers rejected the idea that Christ committed to men an office which carried with it the notion of sacrificial functions. According to Father Hebert, the ministry is held not only to share the general prophetic, priestly, and royal character of the Body but, as representing Christ, to have prophetic, priestly and royal functions to perform on His behalf which are not common to the whole body.³ Commenting on this view J. P. Hickinbotham writes:

> This does not follow; the point of the analogy of the body is to emphasize specialization of function as between members; this implies limitation of function for each particular member and it militates against rather than for the view that the ministry of Word and Sacraments has a special function in relation to all the work of our Lord and His Body. It is notable that the New Testament itself, while emphasizing the priestly character of our Lord and of the Church, never attributes this character to the ministry in particular. ... the New Testament is unanimous in holding that in so far as priestly functions are not exhausted by the work of Christ Himself, *they are now fully open to all members of the Church.*⁴

This is indeed what Protestants mean by the Priesthood of all believers; all members actively participating in the Priesthood of the Lord.

¹ K. E. Kirk (ed.), *The Apostolic Ministry*, p. 299.
² Ibid., pp. 299–300.
³ Ibid., pp. 512–13. For further discussion see the whole of chap. IX by Father A. G. Hebert.
⁴ S. Neill (ed.), *The Ministry of the Church*, p. 69.

5. Royal Priesthood and the Church's Universal Mission

It is an important part of Roman teaching that conversion involves vocation, that vocation constitutes a universal mission, and that the Church's Eucharistic action is only properly fulfilled in the witness of the common priesthood in the world.

(a) Conversion is a Vocation

In de Lubac's words: 'The rest of the world is bound up with us, and it cannot be saved without us. This being so, are not our personal responsibilities tremendously increased?'[1] Again, he says: 'They (Christians) do not belong to themselves but owe service to all men. Let him who is greatest among you be as he who serves.' Christ's great lesson is aimed not only at those who hold some authority; it is a commandment envisaging all who enjoy greatness of any kind. Those who, by receiving Christ, have received all, have been raised up for the salvation of those who could not know Him. Their privilege constitutes a mission.

(b) This Vocation constitutes a universal mission

Such a vocation is inescapable and it belongs to every Christian. It is incumbent upon every Christian to embody and express in his own life this universal mission. By example, intercession, witness and service, Christians become, as Origen says: 'a house of God built of living stones, a spiritual house for a holy priesthood'. In fact, the Christian cannot hold the faith without confessing it. 'Every individual member of the community should have this living faith and should exercise this confessorship. It will be exercised in infinitely various ways according to each one's particular qualities, according to his bent of mind, the grace he receives, his special vocation, his environment and fortunes.'[2]

Commenting upon St Paul's words to the Galatians: 'That I might preach Him among the Gentiles,' de Lubac says:

> His *conversion* is a *vocation*. He cannot remain in quiet recollection with the Christ whom he has just discovered within himself. By the same token, and with the same urgent need as the service of the Christ, the service of men, his brethren—of all men without respect of persons —calls him. 'The whole human race can find room within his heart.'[3]

---

[1] H. de Lubac, *Catholicism*, p. 122.   [2] K. Adam, op. cit., p. 131.
[3] de Lubac, op. cit., p. 186.

(c) The Eucharist and universal mission

The faithful Catholic does not merely hope that Jesus will come to him in the Eucharist. He knows that He does. The believer's horizons are widened because he meets with Christ. He does not seek Christ merely for his own edification; from this focal point of Catholic worship he is 'sent' into the world. This intensive experience makes everything about him more comprehensive. He prays with Angela of Foligno: 'May your love embrace all nations,' and makes his own the words of Methodius of Olympus, 'The Church is in the pains of childbirth until all peoples shall have entered into her.' The real challenge of the Mass is that not only is the believer united with Christ but the whole world is to be renewed through it. The following description of the conclusion of the Mass which is given by Gerald Vann, O.P., makes this point clear:

> The Sacrifice is ended: the official act is over; but if the *Ite, missa est* is an end it is also a beginning: the work of the official priesthood is over, but the work of the 'common priesthood' of the laity must now begin. The Mass is a corporate act, the offering of all the faithful; it is also a cosmic act, the renewal of the world; and it is through the laity that that cosmic effect is to be fulfilled, it is through the laity coming down from the altar to the world and the work of every day, that the power and blessing of Christ are to be diffused and the face of the earth is to be renewed.[1]

Their duty is now made clear to them and they are involved in the universal mission of Christ from which there is no escape. Like St John of the Cross they know that 'the Father's business is the redemption of the world'. After they have been individually and collectively renewed, what is their primary task?

> But then they in their turn must go forth into the greater world of men, they must be God-bearers to that world, the world of sin and suffering, bringing it healing in the power of Christ, bringing it integrity in the power of Christ, bringing it the unity and peace of a restored human family. The Mass is fulfilled in them in so far as they themselves put on Christ and are filled with His life; but in so far as they do that they will inevitably fulfil a larger destiny: they will share in His redeeming work in the world, they will share in His sacrifice for His brother men, they will help Him to accomplish the work of love for which He came, the renewal of the face of the earth.[2]

[1] G. Vann, *The Holy Communion*, p. 44.   [2] Ibid., p. 48.

Therefore, when the Royal Priesthood is viewed in the light of the Mass, it means that all Christians share in the sufferings of Christ, in His work of love for all the world and in His ultimate victory, and in this threefold way the universal priesthood finds its fulfilment.

6. *Eastern Orthodox Interpretation of the Royal Priesthood*

Since the teaching of the Eastern Orthodox Church on the subject of the Royal Priesthood differs from that of the Roman Church, it is necessary to examine this difference in interpretation.

(a) *The Church is hierarchical throughout*

Dean Stanley, in his Introduction to the *History of the Eastern Church*, states with great clarity what the Eastern Church means when it says that the whole Church is priestly:

> If the Christian religion be a matter, not of mint, anise, and cummin, but of justice, mercy and truth; if the Christian Church be not a priestly caste, or a monastic order, or a little sect, or a handful of opinions, but 'the whole congregation of faithful men, dispersed throughout the world'; if the very word which of old represented the chosen 'people' (*laos*) is now to be found in the 'laity'; then the range of the history of the Church is as wide as the range of the world which it was designed to penetrate, as the whole body which its name includes.[1]

According to the Eastern Church hierarchical powers belong to the whole people of God: 'Episcopal grace is given to the community and not to a separate individual, and can only be realized by the individual *in connexion* with the community.... Being the Body of Christ and the temple of the Holy Spirit, the Church is hierarchical throughout, and holy orders are not the basis, but an expression of its hierarchical character.'[2]

(b) *Does the Orthodox Church offer a synthesis between Roman Catholic and Reformation views?*

The claim has been made that the conflict which arose in the sixteenth century between the clericalism of Rome and the universal priesthood of the Reformers would have been greatly modified if the contending parties had been acquainted with the

---

[1] A. P. Stanley, *History of the Eastern Church*, Intro., p. 25.
[2] S. Boulgakoff, 'Orthodox Church' (in R. Dunkerley and A. C. Headlam, *The Ministry and the Sacraments*, p. 103).

Orthodox conception of the sobornost and not simply with Western formularies.[1] Can such a claim be substantiated? The Orthodox position is as follows:

All Christians are priests in the temple of their own soul, which is at the same time the temple of the Holy Spirit. The practical expression of this lies in the laity taking part together with the celebrants in the divine liturgy and other Sacraments. In the Eastern Church all Christians are clothed with the sacred rank of *layman*.

This sacred rank is recognized by the Ordination of the laity.

> One special rite—that of the sacred unction of Confirmation, which, as we have seen, is conferred simultaneously with baptism—has been explained with a force and eloquence which, on such a subject, rings with the tone of a Tyndale or a Luther, as symbolizing the royal priesthood of every Christian. It destroys the wall of separation that Rome has raised between the ecclesiastic and the layman, for we are all priests of the Most High—priests though not pastors—in different degrees.[2]

In this respect the Orthodox Church differs from the rest of Christendom. Initiation into the Royal Priesthood is by the combined ceremony of Baptism by immersion, anointing with oil, and the laying on of hands in Confirmation.

> It is worth observing that the conferring of the rank of layman is an episcopal sacrament similar to Ordination. In the Western Church it takes the form of laying on of hands by the bishop; and although in the Eastern Church, it is performed by a priest, the oil used in the Sacrament must have episcopal consecration. In that sense Confirmation is the sacrament of the Universal priesthood.[3]

Members of the Western Church may be forgiven for wondering why such an impressive initiation into the Royal Priesthood should have so little effect upon the practical witness of the Church, and should signify no more than the granting of permission to the laity to take part in the liturgy of the Church. Also, a more dynamic conception of the Royal Priesthood must inevitably result in a stronger grasp of the Church's universal mission and this is notably lacking in the outlook of the Eastern Church. 'In regard to missions, the inaction of the Eastern Church is well known . . .

---

[1] 'sobornost' = the common mind both of clergy and laymen.
[2] A. P. Stanley, op. cit., p. 3.
[3] R. Dunkerley and A. C. Headlam, op. cit., p. 103.

whilst many Protestants pour the whole of their religious energy exclusively into missionary enterprise, the Eastern Churches, as a general rule, have remained content with the maintenance of their own faith.'[1] In vain is it argued that this attitude has at least exonerated them from the curse of proselytism and persecution, for while the Church may fail in the fulfilment of her mission, it is a greater failure to pretend that she has no mission. Moreover, in respect of her universal mission, the Church is judged by her attitude to the words of Christ: 'Go ye into all the world and preach the Gospel,' and nothing can exempt her from this obligation.

Further observations will show that it is possible to believe in the doctrine of the Royal Priesthood and to mean something far different from what is believed in Protestantism. Professor Boulgakoff writes:

> Hierarchy may be and must be understood as the organization of the universal priesthood. It is a mistake to interpret the principle of the universal priesthood literally. A practical application of this principle leads to hierarchy, the power of priesthood being delegated to and concentrated in certain organs. How is the universal priesthood made real? This is achieved through the Sacrament of Ordination, which is, as we have seen, a Sacrament of the whole Church, the realization of the Universal priesthood.[2]

Two statements may now be added to show whether real importance can be attached to the doctrine of the royal priesthood as it is interpreted by the Orthodox Church. In each case the statement is made after the firm affirmation that Confirmation is the sacrament of the Universal priesthood. Professor Boulgakoff says: 'And so this principle (the universal priesthood), rightly dear to Protestantism, finds proper recognition, *at any rate theoretically*, in Orthodoxy.'[3] Dean Stanley writes: 'This explanation of the ceremony may be doubtful; *but that it should be put forth at all in connexion with one of the most peculiar and significant of the Oriental ecclesiastical rites, is an indication of their general spirit*.'[4]

On the whole we are bound to conclude that the claim of the Eastern Church that it offers through its organic conception of the Church and the hierarchy, a synthesis between Roman and Protestant teaching, cannot be sustained. In theory the doctrine

[1] A. P. Stanley, op. cit., p. 32.
[2] R. Dunkerley and A. C. Headlam, op. cit., p. 103.
[3] Ibid., p. 105.   [4] A. P. Stanley, op. cit., p. 37.

is accepted, but in practice it is rejected. The initiation ceremony is important, but its practical outworking in the life of the Church is negligible. It simply will not do to say: 'All that is required is to admit the supremacy of the principle of the universal priesthood entrusted to the Church and realized by it in a certain form ... that form, hallowed by antiquity, is the episcopal hierarchical succession.'[1] Protestants reject this interpretation on the ground that it is ambiguous and fanciful. The orthodox position is that the belief in the organic conception of the Church necessarily implies the priestly prerogative of the whole Christian community. It also affirms that the sacrament of Confirmation conferred by the bishop means a consecration of *all* the faithful. The implication is that the Confirmation of one person is *ipso facto* the renewal of consecration for the whole Church. Furthermore, the Orthodox view is that the hierarchy is the universal priesthood organized in a particular way. All these statements give the impression that the Eastern Church is bending over backwards to make a point. However, each statement is conditioned by a word which occurs too frequently in Orthodox writings, namely—'theoretically'. It is for this reason that some of these high-sounding phrases have sometimes been regarded as examples of Orthodox Latitudinarianism.

At the same time, it must be conceded that within the limits of a Church strongly influenced by the past and untouched by the challenges of the Reformation, a genuine attempt is made to understand and express the meaning of the universal priesthood. This attempt is made in several directions:

(*a*) Clergy and laity together make the fulness (pleroma) of the Church. The authority of the Church is expressed by the 'conscience' of the Church, which is the common mind of clergy and laity together.

(*b*) In the East there is no distinction between clerical and lay. The dominating truth is that the Church is an ordained community. Confirmation, for the Orthodox Church, has nothing to do with the renewal of baptismal vows, it means that the believer receives a special grace by which he is able fully to participate in the sacraments of the Church and to be spiritually equipped as well as commissioned for service.

(*c*) Because the Church is a universal priesthood she is one and

[1] R. Dunkerley and A. C. Headlam, op. cit., p. 103.

must be one. In Orthodox teaching the one Church as created by Jesus exists even now intact and is preserved undivided and whole, unchanged and uncorrupt. Tensions and divisions do not alter this fact, for the oneness of the Church is absolute. The Church is essentially the universal priesthood of the people of God.

(*d*) Special spiritual power belongs to the whole Church and not to any individual in it. In Ordination the Holy Spirit works through the unanimous decision of the congregation, and the Eucharist administered by a priest without the participation of the congregation, is null and void. Even if these concepts appear to remain in the sphere of dogmatic theory and are not given full expression in the everyday life of the Church, it is noteworthy that they have persisted in the Church from ancient times until now. Moreover there are now signs of a deeper understanding between Eastern and Western Churches. In this connexion the recent meeting of the World Council of Churches in New Delhi is significant. The integration of the World Council of Churches and the International Missionary Council is indicative of a new realization of the need for unity and mission. The fact that observers from the Roman Catholic Church, as well as representatives of the Russian Orthodox Church and from the Orthodox Church from countries in the Middle East, were present at New Delhi, shows that the desire for unity is growing. Perhaps for the first time there has been held a *World* Council of Churches in the truest sense and this gives great hope for the future. Dr Ramsey observes: 'It is hard to guess what might be the effect on Christendom if the stores of spirituality in Eastern orthodoxy, long isolated from the West, and repressed by historical experiences utterly unlike our own, came into vigorous contact with other parts of Christendom.'[1] Three important facts have emerged from New Delhi: the desire for a real unity in Christendom; a new appraisal of the Church's duty and mission in the twentieth century; and the emphasis upon the witness of the laity in the world. A thorough understanding and appreciation of the doctrine considered here may point the way to the fulfilment of the aims and hopes so trenchantly expressed by representatives of all the Christian Churches in New Delhi.

[1] A. M. Ramsey, Presidential Address to Upper House of Canterbury Convocation, 1962.

CHAPTER SEVEN

MARSIGLIO OF PADUA AND JOHN WYCLIF

MARSIGLIO OF PADUA, 1270–1328

MEDIEVAL philosophy is still a matter of great interest and importance because the clash between Church and State is an ever-recurring problem. It was not only that a Church-controlled State was a widely accepted idea, but that it was propounded as a philosophic theory as well. This philosophy had three main sources: the Old Testament, Augustine and Dante. There was a common belief that theocratic government was right because of its ancient origin and its connexion with Hebrew religion. The Augustinian theory which assumed that eventually the City of God would overcome and absorb the Earthly City was firmly accepted, and this was buttressed by the idea, often associated with the name of Dante, of *preparatio evangelica*, which assumed that the function of the State was to prepare the world for the Gospel. Apparently this was possible only in a universal empire governed by a universal monarch. Dante conveniently attributed this imperium to the Empire of Rome. The concept outlined in *De Monarchia* was not new, and Dante took his thought-forms from the past. In any case it is dangerous to identify the Kingdom of God with any earthly empire, and Constantine's attempt to do this does not provide one of the finest phases in Christian history. Dante was, in fact, a prophet looking the wrong way, or, to be more accurate, he was an historian rather than a prophet. He took a picture from the past and tried to frame it in the present. Whatever may be said of those notions as philosophic theories, there is no doubt that when put into practice the idea of fusion brings only confusion. The old idea that God had provided universal peace in the Roman Empire so that it might be a cradle for His Son was no longer tenable in the fourteenth century. A revolutionary change had taken place. As Dawson has observed, in the Roman Empire the Church was in the State. 'But in the

Middle Ages this relation was reversed, and it could really be said that the State was in the Church.'[1] It was essential that the situation should be clarified and that the lines of demarcation, no longer visible, should be clearly drawn. Marsiglio of Padua set himself this task and it could only be accomplished by a thorough examination of the whole question of the relation of the Church to the State.

He began with the assumption that sovereignty rests with the people and that the ideas of divine right and hereditary principle had been introduced from false motives. But this is true of the Church as well as the State, and it is on this subject that Marsiglio makes an entirely new approach. For this reason it may be affirmed that in him the voice of Protestantism is heard for the first time. He asserts that Christ is the Rock on which the Church is built and all apostles and ministers of the Church are but His members. 'The name "Church" he would recall to its first and apostolic, its truest and most proper signification, as comprehending the entire body of Christian men: all, he says, are alike churchmen, be they laymen or clerks.'[2] It will be noticed that he sweeps away at one stroke the pretensions of a sacerdotal order. The Church as a universal spiritual society is distinct from the State—this basic fact underlies his thesis.

If the Church is different in nature, it is also different in function. The function of the Church is to proclaim the Gospel of eternal life, and to fulfil this function the evangelical law is sufficient. The civil law is concerned with the earthly life and its interests and therefore has no jurisdiction over the affairs of the Church. The fact is that the Church's supreme loyalty is given to something beyond the State, for, as far as the Church is concerned, the evangelical law is always transcendent. Karl Barth suggests this simple principle of Christian politics: 'All that can be said from the standpoint of divine justification on the question of human law is summed up in this one statement: the Church must have freedom to proclaim divine justification.'[3] The freedom of the Church to proclaim God's righteousness by which every state is judged is an essential element of the Christian message. Whether

---

[1] C. Dawson, *Medieval Religion*, p. 26.
[2] R. L. Poole, *Illustrations of Medieval Thought*, p. 270.
[3] K. Barth, *Church and State*, p. 83.

this freedom exists in a Church which is controlled by the State is a debatable point. On the whole, and taking into consideration man's sinful nature, it is extremely doubtful, and there may be occasions when it is impossible.

Marsiglio's contention is that man's sinful nature is at the root of the whole problem. He goes so far as to say that the civil law became necessary in order to counteract sin. Indeed, had man continued loyal to the divine will, no such institution would have been required. At the same time he will not allow that it is the Church's business to enforce civil law, and he dismisses the argument of the 'two swords' with the text, 'My kingdom is not of this world'. The Church can have no temporal sovereignty or jurisdiction and the attempts to enforce these have brought corruption and disorder in their train. On this fact Marsiglio is emphatic: 'The power bequeathed by Christ to the priesthood can only concern religious affairs; it is idle to suppose He gave temporal jurisdiction. The keys open and close the door of faith, but faith is the act of God, determined by the penitence of the sinner. The turn-key, claviger, is not the judge.'[1]

If the Church consists of the entire body of Christian men, it follows that it possesses certain prerogatives which must not be usurped. The power of the priest to excommunicate offenders Marsiglio flatly rejects. The sole business of the priest is to preach the Faith and administer the sacraments. Excommunication can only be decreed by the congregation to which the believer belongs. It is permissible and perhaps desirable that the priest or a council of priests should be consulted but the actual decision rests with the congregation. It is important to note that in all questions of discipline Marsiglio calls for the whole Church to act in her priestly capacity. A function which for so long has been the prerogative of the sacerdotal order was transferred in his teaching to its proper place—to the priesthood of the Church.

Marsiglio's Protestantism is revealed even more clearly in his observations on the position of the Pope. Workman draws attention to this: Though in theory all priests are equal, the Pope, he (Marsiglio) held, is convenient as a symbol of the unity of the Church, and as providing a necessary president for its councils.[2]

[1] R. L. Poole, op. cit., p. 270.
[2] H. B. Workman, *The Dawn of the Reformation*, Vol. I, p. 83.

Marsiglio, however, was not content to leave the matter there, and he goes on to doubt whether Peter was ever Pope of Rome, to challenge his superiority over the other apostles, and to question his power to hand on his gift to his successors. Such statements indicate how far Marsiglio was ahead of the thought of his time.

He also objected to the attitude of the priesthood in monopolizing the term 'spiritual'. There were two reasons for this objection: first, if the word 'spiritual' were used only of the priests, it implied that all other members of the Church were not included in the spiritual society. But the second reason was that the term 'spiritual' was often used by the clergy as a cover for evil actions and to exempt them from the penalties of the civil law. The Church was a universal spiritual society and fulfilled her true function when she aimed not at evading the law but at reforming it. The Church stood in relation to the world as a spiritual priesthood, cleansing, guiding and instructing, so that ultimately all laws would become the expression of the divine will. The universal spiritual society was committed to a universal spiritual task.

Further, Marsiglio had no room for the ascending orders of dignity and authority in the ranks of the priesthood. He claimed that such distinctions had no scriptural warrant. As Neander observes:

> The author of this work (*Defensor Pacis*) perceived already the baseless, unsubstantial character of the whole hierarchical system; and with a boldness and freedom from all bias, truly worthy of admiration, showed his ability to distinguish the original truth from later impositions. He discovered, already, that originally there was but one priestly office, and no distinction of the office of bishops from that of presbyters.[1]

Later research has confirmed Marsiglio's discovery but it is significant that he should state it so plainly in the fourteenth century.

Nor is he silent about the specific function of the priest. It is God alone who forgives and the priest declares the forgiveness which God offers. The confusion of these two facts has resulted in much misunderstanding in the course of Church history.

Perhaps the most fruitful of Marsiglio's contentions was his definition of a general council as the final authority in the life of the Church.

---

[1] Neander, *Church History*, Vol. IX, Pt. I, p. 44.

The supreme power in the Church is the Church itself, i.e. a general council formed of clergy and laity alike. Thus constituted, a general council may not only decide ecclesiastical questions but even proceed to excommunicate the temporal ruler and place his hand under an interdict, just because it represents the universal Church and speaks the voice of the entire community both in its spiritual and temporal capacities.[1]

It is at this point that the originality and power of Marsiglio are most evident. Ockham, not less than Marsiglio, is hostile to papal sovereignty, but he has no desire to transfer that sovereignty elsewhere. Marsiglio, on the other hand, does not hesitate to transfer it to the place where he believes it properly belongs—to the general council which is the organ of the Christian community. While Ockham draws the line at the transference of sovereignty he concedes considerable authority to the general council, and its composition is even more universal than in the pages of Marsiglio, for he argues with much cogency that women are equally entitled with men to represent the laity upon it.

We must now consider why Marsiglio rejected the theocratic ideal of the Hebrews, the Augustinian ideal and the Ghibelline ideal of Dante.

It is commonly held that as long as Israel remained a holy community the problem of the existence of two distinct communities did not arise. The religious community and the political community were not separate until the prophetic word distinguished a remnant of the people as the true Israel of God. When Israel forfeited her political independence under the dominance of imperial powers, she lost her religious independence as well. But even before the significance of this loss was fully realized, the theocratic ideal was known to be an illusion. For a long time the word 'theocracy' has been used to express the difference between the constitution of Israel and that of all other nations. In fact, it was precisely the idea of theocracy which Israel had in common with the faiths of surrounding nations. The gods of other nations—Moloch, Melkart and Chemosh—were regarded as divine kings to whom the people brought their tribute. Therefore the idea of kingship and theocracy in Israel was not unique. The real difference between Israel and other nations lay not in an abstract

[1] R. L. Poole, op. cit., p. 273.

formula but in their concept of the difference in character between Jehovah and other gods. Now Marsiglio rejected the theocratic ideal because it was not the unique characteristic of Hebrew religion. This does not mean, however, that he was striving to establish secular supremacy, he was seeking secular independence. Equally clearly, he was striving to establish the independence of the Church. The idea of supremacy whether papal or royal was under condemnation. The gravamen of his charge was that papal supremacy had come to mean supremacy over Church and State whereas the two were separate organizations. In the end, Marsiglio's protest was a denial of papal claims, of divine right as well as hereditary principle. In his view, the idea that the two swords, the temporal and the spiritual, were to be wielded by the Pope was due to a misapplication of the ancient theocratic ideal, and he never ceased to emphasize that the Church was a separate organization—a fellowship of the faithful, within which the special functions of the priestly element were to be carried out as an organ of the whole body. It is conceivable, however, that Marsiglio did not fully realize the danger implicit in his theory. A denial of papal supremacy involved also a denial of the authority of Canon Law and this might have led to an undue exaltation of the State.

With equal firmness, though for a different reason, Marsiglio rejected the Augustinian ideal. According to this ideal the power of the State might be called in at any time to further the aims of the Church. But this assumes too much: it assumes that the State is no more than a vassal of the Church and that the State will always be content to function in that capacity. It also assumes that the acts of the Church will always be right. Further, it assumes the equation of the kingdom of God on earth with an omnipresent Church. In short, the Augustinian ideal is applicable only in the light of an infallible Church, and this formed no part of the teaching of Marsiglio. In any case, is there any reasonable warrant for such assumptions? Marsiglio is not sure that a Pope will always make the right decisions. 'How in case,' he says, 'that a heretic should be elevated to the papal dignity; or that one after having attained to that dignity, should from ignorance or from wickedness fall into some heresy; ought the heretical decisions of such a pope to pass for valid?'[1]

[1] Neander, op. cit., Vol. IX, Pt. I, p. 47.

Again Marsiglio rejected Dante's Ghibelline ideal because it posed an equation between Church and Empire. Once more the two concepts had become fused into one. The whole notion was too vague and unrealistic for Marsiglio's practical approach. At the same time Dante's view was much more acceptable to the medieval mind and it was certainly much more acceptable to the Papacy. Dante was medieval in thought in the sense that Marsiglio was not. In *De Monarchia* he envisages a divinely appointed universal monarchy. 'In the first book he shows that this universal monarchy, thus conceived, is necessary for the well-being of the world; in the second he attempts to prove, first from arguments based on reason and then from arguments based on the Christian faith, that the Roman people acquired the dignity of empire by divine right.'[1] For instance: in the *de Monarchia* the supreme historical moment is reached in the reign of Augustus when universal peace is established and the Saviour is born. He goes on to describe Constantine as founding the city in the East which is called by his name, so that 'he might give the Shepherd room,' but Marsiglio had no such naive opinion of the motives of the rulers of States. Dante's theory left too many questions unanswered such as the character of the rulers, the beliefs of the people, and the aims of the State.

Further, Marsiglio did not argue, like Dante and the orthodox Ghibellines, that a universal monarchy was a necessity. For him the essence of kingly rule was the popular right of deposition. Indeed he went as far as to say that the will of the Christian community was the effective power in the State. But Dante's view did not leave any room for the exercise of the power of deposition. Since the Emperor was deemed to receive his office immediately from God, there was no possibility of deposition by man. In such circumstances the voice of the Christian community was effectively silenced. From this grandiose assumption of a divinely appointed emperor there could be no appeal. Despite this, Marsiglio held tenaciously to the view that the temporal functions of government could be discharged by laymen in the interests of the *civitas Dei* without assuming a direct appointment of the Emperor by God. Dante's view was strongly supported by the hierarchy, and indeed, it was based on the hierarchical concept of the Church. It is at

[1] Hastings, *Enc. of Religion and Ethics*, Vol. VI, p. 396.

this point that the root of the difference between the two men emerges. For Dante universal authority is invested in one man—the Emperor; for Marsiglio universal authority is invested in the universal body of believers. From this point of view he never deviates. By virtue of their faith and calling believers possess inalienable privileges and functions, and failure in the recognition and exercise of these was a failure in their Christian duty. Marsiglio's approach to the problem was a practical one. He deemed it his task to lay down certain workable principles though he could not have realized that his views would receive such careful attention and implementation in later years. His influence has been adequately assessed as follows:

> Marsiglio, doubtless, was far in advance of what his own age would attempt. But the horror he inspired in the papal camp, the constant references to him in literature, the recollection of him at the Reformation as the greatest of its precursors, are all testimony to the fact that he stated boldly and in detail what was already implicit in the minds of thousands dissatisfied with the moral condition of the Church.[1]

It is possible to summarize the ideas of Marsiglio in one phrase. His attitude to the papacy, the restraints he places upon the powers of the hierarchy, the dignity and responsibility which he attaches to all believers, the power of decision in matters of faith which he regards as the right of a General Council, as well as the cogent reasons which he gives for rejecting the prevalent ideas on theocracy, the Augustinian and Ghibelline ideals, may be epitomized in the phrase—the priesthood of all believers. Although the phrase was unknown to him it is unquestionably the pivot around which all his ideas revolve. The principles which he laid down have played a much more important part in the development of the State as well as the Church in Europe than is generally recognized. Some of these principles were adopted by Wyclif and later applied by Luther but there is no doubt that Marsiglio was the pioneer. While it is true to say that in the fourteenth century these ideas were not popular and therefore met with little response, it was no small achievement to have stated them with such clarity and vigour. The truths which had been so cogently stated by the philosopher-statesman of Padua were soon to be emphasized in

---

[1] C. W. Previté-Orton and E. N. Brooke (eds.), *Cambridge Medieval History*, Vol. VIII, p. 630.

another part of the world by Wyclif the theologian. In their approach to these momentous questions and in their interpretation of them, they were very different, but the subject was the same. It is this significant fact which we must keep in mind, for although the voices of protest came from different quarters their message arose out of the same doctrine as we shall now see.

JOHN WYCLIF, 1320-1384

The task of maintaining religious liberty is always a difficult one, and there are times in the history of a nation when this responsibility seems to have rested on one man. Wyclif was such a man. He knew that liberty required for its preservation something more than ruthless external measures lest the remedy should be more obnoxious than the disease. If Wyclif's teaching had been heeded in the fourteenth century, much of the conflict and bloodshed of the seventeenth would have been avoided. The fact that his teaching was disregarded by many of his ecclesiastical contemporaries does not affect in any sense the importance of his achievement. It is true that he gathered around him a number of faithful followers, but the constant pressure of the official Church soon stifled Lollardy almost out of existence. John Foxe's description of them as the 'secret multitude of true professors' is only partly true, for, while it is correct to say that they were true professors of the Christian Faith, they cannot be regarded as a multitude even at their greatest strength. Their influence, however, was out of all proportion to their numerical strength, and this was largely due to the intellectual power and skilled leadership of Wyclif himself. Like Luther he not only criticized the practical abuses in the Church, but he set himself the task of examining the theology on which they rested. His research produced a Biblical theology which, although in many respects distasteful to the Church of his time, could not be ignored because it was the work of the foremost Schoolman of his age. We must now consider some of the important aspects of his teaching.

A prevalent theory of his day was that 'dominion' or lordship either spiritual or temporal was derived from God through intermediaries. Land was let out to tenants not directly by the owner of it but through intermediate or 'mesne' lords. The subtenant may not even know the owner of the land, and certainly no direct business transactions took place between them. All transactions were in the hands of the tenants-in-chief or intermediaries. In this respect the Church learned a rather dubious lesson from the world. The feudal system was applied to the relationship between God and man. Consequently, all divine blessings were dispensed through the tenants-in-chief who were the Pope and the hierarchy. Wyclif subjected this widely-accepted view to the most penetrating examination and then expounded his own view with remarkable originality and power.

1. *Lordship and Service: Basis*

The basis of his doctrine was Scriptural, for every system had to be scrutinized in the light of Scripture. All God's actions are self-determined, for only God creates out of nothing. God creates because He is free to create. This is the first divine claim—the claim to power. The act of creation is also the claim to possession. God is the sole possessor of the universe He has created. 'The heavens are Thine, the earth also is Thine: as for the world and the fullness thereof, Thou hast founded them' (Ps. lxxxix. 11). Under a picture depicting God in the act of creation, the artist adds the caption: 'If about to create such a world, stay Thine hand.' But the fear is without foundation because the One who creates and possesses the world also makes a further claim—the claim to rule. This three-fold truth—that God is sole Creator, Possessor and Ruler—is the basis of Wyclif's doctrine of lordship. Lordship is necessitated by the creation of man. Man is not only God's creature but His servant also. God is Creator and Lord. The assertion of lordship is essential. Hence the continual refrain of Scripture: 'God is Lord, the Lord, He is God.' God Himself decides how and to whom His gifts shall be given. No one has any power to determine this except God. God is Lord, and man is servant, and it follows from this that lordship and service are correspondent terms. This lordship is immediate and independent, and must not only be recognized by man but must also receive his unqualified response. 'God,' says Wyclif, 'rules not mediately, through the rule of subject vassals, as other kings hold lordship, since immediately and of Himself He makes, sustains all that which He possesses, and helps it to perform its works according to other uses which He requires.'[1]

2. Lordship and Service: Meaning

According to Wyclif, 'All authority is founded in grace,' for power is only safe when ruled by love. Grace operates in personal relationships and therefore God deals with people individually and immediately. God demands obedience and service and the man who offers these to God is under the dominion of grace. The wicked man may have 'power' by God's permission, but the righteous man possesses 'dominion' as his true inheritance. So the righteous are called to be kings and priests unto God, sharing His dominion.

Wyclif takes this thought a step further, 'God gives not any lordship to any except He first give Himself to them.'[2] Commenting on this statement Dr Workman says, 'The reader must not be misled by the feudal phraseology into undervaluing the consequences of such teaching. For Wyclif, every man had an equal place in the eyes of God; priests and laymen become one, each "hold" of God, and on the same terms of service.'[3]

By the immediacy of this relationship of grace all men—Pope and layman, Prince and peasant—owe the same direct allegiance to God. In respect of their 'tenure' all are equal.

> It is this principle of the dependence of the individual upon God and upon none else that distinguishes Wyclif's view from any other system of the Middle Ages. He alone had the courage to strike at the root of priestly privilege and power by vindicating for each separate man an equal place in the eyes of God. By this formula all laymen become priests and all priests laymen.[4]

The fact of sin has to be reckoned with, for every man does not by nature render service to God. Yet lordship is conferred upon man only on the explicit understanding that he renders service to God continually. When, by sin, he refuses to do this, he defrauds God of the service that is His due and thereby forfeits all lordship whatsoever. By disregarding God's command, man is *ipso facto* dispossessed. Sin deprives God of the service which He requires, and man of the lordship which by grace he possesses. It is along

---

[1] R. L. Poole, op. cit., p. 291.   [2] Ibid., p. 292.
[3] H. B. Workman, op. cit., p. 162.   [4] R. L. Poole, op. cit., p. 292.

this road that Wyclif reaches the same conclusion as St Augustine who says that when men sin they become nothing. On the other hand, 'the faithful man hath the whole world of riches: for him all things work together for good. Each faithful man is therefore lord of the universe; and it follows that all faithful men must hold their goods in common. So he interprets "Charity (i.e. Grace) seeketh not her own"—seeketh not to be a proprietor.'[1] In Wyclif's opinion, this was precisely what the Pope and hierarchy had tried to do: they sought to be the proprietors of God's blessings. Nothing roused the opposition of Wyclif more than this. It is therefore essential to consider the effect of his teaching upon the Church of his day.

3. *Lordship and Service: Consequences*

(a) *It affected the position of the Pope*

Although Wyclif was a child of Medievalism, he was not blind to the humanistic tendencies of his age. If he could not always free himself from them, at least he was aware of their presence. Man loomed large in medieval thought; so large sometimes that God could not be seen. Man had become the determining factor in all affairs of religion. He possessed power to dispense pardon, to re-offer Christ in the sacrifice of the Mass, to withhold divine grace from those who sought it. Everywhere Wyclif found that religion was centred on man and not on God. Not only did he realize that religion was humanly controlled, he also realized that the controlling factor was the Roman Priesthood. As Dr Payne has pointed out: 'The Pope had assumed supreme authority throughout Christendom. Canon Law was the basis of society. The elaborate system of medieval Catholicism, its forms and ceremonies, its orders and hierarchy, controlled all human activities.'[2]

It is against this background that we must consider the effects of Wyclif's doctrines. Lordship is of God, and Christ is the Lord paramount. Since the Pope is a fallible man, he must lose his lordship in the event of his falling into mortal sin. Forfeiture of lordship applies to all irrespective of office or position. We all of us hold our kingdom immediately from Christ.

[1] H. H. Smith, *Pre-Reformation England*, p. 269.
[2] E. A. Payne, *The Free Church Tradition in the Life of England*, p. 24.

Wyclif carries this argument still further, for he begins to question with Ockham whether the Papacy was an indispensable element in the fabric—a more daring suggestion it is difficult to imagine.

Wyclif's position hitherto would seem to have been this: we must obey the Pope as the vicar of Christ, only the vicar of Christ must be the holiest, the most God-enlightened man in Christendom. This obedience to the Papacy was rather a matter of convenience and Church order than principle. Wyclif had already questioned whether one day 'the ship of Peter may not exist exclusively of laymen,' and whether, when that day comes, 'Christ will not be *per se* sufficient for the rule of His own spouse'.[1]

(b) *It affected the authority of the Church*

Wyclif again shows his originality when he considers the question of Authority. In his view Authority did not belong to the Pope, or Tradition, or the Councils, but with Scripture. Not with Scripture *and* anything else, but with Scripture alone. His doctrine was grounded in Scripture, and just because he was far ahead of his contemporaries in his understanding of the Bible, his message seemed not only uncongenial but revolutionary in the eyes of his opponents. The appeal to Scripture was the final appeal, and nothing would shake him from this principle. In this respect also he was following in the steps of William of Ockham, 'The Pope may err, a general council may err, the doctors of the Church may err; only Holy Scripture and the beliefs of the Church are of universal validity, and with these to guide him the meanest peasant may know the truth.'[2] When Luther adopted the formula 'Sola Scriptura' many rallied to his support, but in Wyclif's day the time was not ripe, even though his message was the same.

Every man was responsible for keeping God's law, and by 'God's law' Wyclif meant the Bible. The emphasis was on dominion by grace. There could be but one inference about Church organization drawn from the Scriptures: Wyclif had thrown overboard the appeal to the visible and historic Church as the final authority, and he found an alternative one—the written Scripture.[3]

[1] H. B. Workman, op. cit., p. 172.
[2] H. B. Workman, *Christian Thought to the Reformation*, p. 217.
[3] M. Deanesly, *A History of the Medieval Church*, pp. 230-1.

(c) It affected the function of the priesthood

There was a further outcome of Wyclif's relentless logic. If the only valid Law for the community of believers was the Law of God, it follows that the laws of the Papacy which were associated with an historical human development, were to be rejected. Consequently all the rules concerning worship, penance and pilgrimages were denounced. This meant the virtual end of consecrations, blessings, indulgences, fraternities, worship of saints, pictures and relics, and it challenged the organization of the Church and Priesthood. It is clear, therefore, that Wyclif was aiming at an evangelical lay religion.

Wyclif did not discover the peculiar formula—justification by faith—but his original formula 'dominion by grace' is very close to it, and in feudal language he was saying what Luther said later in his doctrine of justification. Wycliff's doctrine of Lordship and Service was a clear denial of a mediatorial Church and a mediating priesthood. We may safely say that it was left to him to interpret for the Church of the fourteenth century the meaning of the priesthood of all believers. Workman truly sums up Wyclif's achievement, 'Thus Wyclif left no place for the mediating priesthood and the sacrificial masses of the Medieval Church. The personal relationship between a man and God is everything; character the one basis of office.'[1]

(d) It affected the status of the individual believer

Perhaps this was the greatest gain. To be sure, it was Wyclif's main objective. If the Law of God is paramount and the rule of God direct, His Law must be known personally and His rule must be operative directly. Each man is responsible to God alone: his primary obedience is to God. The throne of God to which, in his new grace relationship he has direct access, is his true and only tribunal. In this sense Wyclif may be regarded as the first existentialist, for he believed that man lived in an immediate and inescapable relationship to the Law of God. It is worthy of note that Ritschl made the idea of spiritual dominion the governing thought of his theology: 'The conception of God which is given in the revelation of God received through Christ . . . is that of a loving

---

[1] H. B. Workman, *The Dawn of the Reformation*, p. 162.

will which assures to believers spiritual dominion over the world, and perfect moral fellowship in the kingdom of God, as the summum bonum.'[1] In this study of Wyclif's doctrine of Lordship and Service we have reached certain important conclusions. Having examined the basis, meaning and effects of his doctrine, we may say on the negative side that he challenged the position of the Pope, questioned the accepted view of Authority, and rejected all human intermediaries of 'dominion' whether in the secular or spiritual sphere. On the positive side, he proclaimed the Authority of the Scriptures, inaugurated a prophetic ministry, emphasized the spiritual privileges of all believers, and asserted that all things, and systems and institutions are subservient to the Law of God. As further evidence of his positive contribution we must now consider his conception of the Church and the Ministry.

The Church and the Ministry

His ideas of the nature of the Church are expressed in the following passage:

> When men speak of the Holy Church, anon, they understand prelates and priests, with monks and canons and friars ... though they live accursedly and never so contrary to the Law of God. But they call not the seculars men of Holy Church, though they live never so truly, according to God's Law, call Holy Church the congregation of just men, for whom Jesus Christ shed His blood, and not mere stones and timber and earthly dross, which the clerks of Antichrist magnify more than the righteousness of God, and the souls of men.[2]

Life lived under the Law of God has a further corollary: it means that life is lived in a spirit of love, which expresses itself in every kind of vocation or calling within Christian society. Certainly it could brook no distinction between clergy and laity. For this reason gradation of rank or official pre-eminence among ministers was rejected. 'It were better for the clerks to be all oʌ one estate.' Wyclif was determined to make these truths widely known, and, as he had discovered them in the Bible, he proceeded to make it possible for others to make the same discovery by translating the Bible into his own tongue. The Scriptures became available to the laity and this meant that the power of the clergy was in some measure minimized.

[1] A. Ritschl, *Justification and Reconciliation*, Vol. III, p. 326.
[2] J. A. Wylie, *History of Protestantism*, Vol. I, p. 128.

But it was not enough that the Bible should be translated, it must be expounded and taught. Hence Wyclif sent out his 'poor priests' to preach. It is significant that he appointed laymen, and he laid down that their principal duty was to preach the Gospel. These men had no *character indelibilis*, and they were in no sense a hierarchy; their priesthood consisted in fulfilling the missionary tasks laid down in Matthew x, and their Head was Christ alone. This radical procedure clearly indicates how Wyclif prepared the way for the Reformation. 'Apart from Friars, preachers needed a licence from the bishop, but Wyclif maintained that Christ was sufficient authority, and that a licence might come immediately from Him.'[1]

The Church had become a wealthy and elaborate organization and needed to be reminded of its original spirituality and its unique mission. It was at this point that Wyclif introduced something entirely new into the medieval world—he called upon the state to reform an unwilling clergy.

> Wyclif had demanded that the employment of the clergy in secular business should cease; neither prelates, priests nor deacons should have secular offices. Above all, as Wyclif insisted with wearisome reiteration, by the restoration of the Church to its original poverty, when the priests should live on 'dimes and offerings' there would be a return to the primitive spirituality.[2]

In much of his teaching he proclaimed what Luther meant by the priesthood of all believers, but perhaps he was not sufficiently constructive in his approach to the subject, and perhaps he came too soon to win a widespread response. All the same, he did a good day's work for Christendom, and by his constant demand for a return to the doctrines and practices of the Patristic period he forms a strong link with the Early Church. If Hardwick's estimate of the Reformation is true that 'above all, the Reformation vindicated for our blessed Lord the real headship of the Church, exalting Him as the One source of life and righteousness, and thereby placing saints and priests and sacraments in their true subordination,'[3] who shall assess Wyclif's part in this tremendous achievement?

[1] H. H. Smith, op. cit., p. 272.   [2] H. B. Workman, op. cit., p. 156.
[3] C. Hardwick, *A History of the Christian Church during the Reformation*, p. 10.

CHAPTER EIGHT

THE MONKS AND FRIARS

THE ability of any outstanding leader in the Church from the fifth to the thirteenth centuries to bring his projects to a successful conclusion largely depended upon his success or failure in enlisting the support of the monks. The exceptions are those occasions when the leadership itself had passed to the monasteries. Any attempt to interpret the developing life of Christendom without reference to the monastic movement would be a distortion of the facts. 'The whole history of the Church,' says Jacques Ellul, 'is the history of the reformation of the Church by the Spirit.'[1] If obedience to the Spirit is the condition of Church reform, the monks must be placed among the reformers. It is true that often in the East and sometimes in the West those who have followed the monastic way of life have succumbed to an unwarranted individualism and isolation. It is all too easy to reject a false objectivism and fall into an equally false subjectivism. Yet even men like Anthony and Basil, Jerome and Martin of Tours fled rather from a secularized Church than from a hostile world. It is important to know what really happened, and Harnack has said with rare insight: 'They fled not the world only, but worldliness in the Church; yet they did not therefore flee *from* the Church.'[2] Even so the anchorite type of monasticism was short lived and it was soon realized that the soul requires something more than individual discipline if it is to grow in grace. Benedict of Nursia (480–543) has the distinction of perceiving the need and the answer to it when he formed the first monastic community in the West and provided the Rule by which it should be organized. Although Basil had founded a similar community with a far more rigorous system in Asia Minor, the fact remains that in combining worship, work and study in the orientation of a Christian community, Benedict had laid down a Rule which was to characterize

---
[1] Quoted in W. A. Visser 'T Hooft, *The Renewal of the Church*, p. 84.
[2] A. Harnack, *Monasticism*, p. 36.

monasticism in the West until the appearance of the Mendicant Friars in the thirteenth century.

Throughout the Middle Ages monasticism was a force to be reckoned with. Father Congar has drawn attention to the fact that in the development of Christian history two notions have been prevalent—the Canonical Notion and the Monastic Notion. The first is interpreted along the lines of function and competence and the second refers to a way of life. Congar's sacramental emphasis is clear in the following statement: 'There are three states in respect of faith, according as that faith is simple, forceful and fruitful. Baptism distinguishes the faithful from the non-faithful; among the faithful Confirmation denotes the strong; by Holy Orders a minister of the Church is separated from the laity.'[1] This view is more juridical than the monastic notion and pre-supposes the priesthood of the clergy. By calling and training, competence and function, the clergy are set aside to rule, shepherd and teach the flock of Christ. The position of the laity is described by Congar as follows:

> The laity lives among earthly things. Gratian's text says: 'There is another sort of Christians who are called lay folk. LAOS means people. These are allowed to possess temporal goods, but only what they need for use. They are allowed to marry, to till the earth, to pronounce judgments on men's disputes and to plead in court, to lay their offerings on the altar, to pay their tithes.' From our angle of interest here two things are particularly noticeable in this passage: the lay position is presented as a concession, and its general tendency is to deny that the laity, concerned in temporal affairs, have any active part in sacred things.[2]

The monastic movement is the most emphatic protest against the view that the lay position may be regarded as a concession. Benedict, the Father of Western monasticism was himself a layman, and his strenuous labours which far outstrip the functions conceded to the laity in Gratian's text, may not unreasonably be regarded as fulfilling the *essential* function of the Church. Benedict founded the monastery of Monte Cassino in 529.

> Here he laboured fourteen years, till his death. Although never ordained to the priesthood, his life was rather that of a missionary and apostle than of a solitary. He cultivated the soil, fed the poor, healed

---

[1] Yves Congar, *Lay People in the Church*, p. 13.
[2] Ibid., pp. 7–8.

THE MONKS AND FRIARS

the sick, preached to the neighbouring population, directed the young monks, who in increasing numbers flocked to him, and organized the monastic life upon a fixed method or rule, which he himself conscientiously observed.[1]

Not only in the time of Benedict, however, but throughout the Middle Ages, whenever there was a revival of monasticism, it was due primarily to the energy and initiative of laymen. Kraemer is explicit on this point:

> It seems therefore right, although monasticism as such has become wholly ecclesiasticized, to say that a great amount of lay inspiration has been channelled through this movement. The 'wandering' preachers in the Middle Ages in France; the preaching of the Mendicant Orders, which happened till the fourth Lateran Council in 1215 without episcopal consent to a great extent through lay people; the Terteriai who lived as secular people attached to one of the great monastic Orders ... are well known examples. The monastic knight-orders which arose also in the Middle Ages are another aspect of the specific lay-expression in the life of the Church.[2]

The part which the laity have played in vital movements in the history of the Church should not be underestimated, and monasticism in particular provides many examples of laymen of marked initiative, spiritual insight and intellectual power. On the whole, the monks did not wish to take Holy Orders and at least three of them were made priests against their will. These were Augustine, Jerome and Hilary of Poitiers. Indeed, St Anthony and Tertullian resisted all attempts to make them ordained priests. Why did they refuse what was so obviously an honour? It is facile to assume that personal idiosyncracies were accountable. On the contrary, there were definite and well-considered reasons for their reluctance.

First, there was the conviction that communion with God was not dependent upon the presence of a priest. In the desert where the early monks lived there was no priest, and in those circumstances the priesthood of believers was accepted and practised even though its theological implications were not worked out. Tertullian's insistence on the application of rules of spiritual discipline to the laity as well as the clergy was based on the concept of the universal priesthood. It is clear that St Anthony shared the same views.

[1] P. Schaff, *History of the Christian Church*, 311–600, Vol. I, pp. 218–19.
[2] H. Kraemer, *A Theology of the Laity*, pp. 21–2.

Monasticism, especially in its early days, was the protest that the laity also are priests unto God. The earlier monks were generally laymen. St Anthony, the founder of monasticism, was a layman to the end. He neither goes to Church nor receives the Eucharist for years, and yet continues in the closest intercommunion with God. . . . In the Rule of St Benedict confession was not made to a priest, nor to the monastic chaplain, but to the abbot or to the whole brotherhood, even though they were laymen.[1]

Secondly, the monks were concerned with a perfectionist ethic and in their view priesthood was regarded as a way of life rather than an office. They learned lessons in the cloister which later many of them put to the test beyond its walls. Indeed the farther they moved away from the cloister into the life of the world, the more their holiness shone forth. This is particularly noticeable in their witness in the thirteenth century. 'Franciscan piety . . . has the distinction of being the final flower of monastic perfection and the beginning of a new sense of historical fulfilment.'[2] It was very necessary that their holiness should be revealed amid the conflicts of the world as well as in the more sheltered cloister, and it cannot be doubted that this was one of the great achievements of the friars. It was the aim of the Franciscans 'to follow naked the naked Christ' and by following the way of poverty, simplicity and self-renunciation they pointed to a holiness which is not dependent on a mediating priesthood or upon prescribed channels of grace but upon personal faith and unqualified obedience. Holiness of life pleaded the validity of their cause. Yet by this means they came nearer to the historical fulfilment of the New Testament ideal than their fellow Christians in any age. Beet has pointed out that it was their dissimilarity to the accepted Catholic pattern which gave them their unique appeal. 'In utter contrast to the more than regal splendour which surrounded the papal throne was the absolute poverty of the begging friar. But the mere fact that the friar was the very antithesis of Pope-King and Prince-Bishop perhaps lent to the mendicant movement its greatest power to serve the Church.'[3] If, in fact, the Franciscans had been persuaded to take Orders the strongest ally of the Church would have been swallowed up in Catholic orthodoxy and officialdom. Identification with the

[1] H. B. Workman, *The Place of Methodism in the Catholic Church*, p. 63.
[2] R. Niebuhr, *The Nature and Destiny of Man*, Vol. II, p. 167.
[3] W. E. Beet, *The Medieval Papacy*, p. 184.

hierarchy would have meant the surrender of their distinctive witness. It is therefore important to note that the real strength of Catholicism in the thirteenth century lay in the witness of those whose priesthood consisted in holiness, spirituality and a sense of mission.

Thirdly, there were occasions when the success of the missionary labours of the monks and friars accentuated their dilemma. Their zeal took them into regions where the usual ministrations of the Church were not available. The people to whom they were sent, impressed by the holiness and faithfulness of their missionaries, begged of them to fulfil the duties of the parish priest. Where all other arguments had failed, the pressing needs of their new converts persuaded them. There is little doubt that this is the principal reason why monasticism did not remain entirely a lay movement throughout the Middle Ages.

There was, however, one other reason why the monks and friars were reluctant to take Orders. It was a long-standing conviction that the order of clerics and that of the monks were essentially distinct. The difference between the two in both calling and function had long been accepted. Deanesly quotes Gregory the Great to prove that the monastic and clerical vocations were regarded as separate: 'No one can perform ecclesiastical (clerical) duties, and remain by due order under monastic rule. The duties of each office separately are so weighty that no one can rightly discharge them. It is therefore very improper that one man should be considered fit to discharge the duties of both.'[1] There were exceptions to the rule, and sometimes monks were persuaded to become clerics for the reason already given, but for the most part monasticism remained a lay movement. There is no indication that they were deprived of grace because they remained in the ranks of the laity, nor was their service to the Church as a whole jeopardized because they were not ordained. On the contrary, the work and witness of the monks provide one of the most thorough applications of the doctrine of the priesthood of all believers that is known before the Reformation.

The doctrine is clearly revealed in the attitude of the monks to secular toil, and in support of this we must turn to the work of St Benedict whose achievement cannot be overstated.

[1] Quoted in M. Deanesly, *A History of the Medieval Church*, p. 41.

For Benedict accomplished that most difficult of all tasks, a revolution in the moral attitude of man, and that in more ways than one. Compared to this profound issue a revolution in monasticism is a small matter. We see this moral revolution most clearly in the change which the Rule brought about in men's conception of the place of toil.[1]

It is remarkable that knowing the Rule of the Monastery, noblemen should apply for admission. They were not always accepted. In the East when a nobleman applied for admission into St Basil's monastery and had not obeyed the injunction to sell all his possessions, he was rejected with the words: 'Syncletius, you have spoiled a senator without making a monk.'

It is even more remarkable that free-men were content to work alongside slaves. It should be remembered that in the Roman world manual labour was reserved for slaves but within the walls of the monastery men were equal in honour because all were brothers in Christ and all shared a common servanthood. Indeed to take the role of a servant was the first condition of their acceptance. It was Benedict's aim and desire that the brethren should render all work as a service to God.

> So he laid it down that in his 'school of divine servitude' six hours each day should be given to manual toil and two to reading. The sons of Benedict, freemen be it remembered, often men of high degree, as they laboured in the field clad in the dress familiar to the pagan world as the dress of slaves, or took their share in the work of the house, cooking the meals or cleaning the rooms, sanctified industry by consecrating it to the lowliest tasks.[2]

Nor should it be thought that the life of the monastery was self-centred and that every exercise was done with a view to self-discipline and self-edification. The loving outreach to those in need was not overlooked. Therefore the following observation by Stephen Neill requires modification: 'The task of the monk was to make an island of salvation in the midst of a world doomed to destruction. His purpose was to save himself and not to save the world.'[3] Whether in the sphere of secular work or in missionary labours or in the observance of canonical hours of prayer, theirs was a true liturgy—a work done unto God, on behalf of others, without any thought of personal gain. Far from being narrowly

---
[1] H. B. Workman, *The Evolution of the Monastic Ideal*, p. 154.
[2] Ibid., p. 155.   [3] S. Neill, *The Christian Society*, p. 55.

individualistic the broad scope of monastic service may be seen in the following statement of the Benedictine Constitution:

> He (the monk) may follow the contemplative life or the active ministry of the Apostolic mission. He may teach or may write books. He may plant trees or till the soil, or he may follow art in any of its many branches. He may convert the heathen or preside over the welfare of the universal church from the Chair of Peter. Any work a Christian may do, he may do. . . . He is still a benedictine. He works for work's sake; for the discipline it gives to the soul; for the avoiding of idleness; and for his own support; for then, says St Benedict, 'we are true monks when we live by the work of our hands'.[1]

It is not always appreciated how much light the monastic life throws on the biblical doctrine of work. Even allowing for the sheltered atmosphere of the cloister, its congenial fellowship and the absence of the pressures of a competitive world, there is no doubt that new insights concerning the attitude to daily work came from the cloister. One of these was that daily work, so far from being a hindrance to Christian living, is a necessary ingredient to it. The astonishing thing about the secular work done in the monasteries is that it was done without any obvious incentive. For monks under the Benedictine Rule the incentive and the end of their labours was the glory of the Lord. Windgren makes a curious accusation against the monk when he says: 'All his life the monk is supplied with food, clothing and everything else, provided by the labours of others out in the world, and put at the disposal of the cloistered inhabitants in the form of gifts and endowments. So the monk is secure, without perils or cross.'[2] But the monk was not as secure as this statement might lead us to suppose. The description of the life of the Cistercians who first came to Fountains tells a different story.

> The inside (of the loft) was strewn with chaff or dried leaves, which, with the wood-work, seem to have been the only covering permitted. The monks had thus got a house over their heads, but they had got very little else. Autumn and winter were approaching, and they had no store laid by. Their food during summer had been a compound of leaves intermixed with coarse grain. Beech-nuts and roots were to be their main support during the winter. And then to the privations of insufficient food was added the wearing out of their shoes and clothes.[3]

[1] E. L. Taunton, *English Black Monks of S Benedict*, pp. 47-8.
[2] G. Windgren, *The Christian's Calling*, p. 32.
[3] In a MS. in the possession of the Royal Society, published *in extenso* by Dugdale in his 'Monasticon'.

This is not a picture of opulence and, in any case, Luther's criticism of the monks was not, as Windgren supposes, that they were lazy, but rather that their very hard work was merely a form of works-righteousness. But even this criticism is open to question. The disciplined daily work of the monastery was done partly because the monks were under a vow of obedience and partly because this aspect of their calling was as much a part of the life of the Evangelical Counsels as prayer and praise. Moreover, this attitude to daily work gave them a spiritual as well as an economic repose. The fulfilment of a task was spiritually rewarding as well as helping to provide the material needs of the monastery. But perhaps the greatest reward was the knowledge that they were sharing a priesthood which was common to all and without which the monastic movement could not have survived.

The comprehensiveness of their view of priesthood is altogether striking and has not been sufficiently realized. It extended to all the interests of life, to work in the fields, to the home-life of the cloister, to the works of charity for their neighbours and their missionary labours. All these activities were varying expressions of their priesthood.

It is not without significance that this comprehensive idea of priesthood characterized monasticism from the fifth to the thirteenth centuries. The idea is broadened by St Francis who wished to include those who, while remaining outside the monastery, were willing to accept conditions of spiritual discipline and look upon their secular occupation as a priestly vocation. This extension of the monastic principle beyond the bounds of the monastery marks a turning-point in the history of monasticism. Its repercussions were felt throughout the whole church. Perhaps even St Francis was not fully aware of the far-reaching consequences of his action. Harnack places the Franciscan movement in its true setting:

> The church had attained to political world-dominion; she had actually overcome, or was on the point of overcoming, the Empire and the old State order. The aims and results of the mighty efforts put forth by the church in the eleventh and twelfth centuries had now been made manifest; but now a movement began among the laity and in the nations to emancipate themselves from the tutelage of the hierarchy.[1]

[1] A. Harnack, op. cit., pp. 91–2.

The full impact of the Franciscans covers a very wide range and it is necessary to consider the effect of their work upon the laity, the hierarchy, monasticism itself, and to show how the ideal of service epitomized the movement.

The originality of some of the reforms of St Francis marks him out as a great leader of men. His genius lay not only in founding the Third Order but in the successful application of it. This Order meant that men and women, peasants and artisans, professional men and rulers, while living an ordinary life in the world, were committed to a holy life, to specific acts of service, to the Christian education of children and to the world-wide mission of St Francis. The Tertiaries opened to the laity doors of opportunity which had been closed too long. Living in the world, they lived unto God; serving their neighbour, they served their Lord; pursuing their secular occupations, they sanctified them to the service of God. For the first time there was a large-scale realization that theirs was a high calling. Time and thought, work and leisure, wealth and possessions, natural endowments and spiritual gifts were irrevocably offered as a service to God. With this vow or commitment there came into their lives a lofty aim, a new dignity and a spiritual elation which they had not previously known. The emergence of the Third Order marked the awakening of the laity of Christendom, and with this awakening there came a new consciousness of vast spiritual resources which previously had been unknown and unused. The importance of this is aptly stated by Workman:

> The founding of the Order ... was the beginning of a social revolution the depth of which was hidden by our older historians. For centuries the laity had had little place in the organization of the Church. Now Europe was filled with a host of earnest laymen, bound together in social service and Church work, most of whom earned their own living, like St Paul, by the labour of their hands. Francis realized that his own life could never be the life of all ... but the life and labour of love was open to every Christian.[1]

And that is the crucial point, the pivot of this new revolution: in the hands of St Francis the theory of the priesthood of all believers was turned into fact and it was now realized that the life of holiness, witness, service and sacrifice was open to every Christian. This knowledge enriched their experience, deepened their churchmanship, clarified their vision. At last they knew that theirs was

[1] H. B. Workman, *The Evolution of the Monastic Ideal*, pp. 298-9.

not only a high calling, it was the highest. The Tertiaries became the leaven of the whole community. No movement has stirred the imagination in quite the same way or inspired men to greater acts of piety and charity. The friars were also apostles and as they pressed on in their travels, so the frontiers of the kingdom were extended. 'The interest of the laity in the life and sacraments of the Church was awakened by them; through them the idea grew slowly effective that a layman, sincerely obedient to the Church and inwardly pious, has a right to share in the highest good which the Church can communicate.'[1]

St Francis appeared to be naively unconscious of the radical nature of the reforms which his new movement involved, and sometimes he seemed to be oblivious of the fact that alongside the friars there was a Church which was seeking to do precisely the same kind of work. But perhaps he was not convinced that the aim of the Church was the same as his, so while others wrangled about the rights and wrongs of his new system, St Francis pursued, meekly and effectively, his appointed task. All in all, Harnack's tremendous claim is justified: 'He wished not to found a new Order but to revolutionize the world.'[2] On the whole the clergy missed the point of his purpose, for it is, of course, impossible to revolutionize the world without reforming the Church. By a curious blindness the clergy did not appreciate that wherever St Francis went there was a harvest waiting to be reaped. But whether they realized it or not, it remains true that the strength of his movement was the strength of the whole Church.

> He taught that men should seek a higher perfection than that set forth by the Church, without realizing that this involved the reformation of the Church on the lines that the Church, with its vast legal, almost commercial, certainly secular, interests would not have welcomed. He preached that society should go back to the Sermon on the Mount, at the time when Innocent III was making the Chair of the Fisherman into the most powerful throne since the days of the Caesars. In an age when a dominant sacerdotalism had established impassable gulfs between clergy and laity, he attempted a revolution whose ideal, at any rate in its earlier forms, was the priesthood of all believers.[3]

Perhaps it was the simplicity of the friars, their single aim, their

---

[1] A. Harnack, op. cit., p. 97. [2] Ibid., p. 95.
[3] H. B. Workman, *The Evolution of the Monastic Ideal*, p. 308.

gentle disregard of all opposition, which eventually won the day. But it is more likely to be something else. In their teaching they gave to priesthood a new interpretation and in their lives a new exemplification which have undoubtedly influenced the universal Church. Without argument or legislation or written work, they demonstrated in their life and witness the difference between the priesthood of the pope and the priesthood of the friar. Beet has drawn attention to this difference:

> A universal ruler and busy statesman, the Lord Innocent was a man apart, and had but few points of contact with the common life of ordinary men. With that common life the Friars, on the other hand, were in contact at every point. . . . As we consider the contrast in outlook and aim, as between the pope and the friar, we wonder the less that the latter owed little even to a Pope so really great as was Innocent III.[1]

The bishops and parish priests shared the discomfiture of the Pope but for different reasons. The Pope was disturbed because he did not know what was happening; the bishops and priests were disturbed because they knew. Reluctantly the Pope had given his blessing to St Francis without realizing the implications of his action. This blessing, whether given in knowledge or in ignorance, was of immense value to the Franciscan movement. The bishops saw their authority dwindling before the authority of a holy life, and the priests were dismayed to find that their erstwhile distinctive duties were undertaken by the wandering friars. The Franciscan movement produced the utmost confusion in the ranks of the hierarchy. Yet the permission of the Pope and the personality of St Francis were sufficient to ensure the success of the movement. The issue became more and more clear-cut; it was focused on the idea of priesthood; that of the clergy and that of all believers. The latter were sincerely anxious for full leave to preach the story of Christ's words and deeds and the former no less sincerely convinced that such a permission, since it must encourage private interpretation, could only end in the ruin of souls. But the facts proved otherwise, for souls were saved and not lost, so the friars continued their work, moving from place to place, without possessions, holding all things in common as the apostles did, following naked in the steps of the naked Christ. But the Church which

[1] W. E. Beet, op. cit., p. 187.

had received such great gains from the Franciscans did not realize the doctrine which underlined and inspired the movement. The friars had believed, grasped and applied the doctrine of the priesthood of all believers, and if this movement of the thirteenth century did not actually begin the Reformation, it showed unmistakably the path towards it.

Not the least achievement of the Franciscans was the effect of their work on monasticism as a whole. With the coming of the friars the static expression of the Christian life gave place to the dynamic, and religion was seen to be not only a subject of meditation but a way of life. In St Francis's famous dictum, 'It is useless to walk anywhere to preach unless we preach everywhere as we walk.' A life of selfless service is itself a proclamation of the Gospel. The monastic movement was like a reservoir of culture and spiritual power, whereas the Franciscans were like a flowing stream bringing life, nourishment and renewal over a wide area. Of one thing they were unconquerably persuaded, namely, that not in the forest but in the forum, not in the monastery but in the market-place, not in the void but in the vortex of life, the Lord's work must be done. The success of their new approach is its own justification.

Deanesly gives five reasons for this success:

1. The character of St Francis himself.
2. The fact that the friars' movement was democratic compared with the monastic.
3. The ineffectiveness of the parochial system which was designed to serve country areas and left untouched the poor in the towns.
4. The success of the friars in overcoming the distrust of lay-preaching which was prevalent in the middle ages.
5. The approval of the Pope.[1]

To these cogent reasons there may be added three more: the voluntary nature of their work, their joy in doing it, and the wide scope of their activities. The word 'mendicancy' has often been used to pour scorn on the methods of the friar, but that is to miss the point of an important development. In the thirteenth century the work of the local church was in the hands of temporal vicars and stipendiary clerks who were not always as competent and conscientious as they might have been. Had they done their work

[1] See M. Deanesly, *A History of Medieval Church*, pp. 154–5.

effectively there would have been no justification for Jack Upland's complaint:

> And Christ himself was apaied*
> With twelve apostles and a few disciples
> To preach and doe priest's office
> To the whole world.
> Then was it better doe than is now at this time
> By a thousand dele.†¹

It frequently happened that on the doorstep of the rectory stood an itinerant friar who was as anxious to occupy the pulpit as the rector was to vacate it. The argument was not that there was no room for a paid ministry but that there was no room for an idle ministry. The contention of the friars was that it was better that the Gospel should be preached by them than not preached at all. But this was too modest an estimate, for it frequently happened that they did the work better than anyone else even though they expected no remuneration. The idea of Christian service, voluntarily rendered, which has become widespread and necessary in many lands, received a new impetus from the Franciscans. Their priesthood consisted in the voluntary offering of life and service and by it the Church was greatly enriched.

Not only was their work done without any hope of financial remuneration but it was done in a spirit of exuberant joy. It is, of course, one thing to accept a life of poverty and obedience, but it is an entirely different thing to accept it in such a spirit of gaiety and zeal that others are inspired to follow the example. The sight of men of God filled with joy was not a new experience but it was a forgotten one. The rigorous tortures of the ascetic life had left their mark on the faces of many righteous men. For a long time the sad countenance and wasted frame had been a recommendation of the Christian religion, but this was something different and the world warmed to the rapturous singing and dancing of the wandering friar. What was the reason for this joy? 'St Francis really meant what he said when he said that he had found the secret of life in being the servant and the secondary

---

¹ Quoted in G. R. Owst, *Preaching in Medieval England*, p. 48.
* *apaied* means 'satisfied'.
† *A thousand dele* means 'a thousandfold'.

figure. There was to be found ultimately in such service a freedom almost amounting to frivolity. It was comparable to the condition of the jongleur because it almost amounted to frivolity.'[1] But they did not sing and dance to cheer up a sorrowful world but because they were convinced that to do Christ's work with joy was well-pleasing in His sight. Just because their calling enabled them to sit loosely to the things of earth, they enjoyed a freedom in service which was denied to their fellows. Yet their joy was not the result of evading the stern conflicts of the Christian life but of facing them. They were God's knights as well as God's jongleurs.

St Francis inculcated into his followers that obedience to God and adventure in His service brought unspeakable joy to the soul.

> The ideals of his fraternity were founded on those of romantic chivalry rather than on those of the Benedictine monastery. It was to be an Order of spiritual knighthood, dedicated to the service of the Cross, and the love of the Lady Poverty. The friars were his 'Brethren of the Round Table', 'jongleurs of God', and they were to set forth like knight adventurers on the path of God, performing spiritual deeds of prowess, shrinking from no hardship or danger and finding their reward in the service of love.[2]

To the voluntary and joyful nature of their service we must add the wide scope of their activities. The output and extent of their work are astonishing. It was social, pastoral, educational and missionary. Even the attempt to cover so many fields was remarkable and the achievement of it was due to the inspiration, energy and leadership of Francis himself. He was great in a great century. If Aquinas was the greatest Christian philosopher and Dante the greatest Christian poet, there is no doubt that Francis was the greatest Christian hero and the most loved.

His life was his proclamation because Christ was his life. His own experience of Christ gave to his work a strong evangelical urgency and this characterized all his missionary labours. Perhaps the immediacy of Christ's presence and the consequent joy provide the reasons for his stress on faith rather than order, on Word rather than Sacraments, on joy rather than judgment, and on service rather than conformity. But do not these include some of

---

[1] G. K. Chesterton, *St Francis of Assisi*, p. 82.
[2] C. Dawson, *Medieval Religion*, p. 114.

the basic truths which the later reformers sought to establish? If St Francis had been a theologian it is possible that the Protestant Reformation might have been ante-dated two hundred years. The principles of the Reformation had already been applied to a way of life, but the doctrine which gave them new power and implications for the whole Church, had not yet been fully worked out. The work of the Franciscans in preparing a climate of opinion for the coming Reformation should not be under-estimated. So we have the curious circumstance of the greatest hero of Catholicism showing the way and preparing it for the greatest hero of Protestantism.

Our consideration of the work of the monks and friars, especially as this is revealed in the Benedictine and Franciscan movements, has resulted in certain definite conclusions. We have found that these movements are pre-eminently associated with the laity. In origin and development they were lay movements. Harnack's argument that monasticism itself emerged in the second century because 'the priests and kings of God began to clamour for Priests, and to come to terms with the world',[1] is here corroborated. Workman significantly treats the subject of monasticism under the heading 'The Priesthood of the Laity',[2] and Foster in referring to the doctrine of the priesthood of all believers unequivocally affirms: 'this emphasis was revived by the Franciscans'.[3] Our conclusion is not only that these movements contain the germ of this Reformation doctrine but that they translate it into the everyday life of the Church. They have therefore given to the doctrine special tasks for the Church as a whole.

We have also seen that many of the monks refused to be admitted into the clerical priesthood because of their belief in the priesthood of *all* believers.

The monks' attitude to secular toil re-emphasized for the Church the meaning of priestly vocation in relation to every aspect of life.

The Tertiaries are important because they turned the theory of the priesthood of all believers into fact.

By their emphasis on the voluntary, joyous and comprehensive

---

[1] A. Harnack, op. cit., p. 25.
[2] See H. B. Workman, *The Place of Methodism in the Catholic Church*, p. 62.
[3] John Foster, *World Church*, p. 43.

nature of Christian witness and service, the friars laid firm foundations on which the sixteenth century reformers built with astonishing success. And now we must consider how the way to the Reformation was prepared by the lives and doctrines of the German and Flemish mystics.

CHAPTER NINE

THE MYSTICS

WHAT is Christian mysticism? It is an inward spiritual experience in which God is revealed, known and apprehended. A mystic seeks an immediate sense of the grace and glory of God. St Bernard wrote to Cardinal Haimeric, 'Nothing that concerns the glory of God is a matter of indifference to me'.[1] The words, 'Give what Thou commandest and command what Thou givest',[2] place Augustine in the tradition of the mystics for only the God-conscious and God-possessed soul is truly free. God's commands are not impossible where God is personally known. In a similar strain Luther sums up the meaning of salvation,

> Now these and all God's words are holy, true, right, peace-giving, free and entirely good. The soul of the man who cleaves to them with a true faith will be so completely united with God that all the virtues of the word will become the qualities of his soul. Through faith and by God's word, the soul will become holy, righteous, true, peaceful, free and entirely good, and he will become a true child of God.[3]

Wesley's avowed aim was to seek and know God. He found assurance through encounter and out of this experience he states his interpretation of true religion, 'Thou shalt propose to thyself no end, no help, no happiness, but God. Thou shalt seek nothing in earth or heaven but Him: thou shalt aim at nothing but to know, to love, and enjoy Him.'[4] Wesley affirms with remorseless consistency the dominating aim of the Christian religion which is, 'to know and love and enjoy Him'. He not only translated but experienced Gerhardt's words:

> *O Jesu, nothing may I see,*
> *Nothing desire, or seek, but Thee.*

---

[1] Louis Bouyer, *The Cistercian Heritage*, p. 9.
[2] In Ps. cxviii, Serm. xii, 5.
[3] B. L. Woolf, *Reformation Writings*, I, pp. 361-2.
[4] *Sermons*, xxix. 15.

This is not to say that Luther and Wesley would have subscribed to all the doctrines of the mystics but that the basic truths of mysticism are prominent in their writings. Two characteristics are the inalienable mark of mysticism—the inwardness of the spiritual life and the immediacy of contact with God.

MYSTICISM AND RELATIONSHIP

Mysticism can only be properly understood in terms of relationship. The various schools of mysticism stand or fall by this criterion. This is why the *deus-nihil* theory of Eckhart and the atman-Brahman doctrine of philosophic Hinduism are defective. Both are the negation of relationship. There is no such thing as an unrelated experience of the soul. Buddhism would have held in trust for the world a much more positive and inspiring message had not the 'nay-saying'[1] wrecked any hope of relationship. For, what hope can there be of ultimate salvation if the world is unreal and unrelated? The true mystic assumes the reality of the cosmic order but he also interprets it in the light of spiritual facts. Dr Bett considers that this is the essence of mysticism. 'The mystic believes that the universe of the soul is a spiritual system, every part of which depends upon every other, and he always looks for a continuous and causal relation between spiritual facts.'[2] Whether a man's actions are good or bad, this causal relationship remains. In this concept of relation lies his hope as well as his malady. The first emergence of evil coincides with the revolt of human personality against God. It is summed up in Dante's words, 'He who first upon his Maker turned his back'.[3] Behind this act was a motive of spiritual revolt which nullified relationship. The likeness of God in man was defaced and a way had to be found whereby it could be restored. Christ is God's answer. Yet the work of God in Christ is never arbitrary or magical, it is effective only when certain conditions are fulfilled. The mystic is pre-eminently concerned with these conditions. If the idea of restoration is not a day-dream but an actual possibility, a way must be found. Just because God's way

---

[1] 'There is no being, only becoming. There is nothing that abides; there is no rest, no peace, no satisfaction in aught that is, or can be thought to be' (*Samyutta Nikaya*, Text II, 180).
[2] H. Bett, *Studies in Religion*, p. 137. [3] *Paradiso*, IX. 127.

to man was very costly, no mystic believes that there is any easy way to God. In this, at least, he is not mistaken. The dark betrayal night, the tears of Gethsemane and the agony of Calvary, plainly indicate the cost, and compel a man to cast his dreams of ease away. The Schoolmen did not choose an easy way yet no solution was to be found along juristic lines. Certainly they emphasize a relationship but it is the wrong kind; it is a legalistic and not a charismatic one.

MYSTICISM AND FAITH

The Institutional, the Speculative and the Mystical, these according to Baron Von Hügel's lucid analysis, are the three elements of religion. All of them have been important in the history of the Church but, on the whole, the Reformers and especially Luther, preferred the last. Despite much that has been written to the contrary, there is no doubt that many seeds were planted in his mind by the mediaeval mystics. Hodgson's verdict rings true, 'The mystic's uttermost self-surrender carries him to the sacred Heart, brings him to the immediate Presence of God.'[1]

Authentic mysticism as set forth in the New Testament never under-rates the importance of faith. Roman Catholic writers sometimes fall into the error of quoting only the first part of Gal. ii. 20, which states the union of the two wills but does not state how this experience is brought about.[2] The second half of the verse leaves no doubt of this. 'I live, yet not I but Christ liveth in me'—that is the plain statement of the experience. There then follows the means by which the believer partakes of this experience. 'And the life that I now live in the flesh, I live in faith, the faith which is in the Son of God who loved me and gave Himself for me.' Union with Christ cannot exist apart from faith in Christ. God's revelation to man is only known in an experience of relatedness which is born of faith. Bishop Stephen Neill's claim is important for an understanding of mystical theology, 'Concerning the God who participates in the life of His creation, and who speaks in revelation, the New Testament makes three tremendous affirmations that God is Light, God is Love, and God is Spirit; in these three phrases,

---

[1] G. E. Hodgson, *English Mystics*, pp. 9–10.
[2] Benedictine of Stanbrook, *Medieval Mystical Tradition*, p. 2.

the whole of Christian theology is implicitly contained.'[1] It must be remembered that God is Spirit and Light and Love in relation to man, and the mystics sought to understand this revelation in terms of an ever-deepening personal experience. The very words they use in describing the threefold way indicate the different ways in which they grasp the divine revelation. The Spirit purifies the heart—the Purgative way; the Light enlightens the mind, interpreting the meaning of eternal things—the Illuminative way; and Love unites the soul with God—the Unitive way.

Many writers completely misunderstand mysticism because they will not differentiate between Justification and Sanctification. It may be affirmed that in general the experiences of those in the authentic mystical tradition are post-conversion experiences. It is often assumed that the mystics attained salvation by various stages, each one more advanced than the rest, and much of the criticism levelled against the mystics by the Dialectical Theology School is based on this erroneous assumption. Mystical experience is generally the outcome of spiritual maturity, it is the process of the soul's sanctification. Richard Rolle (1295–1349), perhaps the best known of English mystics emphasizes this very point: 'When I had perceived my especial vocation, and, laying aside my worldly dress, had determined to serve God rather than man, it befell me on a certain night in the beginning of my conversion . . .'[2] We shall avoid many pitfalls if we remember that the mystics were not moving towards their conversion and in no sense were they seeking to earn or win by their deeds the saving grace of God, but on the contrary, their conversion had become the necessary spiritual spur to a deeper experience and holier life.

It is a mistake to imagine that the place of faith is minimized by the mystics. The reason for the emphasis upon contemplation and meditation is in order that they may hear the Word of God. In the typical mystical order faith comes first because only through faith is cleansing of soul experienced—(the Way of Purgation). There follows spiritual illumination in which the divine revelation is grasped—(the Way of Illumination); this leads to the ecstatic love towards God which characterizes the Unitive Way and is the

---

[1] S. Neill, *Christian Faith Today*, p. 248.
[2] R. Rolle, *Emendatio Vitae* (The Amending of Life), translated by H. L. Hubbard, pp. 22–3.

THE MYSTICS

culminating experience. In fact, each 'way' of the mystics is entirely dependent upon hearing the Word in Faith. The emphasis upon the objective Word in the following passage is important because it was written about a disciple of St Bernard who is often accused of an exaggerated subjectivism.

> If a monk needs to go into the desert, it is so that, in the silence of solitude, the voice of the Word may be spoken to his heart. It is by meditation on the Scriptures that he will hear the voice. It may be said that for Guerre of Igny (d. 1157) this was the basis of an entire system of mysticism. His aim was to rise, through meditative reading of Scripture, in faith quickened by a general asceticism which was directed by love, to a true spiritual intuition of the realities which the Divine Word speaks to us.[1]

TAULER'S SPIRITUAL AWAKENING

It will be noted that there existed even in the twelfth century the seed of a doctrine which only came to fruition at the Reformation. But first it had to be tended carefully by the German mystics whose influence upon the theology of the Reformation was remarkable. Among the German mystics John Tauler* holds a prominent place. If there is some doubt as to the identity of the person who is frequently referred to by Tauler as 'the Layman', there can be little doubt that it was under the instruction of a layman that Tauler was converted. It is generally believed that this layman was Nicholas of Basle although Tauler nowhere mentions him by name but refers to him as 'the layman'. Nicholas was a leader among the 'Friends of God' and must have been still a young man when he met Tauler in 1350. Undoubtedly he was associated with Berthold von Rohrbach who was burnt to death in 1356 for preaching that a layman enlightened by God was as competent to teach others as the most learned priest. Tauler was greatly disturbed that he, a priest, should have to receive instruction from a layman, and Nicholas, sensing his feelings said,

> Dear Sir, I fear that I have said some things to you that have vexed you greatly in your mind; it is because I am a layman and you are a great doctor of Holy Scripture, and yet I have said so much to you after the manner of a teacher. But that I have meant it well and kindly

[1] Louis Bouyer, op. cit., p. 192.   * John Tauler (1290–1361).

and sought your soul's salvation in it, and simply the glory of God and nothing else, of that God is my witness.[1]

There is no doubt that Tauler was soon convinced that he had found a man qualified in mind and spirit to be his spiritual counsellor. Nicholas recognized one instructor, the Holy Ghost, and, as it was a fundamental theme of his theology that the wisdom and power of the Holy Ghost are operative in all believers, he had no sympathy with the view that the priesthood possessed an exclusive authority in matters of spiritual direction. 'If a great lord of this world, or a whole district or city should ask me how, as things now stand, men may return to God, and find reconciliation with Him, I would advise that they seek that counsel which comes from the Holy Spirit, whether such counsel proceed from priest or layman.'[2]

The Holy Spirit is primarily operative through the Word of God, and Nicholas regarded it as the greatest deprivation if men were not allowed access to the Scriptures and to early Christian writings. 'Those book-learned men who would keep the laity from reading these, sought their own glory more than the glory of God.'[3] Because of these views which were in line with the whole trend of his teaching, a firm place may be claimed for Nicholas in the Evangelical tradition of the Church.

> The only peculiarity of his belief which I can discover, is his strong confidence in the reality of the visions and miraculous revelations which were imparted to him and his friends; and it must be remembered that even this peculiarity he not only shares with the great Luther who lived two centuries later, but also with the liberal and sagacious Wesley.[4]

Following in a kind of evangelical succession Tauler imbibed such teaching and eventually became the leader of the Friends of God. Two other factors were determinative of this position of leadership, his conversion and his decisive action in relation to his fellow countrymen who were placed by Rome under an Interdict.

If religion in the fourteenth century was lifted out of the sphere of moral philosophy into that of personal experience, it was due to the work of Tauler. Tauler was seeking a Saviour not a sage. A fossilized orthodoxy provided an impersonal scheme of salvation,

---

[1] Susanna Winkworth, *Tauler's Life and Sermons* (later abbreviated as TLS), p. 61.   [2] Neander, *Church History*, IX, Pt. II, p. 566.
[3] Ibid., p. 565.   [4] S. Winkworth, op. cit., p. 136.

and Humanism offered a holy man who, like Confucius, was no more than a reliable ethical guide. But Tauler was asking questions which have troubled men through the ages and they were questions which these systems could not answer. How can I get rid of my sins? How am I to be saved? How can I be certain of personal salvation? Other questions are answered in vain if there is no answer to these. Tauler could neither evade nor suppress them and they cried out for an answer, and his importance for theology lies in the fact that he was asking the right questions. We must now consider whether he found the right answers.

He knew that sin was rebellion against the will of God and that the conflict in his own experience had to be resolved before he could preach peace and reconciliation to others. He writes, 'Put off thine own will and there will be no hell. If there were any person in hell who should get quit of self-will and call nothing his own, he would come out of hell into heaven.'[1] He found the way of deliverance along a path which seemed temporarily hidden, the path of penitence, faith and obedience. Archibishop Trench does less than justice to the German Mystics when he says, 'There was wanting a sufficiently deep apprehension of sin.'[2] It is precisely on account of his profound conception of the nature of sin that Tauler rejects any easy solution. He was no Quietist. The 'dreaming oneself into God' was one of the extravagances of the 'false light' against which he warned his readers. He also rejects the typical solution of Humanism, 'Natural light, compared with the divine light, is less than a lighted taper to the noon-day sun.'[3] After his meeting with Nicholas there followed two years of the most strenuous spiritual conflict, and from this prolonged encounter two vital truths emerged: a clear consciousness of the depths of sin concealed in his own heart and an understanding of the necessity of the utter self-surrender of the soul to God. In this way only could human rebellion in many forms be decisively overcome. Moreover, we may judge Tauler's horror of sin by his emphasis on the need for redemption.

The sentimental perception of the sufferings of Christ did not go far enough for him and he demands a rigorous faith-identification.

[1] H. B. Workman, *Christian Thought to the Reformation*, p. 208.
[2] R. C. Trench, *Medieval Church History*, p. 353.
[3] Neander, op. cit., p. 553.

'Since your great God was thus set at nought, and condemned by his creatures, and was crucified and died, you should, with patient endurance, and with all suffering humility, behold yourselves in His suffering, and have your minds thereby impressed.'[1] On the personal aspect of God's action on behalf of man Tauler was emphatic. Here he strikes a note, rarely heard in his time, against an exclusively objective view of the work of Christ, 'Though God were to take to Himself all men who exist, and to assume their nature, and manifest Himself in them, yet, if the same did not take place with regard to *myself*, the effects of my fall and rebellion would never be destroyed.'[2]

THE SPIRITUAL PILGRIMAGE

In explaining the stages in the spiritual pilgrimage Tauler is relating the story of his own experience. There are three stages:

Listening for the word of Christ.
Resting in Christ.
Being crucified with Christ.

A man listens in faith, rests in faith, and in faith is crucified with Christ. And is not this the plain story of our salvation? The Word is addressed to faith and faith responds to the Living Word and this results in the crucifixion of the old nature. According to Tauler the three stages are based on the work of Christ in the heart. Firstly, the temple courts have to be cleared and the harsh noises of the buying and selling must subside so that Jesus may be heard. Christ must be heard. To be sure the Word is revealed continually but only true faith listens. Even man's own thoughts and desires are anathema if they prevent him from hearing the Word.

> *Oh if mine own thought should on Thy words falling,*
> *Mar the great message and men hear not Thee.*

The second stage is that of faith-union. Like John-Zebedee, he knew the soul must rest on the breast of the Saviour. For if a man rest solely on the work of Christ, he will cease to rely on any works of his own. This rest does not imply immunity from suffering and

---

[1] Hagenbach, *History of Doctrines*, Vol. II, p. 45.   [2] Ibid., p. 45.

THE MYSTICS 203

conflict but rather it suggests a state of soul which is unperturbed and unhurt by these things. Moreover, this rest sets the soul free, imparting new confidence and energy in the service of Christ's kingdom.

The third stage is reached only after 'many a death of nature, inward and outward', when practically Christ lives and repeats His experience. This produces 'a mingled web of joy and grief' in the soul. When Tauler uses the words of our Lord, 'Put out into the deep', he is thinking of the heart's experience of the unfathomable depths of divine love. If God's impress is not found there, it is found nowhere. A man will endure much conflict to find such love and peace.

It were a well spent journey,
Though seven deaths lay between.

It follows then that in listening and resting and dying, life is renewed in the believer till the end of time.

Tauler's Protest

In addition to his conversion which resulted in inward growth as well as outward usefulness, there was another factor which developed Tauler's gifts of courageous leadership. It was the visitation of the Black Death which killed a vast number of devoted priests and left their flocks without a regular ministry. Just when the people were in deep need and longed for the ministrations of the priest, an Interdict was issued by Rome depriving them of the consolations of the Church. As so often happened in the Middle Ages the Church was used as an instrument to exert political pressure.

Many of the Estates in Germany had refused to recognize the kingship of Charles IV because he had been elected at the instigation of the Pope and in defiance of their wishes. On this issue a bitter quarrel developed between the Emperor Louis of Bavaria and Pope John XXII, and Strasburg, along with many other cities of the Rhine, was placed under an Interdict which lasted twenty years. Already distressed by sickness of body, the people were now deprived of succour of soul and were left to die excommunicate. Hence they were denied the mininstrations of the Church just at the point of their deepest need. Tauler's protest consisted in this: he refused to recognize the Interdict. We may imagine the people's gratitude to Tauler for his noble act of disobedience to a Church which had taken from them their only remaining consolation. This was a 'protest' of the most startling significance, and although the world had to wait another two hundred years for stronger and more effective action, the importance of Tauler's action as a pointer for Reformers who followed him, should not be overlooked. But apart from his defiant protest, these events compelled Tauler to examine the whole question of the Church's attitude to sin and the sinner. We must now consider the result of his investigations. At the same time we must not lose sight of an important question: were there elements in Tauler's theology which Luther imbibed and used with tremendous power in later years? Some vital truths were reasserted by Tauler—the divine initiative in the plan of salvation, the place of faith in man's approach to God, and the meaning of Christian vocation. In this sort of teaching, however, Tauler did not stand alone. He had the support of Ruysbroeck,* Groot and the author of *Theologia Germanica*. The authorship of the last-mentioned book has always presented a problem. Norman Sykes thinks the author was Ruysbroeck (*The Crisis of the Reformation*, p. 30). Susanna Winkworth thinks he came from the German rather than the Flemish School of Mystics (Introduction to the translation of the *Theologia*, p. 21). No one can be sure. But if the authorship is a matter of doubt, the value of the book is unquestioned. Luther first discovered its real worth and made it widely known. In this chapter we shall consider it, alongside Tauler and Ruysbroeck, as a source-book for an understanding of mystical theology.

The divine initiative

If healing and restoration are to be brought to the soul, they can never be brought by the work of man but only by the work of God. 'By whom, and on what wise, was that healing brought to pass? Mark this: man could not without God, and God should not without man.'[1] This was the succinct answer which the Friends of God gave to the 'good works' tendencies in Romanism and the

[1] *Theologia Germanica*, p. 8. * Ruysbroeck (1293–1381).

misrepresentations implicit in Augustinian predestination. Salvation is possible by faith alone in God alone.

> And in this bringing back and healing, I can, or may, or shall do nothing of myself, but just simply yield to God, so that He alone may do all things in me and work, and I may suffer Him and all His work and His divine will. And because I will not do so, but count myself to be my own, and say 'I', 'mine', 'me' and the like, God is hindered so that He cannot do His work in me alone and without hindrance, for this cause my fall and my going astray remain unhealed. Behold! this all cometh of my claiming somewhat of my own.[1]

It was against this error of the Mediaeval Church, this 'claiming somewhat of my own' that the Germanic mind made its protest in the fourteenth century. The plain truth is that man has no claim whatever. He seldom realizes, however, that by the very fact of making these claims he excludes the work of grace; for when he approaches God on this basis, he will always seek to strengthen his claim by his works and whoever trusts his own works does not trust the work of God. On this truth Tauler's sermons are explicit:

> With many, when God comes to them with His touch and gracious gifts, He finds the chamber of their souls occupied and defiled by other guests. So then, He must go His way and cannot come into us, for we are loving and serving someone else. Therefore, His gifts, which He offers without ceasing to every man, remain unaccepted. This is the cause of our eternal loss; the guilt is ours and not God's.[2]

Nor is this all, for there is a deeper and more dangerous reason why the insistence upon good works is a false trail. Man's presumption in the matter of salvation is a denial of God's prerogative.

> God saith, 'I will not give my glory to another' (Isa. xlii. 8). This is as much as to say that praise and honour and glory belong to none but God only. But now if I call any good thing my own, as if I were it, or as if anything were mine or of me, or were due to me or the like, I take unto myself somewhat of honour and glory, and do two evil things: first, I fall and go astray as aforesaid; secondly, I touch God in His honour and take unto myself what belongeth to God only. For what must be called good belongeth to none but to the true eternal Goodness which is God only, and whoso taketh it unto himself committeth unrighteousness and is against God.[3]

[1] Ibid., p. 9. [2] S. Winkworth, op. cit., p. 337.
[3] *Theologia Germanica*, p. 10.

Man's response to the divine initiative

1. The way of the true response is not by self-torture

Self-torture is an aspect of self-reliance and all too often these rigorous exercises are strongly tinged with works-righteousness. But more serious still is the implication that the sufferings and Sacrifice of Christ were insufficient for man's salvation. Thus Tauler says:

> Know, that shouldst thou let thyself be stabbed a thousand times a day, and come to life again; shouldst thou let thyself be strung to a wheel, and eat thorns and stones; with all this, thou couldst not overcome sin of thyself. But sink thyself into the deep, unfathomable mercy of God, with a humble submissive will, under God and all creatures, and know that then alone Christ would give it thee out of His great kindness, and free goodness, and love, and compassion.[1]

Further, Tauler addresses those who think to be made God's children by their much watching, fasting and labour, by keeping silence, by singing hymns, by wearing bad and inconvenient clothing, and by great deeds and pious acts. He affirms that it is possible to do all these from a false motive and for the wrong master.

> Alas! how many are martyrs to the Devil. To such as these Isaiah says, 'Bring no more vain oblations: cease to do evil; learn to do well; wash you, make you clean'. Yea, if a man were to suffer himself to be torn to pieces, and did not learn to cleanse himself thoroughly from his sins, to behave towards his fellow-creatures in a spirit of generous love, and to love God above all things, it would all be useless and in vain.[2]

2. The way of true response is not by the worship of images

Images are confined to time and space and true faith is no longer dependent upon these things.

> It was necessary for the disciples to be deprived of all images that they might learn in this school. Where the mind is busied with images, time must necessarily enter into the operations of the imagination, and this has no place in the school of the Holy Spirit; for there neither time nor images can help us, but contact is all that is needed, the which can happen without time within the space of a moment.[3]

---

[1] Neander, op. cit., p. 555.   [2] *T L S*, p. 228.   [3] Ibid., p. 349.

It is not only that images are inventions of the imagination, they are created things and these often hinder rather than help the soul's free, inner response to God. The unknown mystic (the author of *Theologia Germanica*) emphasizes this truth:

> Now mark what may help or further us towards this end. Behold, neither exercises nor words, nor works, nor any creature, nor creature's work, can do this. In this wise, therefore, must we renounce and forsake all things, that we must not imagine or suppose that any words, works, or exercises, any skill or cunning, or any created thing can help or serve us thereto. Therefore, we must suffer these things to be what they are, and enter into union with God.[1]

It is sometimes supposed that such a view implies the wholesale rejection of the means of grace which God has provided in His Church. This is far from the case, for images are provided by man and not by God. They were to be rejected because they were no more than a man-made attempt to achieve a divine end. And if non-Christians are culpable for making an idol of their own invented dream and fancy of a god, how much more culpable are those who presume to make and worship an image of the true God. It was not that the mystics had reached a certain stage when the image could be cast aside, but rather than it was blasphemy to worship an image at any stage.

3. *The way of true response was not by the worship of saints and angels*

The mystics return again and again to the theme of the sovereignty and sufficiency of God alone, and the common notion of seeking solace and hope in anything less than God was regarded as not only undesirable but sinful. Nothing must detract from the paramount glory of God, nothing must be permitted to intervene. Hence Tauler says:

> There are, however, some religious persons who will not be left without solace or stay. For rather than be left simply and truly without a solace, destitute and bare, they set up for themselves heavenly beings, such as the saints and angels, and claim a sort of right to them as a source of spiritual enjoyment, and look to them as a consolation. Thus they will say, 'Such a saint or angel is dear to me before all others;' and if you throw down this prop of their own raising, and say that they ought not to speak thus, you leave them little peace; nay, they are

[1] *Theologia Germanica*, ch. XXVII.

greatly disquieted; and this is worst of all, and doing God a great wrong. Thou must not place thy reliance on any creature in heaven or on earth, nor repose nor lean on any save God alone.¹

4. *The way of true response was not by dependence on feeling*

Mysticism appears in the Medieval Church as the protest of practical religion against the predominance of the dialectical spirit of scholasticism. There is no doubt that many people had grown weary with the distinctions and reasonings and speculations which had characterized scholastic philosophy. Of course it was necessary that Christianity should be subjected to scientific enquiry but the price of this was very high and frequently resulted in rationalizing and externalizing the faith. In their reaction to this situation some of the mystics were in danger of over-stating their case. At the same time, many of them were aware of the dangers implicit in their own simpler and more practical interpretation of religion. Ruysbroeck condemns the uncontrolled sensual ecstasies of the Brethren of the Free Spirit, and Tauler inveighs against a plethora of devotions and vocal prayers and has no room for the elaborate methods, the external and showy exercises of religion which were creeping in at his period. Certainly they were aware that religion must never become a matter of 'feeling' only, but their firm emphasis on the unity of personality, of intellect, feeling and will, was one safeguard against placing too much importance on one faculty. The mystics knew too much about the 'winter' of the soul to be deluded into a reliance on feeling. There were times when all was cold within and the soul was devoid of all heavenly consolation and spiritual sweetness. Few men have been more keenly aware of the stern challenge of Christian conflict or more sensitive to the demands of spiritual discipline. Perhaps this is why Tauler warns those who were luxuriating in sweet feelings: 'Their sweet emotions have turned out a weak foundation on which they have been trusting, instead of trusting truly in God, solely and alone, in love and suffering. There are some who so rest in the sweetness of enjoyment as to fall into an improper freedom.'²

Tauler knew that feeling was an unreliable guide which made religion far too dependent on personal moods, changing circumstances and external events. Faith in the living God is too precious

¹ *T L S*, pp. 263–4. ² Neander, op. cit., IX, p. 591.

a gift to be subjected to fitful factors such as these. Tauler is concerned about the result of this reliance on feeling: the pleasure passes and the soul is left empty and cold.

> As long as they find pleasure in it, they cannot have enough of it; but if this sense of pleasure and interest passes away, their devotion passes away likewise, and they come to dislike their good and holy work, and then they grow lukewarm and careless, performing all they do without devotion. All this is owing to their not having had a single eye to God's glory. They have been prompted and sustained in their labour by the pleasure it has yielded them, and now this has fled. For we must not seek enjoyment and sweetness in the gifts of God, . . . but we must take delight in God alone, and not in His gifts.[1]

5. *The way of true response was not by the extreme methods of the Beghards and Brethren of the Free Spirit*

Ruysbroeck stands forth as the champion of the spirit of tradition and discipline against the extreme individualism and moral anarchy which sometimes resulted from the teaching of the Beghards. He knew that liberty is easily turned into licence and regarded it his duty to combat dangerous reveries by pointing to the true paths which lead to God. All the same, he was influenced more than he knew by the doctrines of those he denounced. One of these was Sister Hadewijck (1305–35) who lived in Brussels when Ruysbroeck was a lay-priest there. She declared that love took the place of all church services, that she had received the gift of prophecy, and that she had seen Christ as the Great High Priest come down from the altar to administer Communion to her with His own hand. The fault here lies more in the phraseology and in the possible implications of her doctrines than in the basic truths which they represent. It is true that church services are nothing without love, but it is surely their purpose to foster the spirit of love. Again, she was not mistaken in affirming that woman may receive the gift of prophecy and exercise it, or in affirming that the believer has direct access into the presence of Christ, but she was unfortunate in her phraseology, and, while Ruysbroeck opposed the manner in which she proclaimed her doctrines, he was undoubtedly influenced by them. In his *The Book of the Kingdom of God's Lovers*, he states the same truths in a more orthodox way. He speaks of the believer's privilege, heritage, and the path of service.

[1] *T L S*, p. 263.

Man is separated from God and returns to Him by means of the redeeming Christ and the seven sacraments. He speaks of Communion as the testament of the Saviour, and the testament is none other than Christ Himself present in all His gifts and pledging Himself to man. 'Can one then wonder that they are in a state of rejoicing who taste and experience such things? He died through love in order that we may live, and he lives in us in order that we may remain living in Him throughout eternity.'[1] There is no doubt in his mind about the certainty of access to God or of the outcome of it, as the following words show: 'God wills to be entirely yours, provided that you will consent to be entirely His, to live and abide in Him as becomes a holy and divine man.'[2]

Such is the privilege of believers, the way to God is open to them and in this sense they are priests unto God. They are kings also, for they inherit five kingdoms which Ruysbroeck distinguishes as follows: theirs is the sensible kingdom or the universe; the universe as seen in the light of grace; the kingdom of the Scriptures; the kingdom of grace; and the kingdom which is God Himself possessed by contemplation.

The believer who is aware of his privilege of access to God and of the five kingdoms which are his true heritage, will now seek by the power of the Spirit of God, to serve others in his every act and in every place. Ruysbroeck dares to call this 'the path supernatural', for it is nothing less than the working of the Holy Spirit in the soul through his sevenfold gifts. But the Spirit must first control the will.

> All virtue and all goodness depend on the will. He, therefore, wants nothing, who truly possesses a right will. ... A good will is born of the Holy Spirit itself; and therefore a good will is the living and free instrument whereby God accomplishes what He wills. A good will, in its internal communion with God, is the spirit crowned with the eternal life; and when it is directed outwards, it is the lord of all external actions; and the same is accordingly the kingdom of God, where God reigns by His grace.[3]

The great blessing which accrues from this is that a man is equipped for service, for his every act will be sanctified by Christ and he will be made free to love and serve.

---

[1] A. W. D'Aygalliers, *Ruysbroeck the Admirable*, p. 200.
[2] A Benedictine, op. cit., p. 129.   [3] Neander, op. cit., IX, p. 585.

We cannot redeem ourselves; but if with all the capabilities we have we follow after Christ, then *our* acts are united with *His* acts, and become ennobled by His grace. Therefore has Christ redeemed us by His own acts and by His own merits has made us free. But if we would possess and feel this freedom, then must His Spirit kindle our spirits to love.[1]

If the true way of response to the divine initiative is not to be found in good works, or self-torture, or in the worship of images, saints and angels, and if this response has nothing to do with dependence on feeling or with the extreme methods of the Beghards and Brethren of the Free Spirit, where is the way of true response to be found? According to the mystics it is to be found in faith, fellowship and service.

I. RESPONSE IN FAITH

The Catholic definition of Mystical Theology will help us at this point: 'This is called Theology because it contains acts proximately referred to God as their object; Mystical because acquired by a secret operation known only to God and the recipient of His divine favours; and experimental, because it is only by personal spiritual experience that such a knowledge of God can be gained.'[2]

That is well said. The believer seeks God, and the spiritual experience wherein God is found is possible only by the secret operations of the Spirit. It is impossible either to understand or appreciate the faith of the mystics apart from this persistent emphasis upon the work and place of the Holy Spirit. They are a continual reminder to the Church that the whole area of life must be brought under the control of the Spirit. Their preoccupation with the need for present inspiration should have acquitted them long ago of any charge of Pelagianism or Scholastic Humanism. The Holy Spirit awakens faith, and there can be no faith apart from His touch. Tauler enlists the support of St Gregory on this:

> The Holy Ghost is an admirable master-workman; He fills a fisherman and makes a preacher of him; He fills a persecutor, and transforms him into a teacher of the Gentiles; He fills a publican, and makes

[1] Ibid., pp. 581-2. For Ruysbroeck's teaching on *The Book of the Kingdom of God's Lovers*, see D'Aygalliers, *Ruysbroeck the Admirable*, p. 83, and Hagenbach, *History of Doctrines*, Vol. II, p. 62.
[2] Addis and Arnold, *A Catholic Dict.*, p. 655.

of him an evangelist ... By whatever means He chooses, so soon as He has touched the soul, He has taught it, and His mere touch is His teaching.[1]

Even Ruysbroeck, who can scarcely be regarded as underestimating the value of contemplation, is emphatic throughout on the importance of faith. 'Christ has obliged us to live on earth amidst all His gifts with a firm faith, and not in bright and glorious contemplation.'[2]

Spiritual preparation is both desirable and essential but no one should rely on it for salvation, and the reason for this is given in Tauler's emphatic statement: 'If you have done all the human works that have ever been done, yet of all this you shall be bare and empty in your ground as those that have done no good work, small or great, other than grace for grace, and what has come from the great mercy of God, without any reservation of confidence in your own preparation.'[3]

Again, Tauler gives prominence to trust in Christ as a means of obtaining victory in all kinds of temptations 'When the devout man cannot overcome the dogs he contends with, nor get rid of them, he should run in great haste to the tree of the Cross and of the passion of our dear Lord Jesus Christ; he there obtains the victory in all his conflicts, and is entirely delivered and rid of them.'[4]

This emphasis on personal trust in Christ raises the whole question of the mystics' interpretation of justification by faith alone. The Schoolmen as represented by Duns Scotus could not get away from the theory that man himself, by his own natural will, could produce selfless love, just as without grace he could avoid all mortal sin.[5] And Aquinas insists that man is justified by faith formed by love.[6]

It is necessary to begin with God's revelation to man, for apart from this, there can be no knowledge of God. Yet no man can understand this revelation without faith. The knowledge of God is revealed to faith and it is by faith that God is seen to be merciful and gracious. This knowledge fills the soul with wonder and

[1] *T L S*, p. 349.   [2] *The Mirror of Eternal Salvation*, ch. IX.
[3] Neander, op. cit., IX, p. 556.   [4] Ibid., p. 594.
[5] See *A Catholic Dict.*, p. 828.
[6] See *Thomas Aquinas: Theological Texts* (ed. Thomas Gilby), paras. 413, 458.

gratitude, and, while it is true that love is the *outcome* of this experience, it is not the cause of it.

The teaching of the mystics is that faith, knowledge and love are different though closely related aspects of man's response to God. It must be stressed that they do not mean the same thing. Of course the mystics agree that love is an important factor in spiritual relationship but they do not regard it as the initial, fundamental ground of it. Moreover, they differ from the Schoolmen who invariably interpreted love in terms of meritorious acts, and this implies a denial of God's free, unmerited grace in man's justification.

Now the mystics had New Testament warrant for their teaching. Peter's confession reads: 'We have believed and know that Thou art the Holy One of God.' The Apostles had believed in Jesus and then they knew who He was. Love for their Lord and for their brethren was the result. The Schoolmen would have had no difficulty in saying, 'Thou hast the words of eternal life.' But one thing more remains to be said: It is not enough for a man to say that the Gospel of Christ is theoretically true; he must confess it existentially, and make his own personal act of faith: 'And we believe and know that Thou art the Holy One of God.' The Schoolmen would have agreed with the first statement; the Mystics would have insisted on the second as well.

There is, of course, such a thing as the theoretical acceptance of a truth, but this has nothing to do with justification by faith. Tillich has shown that justification by faith is not as far removed from mystical experience as is sometimes supposed. He points out that man's initial spiritual experience has a paradoxical character, the character of accepting acceptance.

> Faith bridges this infinite gap by accepting the fact that he who is separated is accepted. Faith is not a theoretical affirmation of something uncertain, it is the existential acceptance of something transcending ordinary experience... It is the state of being grasped by the power of being which transcends everything that is and in which everything participates. In this point mystical experience and personal encounter are identical.[1]

Reason assents but it is faith that accepts. Between intellectual acceptance and existential experience there is a great gulf fixed.

[1] P. Tillich, *The Courage To Be*, pp. 163-4.

And even if we admit, as doubtless some of the Mystics would have done, that faith, knowledge and love are phases in the same mystical experience, we are still left with the primacy of faith. Consequently, Dr Pope is not mistaken when, commenting on the mystical way of Purification, Illumination and Union, he goes so far as to say: 'These may be considered as answering respectively the Evangelical doctrines of Purification from sin, the Consecration of the Spirit, and the estate of Holiness in abstraction from self and earthly things in fellowship with God.'[1]

It is by no means sufficient to say as does D'Aygalliers,[2] that the Mystics did no more than prepare the atmosphere in which the Reformation might develop, although even this were no mean achievement, for they accomplished much more than this. Not only did they focus attention on the central dogma of the Reformation, they also proclaimed it and explained its meaning. And even the later Scholastics realized that the sands were fast running out for the traditional works-righteousness approach to justification as Hagenbach's comment on John Wessel clearly shows: 'Though a scholastic himself, he announced that Scholasticism would soon cease to exist, asserted that Scripture is the only foundation of faith, faith the sole ground of justification without works, and urged the spiritual nature of the religious life.'[3]

II. RESPONSE IN FELLOWSHIP

While the mystics taught that the way of true response to the divine initiative was first by faith, it was always faith exercised within the fellowship of believers. To be sure, faith is essentially an individual act, but it always needs to be nurtured, confirmed and renewed by the corporate experience of the Church. The Mystics were not unaware of this and looked to the Church for spiritual guidance and fellowship, but sometimes they looked in vain. It was just because they did not find the necessary spiritual stimulus which they sought, that the community known as the Friends of God appeared. The authorities of the Medieval Church did not always smile upon them, and, while no useful purpose will

---

[1] W. B. Pope, *A Compendium of Christian Theology*, Vol. III, p. 75.
[2] See A. W. D'Aygalliers, op. cit., p. 307.
[3] Hagenbach, op. cit., Vol. I, p. 420.

be served by a detailed account of the persecution which befell the Friends of God, it is necessary to state the ground of their persecution for this has a direct bearing on our theme. They suffered for the following reasons:

(*a*) For their persistent efforts to free the people from the tyranny of the clergy.

(*b*) For claiming that everyone enlightened by God had a right to teach—a claim antagonistic to the inmost essence of the Roman Church.

(*c*) For affirming the great and essential truth that the Christian life does not consist in outward works, but in the inward union of the spirit with God.

It is perfectly clear that the Friends of God were seeking spiritual freedom and an edifying spiritual fellowship, and it seems strange that this quest aroused very serious opposition. Their efforts to shake off the tyranny of the priest were determined by their fundamental and distinguishing beliefs. They were not opposed to the priesthood as such but to a particular expression of the functions of the priesthood. For instance, they firmly rejected all forms of religion which were based on fear and the hope of reward. In fact, their basic doctrines implied a rejection of any system based on punishment and fear. They believed that this new light had come to them by the illumination of the Spirit, but it was precisely this illumination of the Spirit that was denied them by the Church. Their own experience in the school of the Spirit had convinced them of the continuous activity of the Spirit in all believers, and this they were prepared to affirm at any cost. Again, while they always recognized that the organization of the Church was necessary, and submitted to its discipline, they stressed the fundamental equality between clergy and laity. It is our view that in stressing the fact that true religion is based on faith and not on fear, that the Spirit is active in all believers, and that all Christians are equal in calling and privilege and opportunities for service, the Friends of God were contending for the doctrine of the Priesthood of all Believers.

Their name 'The Friends of God' indicated not an isolated sect, for they would gladly have welcomed all mankind into their movement, but the depth and reality of their fellowship in the Faith. They were persuaded that it was necessary that every

Christian should have a friend who was able to give help and counsel under the guidance of the Spirit. Spiritual fellowship is a prerequisite of spiritual growth as Tauler shows: 'Therefore entreat the beloved friends of God that they would assist you in it, and then give yourself simply and solely to God and to the chosen friends of God, that they may carry you along to God with themselves.'[1] If it is argued that such a friend is fulfilling one of the functions of the priest, we can only say that Tauler would not have thought otherwise, for the paramount task of the priest is to draw men nearer to Christ.

If such a man was a priest by virtue of offering help and counsel to his fellows, he was a priest also in his intercessions.

> The needs of every soul in Holy Church are not beyond his help by counsel as well as by prayer. And yet such favoured souls do not always pray especially for this or that person or object, but with a certain kind of wide-sweeping, universal, and yet most simple prayer, do they embrace all souls of men. They see all in the same divine abyss—God's love; viewing thus, as in one glance, the needs of all Christians.[2]

Such an intercessor exercises a universal priesthood, and in this respect they are at one with an Evangelical of a later age who sang:

> *The arms of love that compass me*
> *Would all mankind embrace.*

Since the work of a priest is to bring men to God, we should expect the evangelistic note to be sounded by the mystics. Master Eckhart sounds this note in no uncertain way:

> That which kindles the warmest devotion in a man's heart, and knits him more closely to God, is the greatest benefit he can receive in this present time; and hence the greatest good work a man can do is to draw other men to God, so that they enter into union with Him. And this is the best work of love to our neighbour while we are in this world.[3]

It must be recognized, however, that this fellowship existed within the Church and not outside of it. All the work of the mystics was done in submission to the Church and its Sacraments,

---

[1] Neander, op. cit., p. 560.   [2] A Benedictine, op. cit., pp. 114-15.
[3] Quoted in *T L S*, p. 225.

THE MYSTICS 217

and in obedience to its doctrines and rules. Ruysbroeck was speaking for them all when, at the end of his life he said: 'For all that I understand or feel, and for all that I have written, I submit to the judgement of the saints and Holy Church. For I wish to live and die in the Christian faith, and, by God's grace, I desire to be a living member of Holy Church.'[1] And this, perhaps, is the most significant fact of all, namely, that in spite of their concept of the Church as a fellowship of believers, and of their priestly responsibility to one another which this concept involved, they were permitted to pursue their activities within the Church. Doubtless they fervently hoped that eventually their beliefs would win the day and become the norm of the life and witness of the Church. That this was not possible was due to the blindness and intransigence of the Roman Church, a situation later corrected by the vision and courage of the Reformers.

We have seen that according to the teaching of the Mystics, the way of true response to the divine initiative was in faith and fellowship. It is also expressed in Christian service, and for an understanding of this aspect of their teaching we must turn to an interpretation of their doctrine of vocation.

III. RESPONSE IN VOCATION

(a) *The office that is common to all believers*

It was Tauler's firm opinion that all kinds of skill were gifts of the Holy Spirit. Teachers had a special office in the Church but there was also an office which belonged to all Christians.

> Let us common Christians look to see what is our office to the which our Lord has called and bidden us, and what is the gift of which our Lord has made us vessels. For every art or work, however unimportant it may seem, is a gift of God, and all these gifts are bestowed by the Holy Spirit for the profit and welfare of mankind.[2]

(b) *The active and contemplative are one*

Eckhart supports Tauler in this view, for he will brook no contradiction between the active and contemplative life. In commenting on the story of Martha and Mary, those favourite types of activity and contemplative, he surprises us by putting Martha

[1] D'Aygalliers, op. cit., p. 198. [2] *T L S*, p. 368.

first. 'Mary hath *chosen* the good part; that is, she is striving to be as holy as her sister. Mary is still at school: Martha has learnt her lesson. It is better to feed the hungry than to see even such visions as St Paul saw.'[1] Tauler goes as far as to affirm that a man may be as surely called of God in his secular calling as one who is called to the priesthood.

> I know a man who has the closest walk with God of any man I ever saw, and who has been all his life a husbandman,—for more than forty years, and is so still. This man once asked the Lord in prayer if he should give up his occupation and go into the Church; and it was assured him, No; he should labour, earning his bread by the sweat of his brow, to the glory of Christ's precious blood, shed for him. But let each man choose some suitable time in the course of every four and twenty hours, in which he can give his whole mind to earnest meditation, each after his own fashion.[2]

Windgren too easily sweeps aside the question of Tauler's influence on Luther's doctrine of vocation when he says, 'Since Tauler accords a monk a higher holiness just because he is a monk, his position and Luther's are certainly not the same. And as far as the idea of vocation is concerned, no evidence of influence is to be found in Luther's marginal notes of Tauler's sermons.'[3] All the same, it can hardly be doubted that the following words of Tauler find a clear echo in Luther's doctrine:

> One man can spin, another make shoes, and some have great aptness for all sorts of outward arts. These are all gifts proceeding from the Spirit of God. I tell you if I were not a priest, but living as a layman, I should esteem it a great gift that I was born to make shoes, and I would try to make them so well as to be a pattern to all. Each must fulfil the office for which God has fitted him, however weighty it may be, and what another could not easily do. There is no work so small, no art so mean but it all comes from God and as a special gift of his.[4]

It is not a levelling down that is envisaged here but a levelling up. All secular callings and activities are brought within the orbit of God's holy purpose. Men are ordained to a God-appointed task. They are trained for their task in the school of the Spirit and all work is the expression of a priesthood which is common to all.

---

[1] W. R. Inge, *Christian Mysticism*, p. 161.　　[2] *T L S*, p. 371.
[3] G. Windgren, *The Christian's Calling*, Intro. p. x.
[4] *T L S*, p. 368.

According to the mystics it is this fact which has preserved and sustained the world through all the centuries. Tauler speaks of

> Those chosen spirits whose every work is divinized: upon them, as a house upon its Foundation, stands Holy Church. If they were not in Christendom, Christendom could not stand. The fact of their existence among us, that they simply are, is of more glory and of greater honour to Holy Church than a whole world of action by other Christians.[1]

(c) *The vocation of neighbourly service*

When he turns to the theme of the Christian's duty of loving his neighbour there is a perceptible urgency in Tauler's words which is rarely found in his other writings:

> But, alas! nowadays nature is so perverted in many, both clergy and laymen, as touching brotherly faithfulness and love, that if they see their neighbour fall, they laugh at him, or stand by and let it go on, or care nought for it. Take heed to your failings, and look how it stands with your inward love to God and your neighbour, and keep ever alive in you the fear of God; for I tell you, that which you fail to obtain here through your own neglect, you will lose forever. After this life nothing will be added to you or taken from you.[2]

Ruysbroeck is following in the steps of Tauler when he says:

> Nor wilt thou suffer the grace of God within thee to be idle, but from true love wilt exercise thyself heavenward, in praising God; below, in all forms of virtue and good actions. And, in whatever outward acts thou art employed, let thy heart be free and disengaged from all, so that as oft as thou choosest, thou mayest be able, through all and above all, to contemplate him whom thou lovest.[3]

The man whose heart is set on God will be free to serve his neighbour, a thought which clearly anticipates Luther's doctrine of loving and serving one's neighbour. It is such teaching which is later enunciated by the Reformers as the doctrine of the Christian's priestly vocation. This is the office that is common to all Christians and in this office the active and contemplative life are conjoined; it is conferred by the Spirit upon all believers and is exercised and expressed in neighbourly service.

[1] A Benedictine, op. cit., p. 114.   [2] *T L S*, p. 364.
[3] Neander, op. cit., Vol. IX, Part II, p. 557.

The Brethren of the Common Life
(Founder Gerhard Groot 1340-1384)

Tauler and his disciple Suso frequently visited Cologne, and on one of these occasions there was among their hearers a young man named Gerhard Groot. Like many others of his day Groot was a frivolous care-free man whose life appeared to consist only in the pleasures of the moment. After hearing Tauler's message Groot's interest in magic and astrology began to wane. At that stage he seemed to be carried away by every wind of doctrine. But even his preoccupation with occult studies clearly indicates his state of mind. He was a seeker. His mind had already been influenced by Ruysbroeck whom he visited at Grünthal. At Grünthal a family spirit reigned which placed all its members upon a level. This fact, together with an atmosphere of peace and assurance, made a profound impression upon Groot. It was there that he first saw the ideal of true brotherhood realized and this ideal became his guiding star for the future. The turning-point of his life was drawing near. He did not expect, however, that when the truth dawned upon his mind and soul it would effect a sudden transformation of his life. Groot experienced a conversion of the evangelical type, and his love of the Bible, his application to study, his effective preaching, and his work as the founder of the Brethren of the Common Life were the direct result of his conversion. 'Being not yet inspired by the Spirit of God, he walked along the broad way of the world, until through God's loving-kindness he became changed into another man.'[1] While standing in a street at Cologne a stranger came to him and whispered: 'Why standest thou here? thou shouldest become another man'.

Soon afterwards he became seriously ill and those words came to him again and again. When he recovered he was indeed 'another man'. He renounced his inquisitive experiments in the sensations of life and ceased to rely on the externals of religion. He had done with vows which may be kept or broken, and was filled with a hunger for the life-giving Spirit. The God who transformed his life also provided him with a task. His message was centred on the Gospel. 'Let the root of thy studies,' he cries, 'and the mirror of

[1] S. Kettlewell, *Thomas à Kempis and the Brothers of the Common Life*, p. 66.

thy life be first of all the Gospel, for in it is contained the life of Christ.'[1]

In founding the community known as the Brethren of the Common Life Groot steered a middle course between the negative way of Eckhart and the antinomian tendencies of the Brethren of the Free Spirit.* The first group practised a mysticism which was altogether quietistic and passive; while the second group gave an unwarranted interpretation to the phrase 'the liberty of the Spirit', turning liberty into licence. If Groot's Community managed to avoid the dangers of Eckhartian pantheism and the heretical tendencies of the Brethren of the Free Spirit, they also avoided the exclusive attitude of the passive mystics as well as the laziness and beggary which were sometimes associated with the later Franciscans.

The Brethren of the Common Life did not neglect the interior life and this is evidenced by that gem of devotional literature, *The Imitation of Christ*. In their reaction against the fairs and feastings, the pageants and pilgrimages of the Medieval Church it would have been easy for them to withdraw into a monastic isolationism. But this was not the case, and perhaps their distinctive contribution to the religious life of the fourteenth century was their ability to relate the spiritual life to the practical tasks and demands of their Community. The one was the spur to the other. They had no room for the 'dreaming oneself into God' attitude, and Christian love was for them not merely an ideal but a life. The spiritual life resulted in a useful life and this was revealed in the work of the Community.

The founding of the Community was an expression of their devotion. It was a Community of service. Their prodigious work of translation, their concern for the education of children, their care for widows and for all in distress, their zeal in spreading the principles of their movement, reveal the emphasis on practical service. This emphasis is clearly shown in a prayer of Thomas à Kempis who was a member of the Community:

> Truly Thou art worthy of all service, of all honour and everlasting praise. Truly, Thou art my Lord, and I Thy poor servant, who am

---

[1] C. Ullmann, *Reformers before the Reformation*, Vol. II, p. 74.

* An antinomian sect which arose in the Rhineland at the beginning of the thirteenth century.

bound to Thee with all my might, neither ought I to be weary of praising Thee. O sweet and delightful service of God, by which a man is made truly free and holy. O sacred state of religious servitude, which makes a man equal to the angels, pleasing to God, terrible to devils, and worthy to be commended of all the faithful.[1]

Groot was not by nature a contemplative although an examination of his thought is always rewarding. He was essentially a man of action, and 'action' was the hall-mark of his movement. Even on those occasions when he desired solitude he was forced back into active life as if some inward compelling power was driving him into the world. Yet he refused to become a priest, not because his estimate of the office of priesthood was low, but because it was very high. 'I would not for all the gold in Arabia undertake the care of souls for a single night.'[2] He agreed, however, to become a deacon so that he might be permitted to instruct his people publicly. As a preacher and teacher he excelled. 'At length by God's good pleasure the time arrived for bearing good fruit; and by the counsel of wise men and the religious brethren, he was called forth to preach the word of Life openly, that by his voice, and through the example of holy conversation, he might inflame the hearts of sinners and profit many souls.'[3]

He did not preach for reward; he did not preach because it was a professional duty, nor did he seek popular applause. He preached because in his heart there was a burning zeal which through his words was transposed into light and flame. He preached and taught till the fire was nothing but light. The effect of his message was intensified because it was delivered in the language the people understood, and equally important, it was written for them in their mother tongue. This meant that the influence of his discourses would remain for many years. His keen interest in the written word brought about the transcription of many books as well as the wide circulation of the Bible in the mother tongue. There is no need to emphasize the importance of this step as a pointer to the Reformation.

Having reached a stage of positive Christian experience himself, he felt bound to point the common people to an approach to God

[1] Thomas à Kempis, *The Imitation of Christ*, Book III, ch. X, pp. 4 and 6.
[2] C. Ullmann, *Reformers before the Reformation*, Vol. II, 63.
[3] S. Kettlewell, *Thomas à Kempis and the Brothers of the Common Life*, p. 69.

which was independent of elaborate ritual or the official priesthood. There was in his preaching an element of passionate denunciation and this applied to the sins peculiar to rich or to poor, to layman or to cleric, and he was commonly known as the 'Martel of the heretics' and he certainly hammered them.

Groot, however, is remembered mainly because he was the founder of a Community. The members of it were drawn from all classes. Labourers and masons, carpenters and millers, indeed all types met under its aegis. There were no monastic vows; they lived under the rule of Christ. There was a time for prayer, a time for translation work, a time for manual labour. There was also a time for confession, but not confession to a priest. It was Groot's wish that the brethren should retire to bed in peace, so he arranged for mutual confession and this became a principle of the Community. No one possessed personal property; in true apostolic fashion they had all things common. They were not permitted to beg so the dangers of the later Franciscans were avoided. They were concerned to show that a small group of Christians may live together in community happily, devotedly and usefully. But they also proved that the principles on which their common life was based could be applied conveniently and successfully in the wider world beyond the boundaries of their Community. Their aim was to spread practical Christianity by awakening faith in the common man, by the education of children, by offering the Bible to all, by fostering the spiritual life, by serving one another and by living together as brothers in Christ. 'All was to proceed from freedom and love. . . . Their whole rule was to be observed not from constraint, but from the sole motive of goodwill constantly renewed, and all obedience, even the most unconditional, was to be paid freely and affectionately, and for God's sake.'[1]

Even if it had stood alone the Community of the Brethren of the Common Life would have offered impressive evidence of a reforming movement in the fourteenth century, but when it is considered alongside the movements inaugurated by Tauler and Ruysbroeck, it provides a religious climate which was bound to be helpful to the reformers of the sixteenth century. The fourteenth century, therefore, offers not only a striking interpretation of the priesthood of all believers but a convincing application of it, and

[1] C. Ullmann, *Reformers before the Reformation*, Vol. II, p. 71.

as long as we can point to men like Tauler, Ruysbroeck and Groot and to the communities which they inspired, we shall not want for evidence that the priesthood of believers was a living issue at least in the minds of some individuals in that century.

Luther acknowledged his debt to the German mystics and to Tauler in particular. What did he find in their teaching which made such a deep impression upon his mind? In the foregoing pages we have endeavoured to find an answer to that question by examining the writings of the mystics themselves. One claim at least is justified: Luther found in the theology of the mystics the germ of Reformation principles. The mystics emphasized the sole glory of God, the divine initiative in our salvation, the soul's response in faith, in fellowship, and in vocation. It is true that Luther exemplified these truths, and drew far-reaching conclusions from them, but it is equally true that the two important doctrines of the Reformation—Justification by Faith and the Priesthood of All Believers—are implicit in the theology of the mystics.

CHAPTER TEN

CONCLUSIONS AND REASSESSMENT

I. THE DOCTRINE IN HISTORICAL PERSPECTIVE

IN surveying the whole picture of the development of this doctrine it must be stated emphatically that it has not meant in history what it has often been supposed to mean. For instance, it has often been supposed that the priesthood of all believers means the right of private judgment, the theological sanction for an egalitarian principle, the so-called 'claims' of the laity, the refutation of the office of Ministry, and that it has been the theological monopoly of a small but radical minority. It is true that some of these notions are sometimes connected with the doctrine but they are not prominent in the period covered by our study. Many of these ideas were grasped and exploited by some of the extreme and obscure sects which arose immediately after the Reformation, but for the most part, they are subordinate factors and are not in the main stream of Reformation thought. The ideas connected with the doctrine of the Priesthood of All Believers in the main stream of the Reformation are: Justification by Faith, the right of access to the presence of God, religious liberty for all men, the duty of Christian witness and neighbourly service, and the recognition that every man has a divine vocation to fulfil. Some of these ideas are to be found in the period that we have covered, but not all of them. Luther's insight and originality, no less than his courage and resolution, should not be minimized. But Luther himself recognized that the ground had been well prepared long before his day, and that his achievement was due rather to a unique emphasis than to a unique discovery. Even so, if we admit that sometimes the doctrine has been distorted by a narrow, individualistic and negative interpretation, and that for this reason it has frequently been regarded as a theological by-path, the onus is upon us to prove that the centrality of the idea of the royal priesthood in Church history is inescapable.

It is found in the Scriptures both by certain precise phrases and by general inference from biblical patterns of thought; it has the unanimous consent of the Early Fathers, and is expounded by theologians up to the eighth century and after the twelfth century in both Eastern and Western Christendom. So prominent is it that it is rare for a Church writer of importance to be silent about it. And even in those periods of history when the doctrine has been less prominent, it has certainly been closely related to the theological conflicts which have characterized those periods. Moreover, it has not infrequently happened that the success or failure of the Church's witness has been judged by the extent to which she has grasped or failed to grasp the significance of her priesthood. The failure is particularly noticeable during the Church's encounter with Islam, and the success in understanding the meaning of her priestly mission is especially evident in the new awakening of the Church and its persistent expansion in the thirteenth and fourteenth centuries. One of the secrets of the triumph of Islam was her ability to learn quickly lessons which the Church had neglected. This was not the only reason but it was certainly an important one. The understanding of their message, regular times of prayer, the obligation of personal witness, and the necessity of absolute devotion to their Founder: these factors helped to ensure the success of Islam. It seems that the Church had forgotten that these very factors, in addition to others, were inextricably bound up with her priesthood. She did not learn these lessons, and in consequence, had a very high price to pay.

But if in the seventh and eighth centuries the Church had forgotten that she was pre-eminently a royal priesthood, she most certainly realized it again in the thirteenth and fourteenth. And this realization came through certain dedicated and able leaders who gathered around them groups of lay followers whose sole purpose was to give practical application to the doctrine of the royal priesthood. Through them it was made known to all men that the ethos of the Church is most truly revealed when she becomes a consecrated, interceding, witnessing and serving priesthood of faithful men. Here is to be found the undisputed secret of the movements under discussion. Tauler's ideas were diffused through his followers, 'the friends of God'; Wyclif sent out his 'poor priests' to proclaim the Gospel in life as well as word; and St Francis won thousands of followers by the plain declaration that 'the life and labour of love is open to every Christian'. This was the Church fulfilling her true function and realizing her priesthood in service for the world.

It is one thing to state that the doctrine of the royal priesthood is centred in the Bible, but it is a very different thing to produce concrete evidence to prove it. We maintain that this evidence has been set forth and that the strongest claim has been made for the biblical basis of this doctrine. In particular phrases, in general thought-patterns, and in the *intention* which characterizes the whole message of the Bible, the universal priesthood is to be found. The great and vital truths of the Old Testament are those which help us to understand and interpret the priestly calling and responsibility of the People of God. All the great Old Testament themes are marshalled to this end: to explain, interpret and elucidate the mission of God's chosen people. The doctrine of the People of God is inherent in the concept of revelation, in Israel's divine election, in their covenant obligations, and in their sacrificial service on behalf of mankind as a whole. It is all there: the promise, the method and the purpose of their priesthood. And even when the other great Old Testament truth is dealt with— the coming of the Messiah, it is another variation of our theme. For His coming gives meaning to all past promises and interpretations, and in Him, as well as in the New Covenant of which He is Mediator, there is inaugurated a new and universal priesthood of which baptism is the sign of initiation, and which is revealed in the Church's consecration, worship, service, sacrifice and mission. By baptismal initiation, by Eucharistic incorporation, by functional participation in the Priesthood of Christ, the Church moves ever forward, her oneness, holiness, apostolicity and catholicity being different aspects of that universal priesthood to which she is irrevocably committed.

We have found ample evidence in the writings of the Early Fathers to prove that they accepted, believed and interpreted, the priesthood of the People of God. These brief references must serve to summarize and represent many similar ideas and statements which we discovered in the writings of the Fathers. Irenaeus refers to 'the priesthood of all just men'; Justin refers to 'the high-priestly race of God'; Polycarp speaks of the 'High Priest through whom all men, being once reconciled to God, are themselves made a priestly and spiritual race'; Origen declares that 'they that are made like unto the Apostles, being priests after the order of the great High Priest are sent out to enlighten those who dwell in darkness'; and Tertullian speaking of that spiritual discipline which is incumbent upon every member of the universal priesthood, asks: 'Are not we laymen priests?' These statements together with the detailed exigesis of so many of the Early Fathers, point to one inescapable conclusion, namely, that in the first two hundred and fifty years of Christian history the concept of universal priesthood was paramount and was widely accepted. And even after Cyprian had introduced two ideas which were foreign to the New Testament and unknown to his predecessors—those of episcopal authority and Eucharistic sacrifice—the concept of the universal priesthood persisted and outstanding leaders of thought like Augustine and Gregory the Great emphasized its importance for the whole Church.

All the same, there followed a period when the doctrine we are studying receded into the background and hardly a voice was raised in its defence. And if attempts are sometimes made to prove that the eighth to the eleventh centuries are not as dark as they have been painted, it must be frankly confessed that as far as this doctrine is concerned they were very dark. It is surely not without significance that the Church suffered some serious losses when she was silent on this theme. It was a time of conflict, controversy, misunderstanding and catastrophe for the Christian Church. The laity, represented by powerful princes and wealthy barons, and not having the slightest clue to the true meaning of their priesthood, resisted the grandiose pretensions of a Church whose temporal aims and claims were far removed from the purity of its earlier Faith. The Church, no less than the State, was wholly involved in the struggle for power, and the ideas of sacrificial servanthood and common priesthood had vanished from her creeds as well as her deeds.

There was another fundamental reason which lay behind this complex situation. A Pelagian view was held which regarded salvation as depending, at least in part, on man's will and endeavour, at best assisted by grace. But even this grace was hard to

CONCLUSIONS AND REASSESSMENT

come by, as it was no longer believed to depend upon penitence, faith and obedience but upon the external acts of the official priesthood. Men, in their pride, had arrogantly assumed that it was their prerogative to command, control and dispense the spiritual power of the world. Pardon was offered in exchange for penances, satisfactions and pilgrimages, and even then it only applied to the consequences of temporal sins. The eternal consequences remained and so salvation itself became a matter of uncertainty. The power and pretensions of the Roman Church, in these centuries at least, had pushed out the notion of the universal priesthood.

Even in the thirteenth century when Marsiglio made his plea that the name 'Church' should be recalled to 'its first and apostolic, its true and most proper signification, as comprehending the entire body of Christian men, be they laymen or clerks', he received little support. But he had stated his case and this was no mean achievement. Doubtless he was far in advance of his time, but the recollection of him at the Reformation as one of the greatest of its precursors, is ample testimony to the fact that he had fearlessly proclaimed what was in the minds of thousands who were dissatisfied with the condition of the Church. Wyclif, the Franciscans and the Mystics followed in his wake, and although the ultimate result of their work was seen only at the Reformation, it was abundantly clear that the time of the Church's true awakening was drawing near. The Lollards attacked the Church as an institution—her wealth and power; the Humanists attacked her theology which had become arid, sophisticated and out of date; the Mystics and the Franciscans attacked no one, but unintentionally undermined the foundations of a sacerdotal Church which expressed itself mainly in sacraments and social ordinances. They made no claim to possess esoteric knowledge but they did claim that their eyes had been opened to understand what every man might know. Their emphasis was on the spiritual life, personal religion and the application of their Faith to every aspect of life. They offered no apologetic but simply gave an example of what the Church ought to be and ought to be doing, and by this means they unconsciously prepared the way for the Reformation.

So the world waited for the man whose message and mission was to make articulate the thoughts and feelings of many people throughout Christendom. When Luther appeared he found a ready instrument of reform—the doctrine of the Priesthood of All Believers. His study of Holy Scripture, his knowledge of the history of the Church and his own evangelical experience combined to convince him that this doctrine was the effective instrument of reform. When he viewed the preceding centuries he did not look in vain for support, for doubtless he saw how the doctrines he emphasized had affected the ebb and flow of the Church in the past. Nevertheless, to him must go the credit of giving them a voice and a direction and a power which they had not received before. Out of his doctrine of the authority of the Word of God and of Justification by Faith alone, there came the Priesthood of All Believers which in his hands was the dynamic formula of reform. We must now summarize those permanent theological ideas which Luther found and developed.

II. PERMANENT THEOLOGICAL IDEAS

A functional participation in the Priesthood of Christ

Experience has shown that the attempt to concentrate power in the hands of a special priestly caste within the Church sets up tensions which are fatal to peace and unity, and hinders the progress of the kingdom of God. The united energies of the whole are essential and it should be one of the tasks of ecclesiastical statesmanship to bring this about. But this can only be brought about if priesthood is viewed as a dynamic function of the whole Church rather than as a static office in the Church. This does not mean that there is no room for the office of Ministry in the Church, but the meaning of universal priesthood is obscured if the Ministry is set above the Church rather than within it. The purpose of the Ministry is to facilitate the functioning of the universal priesthood. While it is true, as Luther said, 'that everyone coming out of Baptism is consecrated to be a priest', it is also true that some are specifically set apart to preach, administer the Sacraments, and to be shepherds of the flock of Christ. Ministers have the responsibility of leadership and administration, of preaching, teaching and caring, but they hold this responsibility in a representative capacity, for they are pre-eminently servants of the Church. We have seen that this conception is in accordance with New Testament teaching. Paul says: 'Not that we have lordship over your faith, but are helpers of your joy: for by faith ye stand' (2 Cor. i. 24). And he affirms the same truth in 2 Corinthians iv. 5: 'For we preach not ourselves, but Christ Jesus as Lord, and ourselves as your servants for Jesus' sake.' These passages set the office of the Ministry in its true perspective, for the Ministry is the focus of the spiritual activity of the Faithful. The work of the Church as it is expressed in the preaching of the Word, the administration of the Sacraments, and the caring for the flock of Christ, cannot be left to fortuitous circumstance, it requires those who are called, chosen, trained, equipped and dedicated.

An illustration from Luther will help us to understand the relation between the universal priesthood and its representatives. When a minister is chosen 'it is as though ten brothers, all kings' sons and equal heirs, were to choose one of themselves to rule the inheritance for them all ... they would all be kings and equal in power, though one of them would be charged with the duty of ruling.'[1] Similarly, in the Christian Church, while all are called to be priests, some are particularly called to be ministers or pastors.

All the same, it must not be thought that because the universal priesthood has its called and appointed representatives, all other members are passive onlookers. This would be the gravest error. In the basic pattern there may be a division of tasks, and there is, so to speak, a conductor of the orchestra but *all play*. All are performers rather than auditors or observers, and it needs to be understood much more clearly that when a person is a member of the Church he joins in a functioning, working group and volunteers for a task.

It will be clear from the foregoing that priesthood is here regarded as the functional participation of all believers in the Priesthood of Christ, and that the Ministry is within the universal priesthood and serves it in particular ways. It will save a great deal of misunderstanding of this doctrine as well as strengthen the witness of the Church if this interpretation is accepted and understood.

> Let it appear that the very object of insisting upon the Church's priestliness is to restore to the Christian laity that sense of their responsibility and privilege which Protestantism hardly less than Romanism,

[1] G. Rupp, *Luther's Progress to the Diet of Worms*, p. 83.

has practically denied them; and let the Church's priesthood be invariably represented as a continuation of our Lord's priestly offices *through* her, not as something deputed to her;—let all this be done, and prejudice against the doctrine would probably be removed.[1]

Priesthood as Capacity for Service

Another notion which has occurred again and again is that of priesthood as capacity for service. It is not sufficient to claim the title priest for every Christian unless it is realized what the title involves. By virtue of his priesthood the Christian is not only incorporated into the Body but simultaneously becomes its servant. Failure to realize this means that his priesthood is only nominal. There is a difference between 'being priest' and 'becoming priestly', and it is a difference which is not always realized. It is really the difference between privilege and responsibility. The Christian's priesthood begins when he recognizes his part in the redemptive purposes of the Body. It is when he has become capable of service that he can claim to be priestly. He may claim to be priest only as he becomes priestly. He will then be less concerned about rights and dues and more concerned about self-offering and self-giving. 'It is more blessed to give than to receive' will become the operative principle in his conception of Christian service. It is precisely in this interaction between the spiritual powers which he has received and their application to specific forms of Christian service that the priesthood of the Christian consists. Having received all from Christ in faith, he offers all to Christ in service.

This service is offered in and through Christ and is therefore divested of any notion of merit or self-effort. It is true that there are diversities of ministration but all are performed through the same Lord. Every member receives his own manifestation of the Spirit (1 Cor. xii. 7) and this enables him to perform his God-given ministry. Yet there is no such thing as isolated service or individual ministry, there is only the service and ministry of the whole body. The Christian's offering of submission and service, suffering and sacrifice, is only properly offered when it is rendered as one man, and this is the 'one new man' of which Paul speaks (Eph. ii. 15) and which is the fruit of Christ's sacrifice.

[1] W. Milligan, *The Ascension and Heavenly Priesthood of Our Lord*, pp. 246–7.

CONCLUSIONS AND REASSESSMENT

Wherever and by whom this offering of service to God is made, it should be recognized in some precise form. Ministers are trained in theology, preaching the Gospel, in pastoralia and in the practical work of the ministry, and then they are ordained. Part of the meaning of ordination is that the Church's seal, sanction and authorization are put upon the service they are to render. But laymen also serve in many ways, and in many cases they also have been trained and equipped for the work they do. They serve as doctors, nurses, teachers, evangelists, deaconesses, agriculturalists, local preachers, youth leaders and social workers. In so far as they are sharers in the total ministry of the Christian Church, and have the desire as well as the capacity for such service, their work also should be sanctioned, authorized and consecrated by the Church. This form of dedication to the lay apostolate already takes place in some Churches, but it is too narrowly based and applies only to those who are engaged in specifically Church work. It requires a much wider orientation. To this extent the whole concept of the lay apostolate and the form of its recognition needs to be re-examined. Moreover, such forms of dedication service as already exist are of differing merit and need to be revised and unified. Further, all forms of service sincerely rendered in the name of Christ require the enabling grace of the Holy Spirit and the blessing of the Church. It follows, therefore, that one of the tasks of the Christian Church of our time is to devise a form of service in which men and women are dedicated to the lay apostolate. All notions of 'higher' or 'lower' service will then be banished, for all those who are prepared to accept the conditions and disciplines of service to God, either as a vocation within the Church or in terms of their secular vocation, will render service within the universal priesthood in which there are no grades or distinctions. If it is argued that this is no more than a revival of the Third Order of St Francis, the answer is that it proved to be a laudable and workable idea. There seems no reason why it may not be applied to-day with the same success. It is almost certain that Canon Liddon had such an idea in mind when he wrote:

> Certainly if Christian laymen would only believe with all their hearts that they are priests, we should get rid of some of the difficulties that vex the Church. For it would be seen that in the Christian Church there is only a difference of the degree in which spiritual powers are

conferred, that it is not a difference in kind. The one priesthood will then be found to be the natural extensive and correlative of the other.[1]

There is no better way of ensuring this than by introducing one form of service by which those who genuinely desire it may be dedicated to their appointed task—that is their priesthood. Such a course will give to the concept of the universal priesthood a meaning and an importance for the whole Church which it has not hitherto received.

The importance of a Christian protology

We find in the Scriptures and the Early Fathers not only an eschatology of the People of God but a protology also. How must this be interpreted and understood? Christian protology envisages a relation between the old creation and the new creation, and between the past and future which can only be understood in the light of the doctrine of the Church. The early Christians believed that they belonged to 'the first Church' which was created before the sun and moon; that they were God's original people; that the world was created for their sakes, and that they were a high-priestly race by their unique election and worship and mission. They were not only a people but a holy people; they were not only a race but an elect race; they were not just a random collection of individuals but by virtue of character, calling and purpose they were the high-priestly race. As Justin said: 'Being set on fire with the Word of His calling, we are the genuine high-priestly race of God.' It was this grand concept of their heritage and hope which they passed on to their successors. Everything in the world —the beginning and course and end of all history was not only revealed to them but fulfilled through them. God chose them from the beginning unto salvation (2 Thess. ii. 13). They were chosen in Christ before the foundation of the world (Eph. i. 4) and were called to reveal the mystery which from all ages had been hid in God (Eph. iii. 9). They were redeemed by the Lamb slain from the foundation of the world (Rev. x iii. 8). Everything here centres on the protological act of God—the initial choice of His people and the pledge of their redemption. Protology presupposes an eschatology, for although Christians live within the time-process, their initial election is consummated only in the final act of

[1] H. P. Liddon, *University Sermons*, pp. 198–9.

redemption and triumph. The first and last acts of God are brought together in the Christian Church. As the race of God, Christians hold in trust for the world two important truths—the certainty of election and the pledge of final redemption. What happens to the world happens through the Church as a divine instrument. This is why the Church is called the genuine high-priestly race. Protology and eschatology derive their meaning from the Church's consciousness of priesthood. This truth was vigorously affirmed by the Early Fathers, and without doubt brought hope and strength in time of bitter persecution. It was the consciousness of a priestly mission to the world which characterized the people of God throughout. We have already suggested that the priestly destiny of God's people must be interpreted in an eschatological setting, and we now affirm that the protology of the people of God reveals their priestly origin and gives them their task.

The doctrine of three dispensations

Another prominent idea which has occurred in our study must now be noted, partly because of the frequency with which it has arisen, and partly because it has a direct bearing on our study. It is mentioned by many writers but especially by Origen, Clement of Alexandria, Augustine, Hugh of St Victor and Joachim of Flora. The subject is treated by them in different ways, sometimes referring to three successive stages in the spiritual life and sometimes indicating the spiritual development of humanity. In the latter case this development corresponds to various stages of revelation. Writers like Origen and Clement who had Greek hearers in mind and were themselves greatly influenced by the Gnostics, viewed the development of the spiritual life in three definite stages. Origen, for instance, draws attention to three classes of Christians: those who were *sarx* (carnal), those who possessed *sophia* (wisdom), and those who possessed *gnosis* (secret knowledge), and were thereby enlightened and advanced. The characteristic of the third class was that they were permitted to go 'straight to the Father'. Moreover, 'as priests of the New Covenant they had access to the sanctuary', and because they were dedicated to the sole worship of God 'they were not unreasonably called priests'. It is clear that the third stage refers to the priesthood of faithful believers.

Augustine applies a similar idea to the history of mankind. There is the stage of childhood when some elements of truth are imperfectly grasped; there is the stage of adulthood when the truth is firmly grasped but not effectively applied, and the third period of age or maturity when the truth is both grasped and applied. There are many variations of this theme in the writings of Augustine, and sometimes the stages are given as faith, understanding and vision, but in all cases the climax is reached in the third stage which signifies the discovery of the universal way. This discovery results in spiritual freedom for all, for it is the way to a direct knowledge of God, to the soul's purification, and to world redemption. It is summed up by Augustine as follows: 'This, therefore, is that universal way of the soul's freedom, that is granted to all nations out of God's mercy, the knowledge whereof comes, and is to come unto all men. This, I say, is the way that will free all believers.'[1]

The same idea is elaborated by many medieval writers but especially by Hugh of St Victor and Joachim of Flora in the twelfth century. These writers dwell a great deal on the doctrine of three dispensations. The former conceives of the first dispensation as a day of fear, under the Law given by God the Father, when power is supreme; the second dispensation is the day of truth, under the revelation of Christ, when wisdom is supreme; and the third is the day of love, under the administration of the Spirit, when love will rule all things.

Joachim elucidated the same idea as follows: the first period is the age of law and fear—an age of mere slavery; the second is an age of faith in which men offer to God filial service; the third is an age of love which is characterized by spiritual liberty. In the first age men live a carnal life, in the second there is a conflict between flesh and spirit, and in the third all men will live a spiritual life under the rule of divine love.

It should be noted that Joachim had already written with great power on the corruptions of the Church and he looked forward in faith to a new and better day. He foresaw that the sacerdotal system of the Church would vanish and a new era would dawn in which the saintly character of all believers would be the distinguishing mark of the Church. Moreover in the new

[1] *De civ. Dei*, V. 32.

age there would appear a full, final and abiding revelation through the Spirit of God—an everlasting Gosepl. We must notice also that in the first age the names of the patriarchs are prominent, in the second age John the Baptist is mentioned, but in the third age no specific names are suggested. Perhaps this means that there will come a time when spiritual privileges, opportunities and duties will be common to all Christians, and an era of universal priesthood will be ushered in. At any rate, the thought of the third dispensation is important because it has so deeply impressed the minds of believers in many communions and at many different periods in the history of the Church. When the writings of Hugh of St Victor and Joachim of Flora are carefully analysed and stripped of all strange apocalyptic notions, there remains a constant theme: it is the resilient hope that there will be a final period when the Spirit of God will rule the hearts of all men, and when that day dawns the theory of the priesthood of all believers will be turned into fact.

Lordship and Service

So frequently have we found the combination of these two words that we must find a place for this concept in our conclusions. It is present in the Old Testament under the messianic and servant forms, and we find it in the New Testament where the corollary of the earliest and simplest creed 'Jesus is Lord' was the servanthood of the disciples. Indeed, the recognition of the lordship of Christ is expressed by their readiness to be 'servants of all'.

We have also noticed that the claims made by the early Christians were astonishing both in their profundity of thought and in the rapidity of their acceptance. They did not hesitate to say, 'The world was created for our sakes,' and, 'All things serve us and our salvation.' Nevertheless they were servants of God, even His 'property' and therefore entirely at His disposal. The sacrifices required of the servants of God were humility, almsgiving, worship, service and even martyrdom. It follows that in the thinking of the early Christians lordship and service were correspondent terms.

It will be remembered that Chrism—the anointing with oil—signified for the early Christians the royal nature of their calling, but this was also accompanied by the feet-washing which reminded them, even at the moment of their anointing, of the necessity of humility and service.

The idea is revived by John Wyclif whose doctrine is based on the assumption that God is Creator, Possessor and Ruler of all things. The creation of man presupposes the lordship of God. But believers are called to be kings and priests unto God and to share His dominion. They hold this dominion immediately from God, and it is expressed by an unqualified response of service to God.

Three broad conclusions may be drawn from this summary of our findings on Lordship and Service:

(a) The lordship of Christ renders all men equal in God's sight. By the immediacy of this relationship of grace all men—Pope and layman, prince and peasant—owe the same direct allegiance to God. In respect of their 'tenure' all are equal. The inference is not that men are equal in all things. The doctrine does not envisage a society in which all men have equal talents. On the contrary it recognizes that there are differences in intellectual gifts, educational opportunities, natural endowments and in many other things, but it does affirm that none of them affects a man's standing before God. In the presence of God all men have one need—the need of the merits of Christ. At this point all men are equal, and they have nought to plead except their own exceeding sin and His exceeding love.

(b) The lordship of Christ renders all men servants. Wyclif sent out his 'poor priests' who impressed others by the marks of their divine servitude—poverty, simplicity and humility. They could afford to sit loosely to all earthly privileges for they shared the lordship of Christ. As Wyclif ways: 'The faithful man hath the whole world of riches: for him all things work together for good. Each faithful man is therefore lord of the universe.'[1] But this notion did not fill them with pride but made them all the more keenly aware of the requirements of their servanthood. Sin is a double-pronged fork and ruins this relationship, for it deprives God of the service He requires and man of the lordship which by grace he possesses.

(c) The lordship of Christ renders all men accountable to God. This knowledge affects their life and work, their thoughts and attitudes. It does not mean that they do not respect their superiors

[1] H. H. Smith, *Pre-Reformation England*, p. 269.

CONCLUSIONS AND REASSESSMENT 239

or obey their rulers for these duties are implied in the higher duty. Their ultimate and final obedience determines and transcends everything. For if the Law of God is paramount and the rule of God direct, His Law must be known personally and His rule must be operative directly. Each man, therefore, is responsible to God alone: his primary obedience is to God.

This doctrine of lordship and service presupposes that all men are equal in God's sight, that all men are equally servants of God, and that all are accountable to God. The distinguishing feature underlying this theory is that those who are called to be 'kings and priests unto God' must face the disciplines of their calling as well as accepting its privileges.

Priestly consecration

Certain interpretations have arisen in the course of our study with regard to the precise meaning of believers' priesthood, and we may now set these down in systematic form. The consciousness of priesthood may conveniently be considered in three separate stages: initiation, realization and representation.

There is no more dramatic symbol of the true meaning of priesthood than that in which a believer is incorporated into Christ by the waters of baptism. Baptism is initiation into the royal priesthood. Only an attenuated form of baptism will claim less than this. What happens to such an initiate? The mark of the Cross is upon him, the sevenfold gifts of the Spirit are vouchsafed to him, the prayers of the Church uphold him, and into the fellowship of the redeemed he is received under the threefold Name and in the presence of the people of God. The outward sign of the Cross and the inward seal of the Spirit mean more than the presentation of a believer to God, they imply his consecration as well. Since the early Christians believed that they had 'an anointing from the Holy One', it is not surprising that they soon learned to refer to baptism as 'priestly consecration'. Moreover, the early use of the metaphors of the family and the army shows that the corporate nature of baptism was clearly understood. To be received as a child of God into His family; to be enrolled in the army of God and to be His pledged servant for ever, is to be initiated into the royal priesthood.

Many of these important truths are not understood at the time of the baptismal event, for the initiation into the royal priesthood and the realization of it are not the same. Confirmation and reception into membership are to be understood as realized priesthood. This realization is possible only if two requirements are met. The first is a full, voluntary and personal recognition of the baptismal vows, together with a readiness to be instructed and trained in the doctrines of the Faith. The second, which follows from this, is a desire to be spiritually equipped for whatever service God appoints. Therefore, personal commitment, corroboration of the baptismal vows, discipline and training, readiness for service and absolute loyalty to Christ are seen to be characteristics of the royal priesthood.

Within this royal priesthood some members are appointed to be its representatives, and this appointment is signified by ordination. Ordination is a divine, creative and irrevocable event. A man who is called to the ministry is called from on high. There is no such thing as a human or earthly ordination; it is essentially a divine event. Moreover, there is nothing arbitrary or automatic about the way in which grace is transmitted, for each ordination is a new creative act of God. The irrevocable nature of ordination is recognized in all Churches—a man is ordained for ever.

We must emphasize the place of the universal priesthood in the act of ordination. A man's divine call is confirmed by the whole Church; he is presented to God by the whole Church; the whole Church supports him in prayer, and it is by the whole Church that he is authorized to preach the eternal Gospel. In other words, God acts in ordination through the universal priesthood. We may claim, therefore, that these are the three stages which have arisen in our study—initiation to priesthood, realized priesthood, and representative priesthood. All are essential if the Church is to fulfil her true function, and it is a mistake to imagine that one is more necessary or more important than the other.

III. THE DYNAMIC FORMULA OF REFORM

Priestly mission to the world

Why must the Gospel be proclaimed to all nations and what lies behind this sense of compulsion which has existed in every age? It is not now sufficient to present the Gospel of love merely as an antidote to the threat of eternal damnation. Nor is it any longer tenable to identify the Christian religion with European civilization, with the accompanying implication that this type of civilization is the panacea for all ills. Nor can the urgency of the Gospel be based, as in apostolic days, on the imminence of the end of the world. The missionary obligation of the Church rests on firmer ground, it arises out of the Christian Gospel itself.

This universal obligation is evident in the Old Testament: 'Look unto Me and be ye saved, all the ends of the earth' is an unambiguous declaration. The Servant of the Lord would proclaim Him to the Gentiles, and Israel is chosen to be the priest-nation to the whole world. The Lord Jesus pronounces judgment on the world; He is the Light of the world and its Saviour. There is rarely any doubt in the minds of the writers of the New Testament that the Gospel is not for the Jews only but for all nations, and the Spirit is given at Pentecost to men from nations far and wide. The time had come when men must worship God not in a particular locality (as the Samaritans did), or in a particular temple (as did the Jews) but they must worship Him in spirit and truth. Justin affirms that Christians meet anywhere to worship Him for 'He made heaven and earth'. Those who truly seek Him may find Him anywhere because He is everywhere. Those who are sent to scatter the seed of the Gospel must observe no boundaries for 'the field is the world'.

Sometimes the early Christians were regarded as arrogant because they would not relinquish this sense of universal obligation. In fact, they were not aware of having a choice; their discipleship involved apostleship. The disciples asked their Lord many questions but not on this subject. They had heard the words: 'As the Father hath sent Me, even so send I you' (John xx. 21), and this was sufficient for them. All down the ages the Church has been conceived as a divine instrument wherewith God would bring all nations into a knowledge of redemption. All their work was set in the context of salvation-history. It could not be otherwise, for, although composed of unworthy and unprofitable servants, the Church bears the marks of holiness, apostolicity and catholicity. She is holy unto the Lord, sent by Him into the world in order to draw all men unto Him. Her priesthood could not be more trenchantly expressed. This obligation is at once her divinely imposed mission and her accepted task. She cannot forsake it or neglect it, for her existence depends upon it. Her priesthood consists in the consciousness and the fulfilment of her mission. The priest-nation, which is the Church, must present to God a priestly race. The objective she must ever keep in view is nothing less than the concept of a universal priesthood. It follows that the duty and the goal of the Christian Church must be understood in terms of her unique and universal obligation.

Priestly service for the world

The Christian serves the world by the living of a holy life. He is called to be a saint. The holiness of the Church is revealed in the holiness of individual Christians. A saintly life is the pulse-beat of the Eternal, and those who are in touch with the Eternal are being priests to their fellows. Their priesthood is understood, developed and exercised through worship. Their worship is a service for the world. But they must accept the conditions whereby their priesthood may be exercised. There is the offering of self, of soul and body, as a living sacrifice into God. This means that all that concerns faith and practice is offered to God. The whole range of life's activities, its work as well as its faith, is a sacrifice. Origen gives to worship its true significance when he says: 'Those who are devoted to the divine Word, and are dedicated sincerely to the sole worship of God, may not unreasonably be called priests.'[1]

The Christian serves the world by the offering of others in intercession. This includes those of our own household, those of the household of faith and those who have yet to be won. Burns has referred to the first of these in the story of the cotter who leads his family in prayer. They 'chant their artless notes' in a psalm, whereupon

> *The priestlike father reads the sacred page . . .*
> *Then kneeling down, to Heaven's Eternal King*
> *The saint, the father, and the husband prays.*[2]

And, in a wider context, St Paul dares to come before the altar of God with the whole Gentile race as his offering (Rom. xv. 16). He includes those already of the household of faith, and those

---

[1] *De Oratione*, p. 28.
[2] J. Hawke (ed.), *Poems and Songs*, p. 103.

whom, in faith's glorious anticipation, he would claim for the kingdom of God. There is a vital work to be done in this way. Every Christian is priest to his own family, to his fellow Christians, and by bearing the burdens of others and interceding for the world, he renders a priestly service for the world.

Then, as a further example of our priestly service, there is the willing acceptance of our part in the ministry of reconciliation 'And all things are of God, who hath reconciled us to himself by Jesus Christ, and hath given to us the ministry of reconciliation' (2 Cor. v. 18). We must remember that the word 'us' in both parts of the sentence refers to all Christians. There is no exemption permitted, for we are all of us committed to and involved in this universal mission. The whole world waits for the Church's realization of this paramount work. Will not a full realization of our priesthood revolutionize our attitude to all our work for Christ and His kingdom? It is the plain duty of the royal priesthood to bring mankind to a knowledge of its spiritual inheritance. It is our belief that when the Church awakens to the full implications of this doctrine, the 'universal priesthood' will no longer be an interesting speculation but a universal fact. A task that is cosmic in its dimensions is too urgent to be neglected. So Origen's words are a timely reminder to us all:

> Every religion will be overthrown except the religion of Christ which will alone prevail. And indeed it will one day triumph, as its principles take possession of the minds of men more and more every day. . . . It is not only possible but the literal truth that all, the inhabitants of Asia and of Europe and of Africa, Greeks and barbarians to the world's end, every soul of man should come to agreement under one law.[1]

Priestly vocation in the world

It must be stated at once that one important result of our investigation is that a man's daily work should be regarded as the exercise of his priesthood. The neglect of this single, basic truth has brought innumerable economic crises, industrial unrest and political tensions in the life of the modern world. There will doubtless be occasions when a man is expected to take a course which is at variance with his conscience and his Christian convictions. Such tensions are unavoidable in the circumstances of

[1] Contra Celsum VII, 68, 72.

an unredeemed world. What course should the Christian take in such a dilemma? His first duty is always his Christian duty, but this will not be done simply by evading the conflict. His ultimate objective, hard and long as the path may be, is to Christianize secular organizations. If this seems an ambitious programme, the record of Christian service and achievement in the past must serve as a spur to Christian action in the present. Christians are in the world and that is where they are expected to be. It is precisely in the midst of the bewildering problems and complexities of the secular world that their priesthood should be fulfilled. St Paul bids us buy up every opportunity of service because the days are evil. In the end it is the charitable and unselfish spirit in which a man does his work that matters most. It is at this point that his priesthood receives its severest test. But there is a priestliness of attitude as well as of action, and the saintly disposition, without cant or hypocrisy, is one of the pressing needs of our day.

It is, perhaps, true to say that the impact of Christian witness in the secular world is pathetically weak, and this is due to some extent to a reduced conception of our priesthood. Laziness, dishonesty, avarice and prejudice are not marks of the Christian character. It is the *differentia* of the Christian Faith which should be evident in all our concerns. If this *differentia* is to be seen, a re-examination and a new understanding of our priestly vocation are required. It is in this area that we must look for the reason for the estrangement of vast numbers of people from the Christian Church. But we shall be on the right ground if we regard the present unsatisfactory situation as a reminder of our unfulfilled duty, and if we approach it in penitence and with a new consciousness of our Christian vocation. Perhaps rarely in the history of the Christian Church has there been a time of greater challenge, and rarely have the times so urgently demanded a vigorous application of the doctrine of vocational priesthood. The answer to this challenge is in relating this doctrine to the society in which we live. Theology is not to be divorced from society but has to provide the message and the means whereby society may be redeemed. Therefore we must learn lessons from the past—from Augustine, Benedict and Tauler, so that they may inspire new hope and show us our task.

CONCLUSIONS AND REASSESSMENT

Augustine maintains that any service faithfully rendered to God is a priesthood: 'I would fain be a doorkeeper, or anything in Thy service and amongst Thy people, for priesthood is put here for the people, to whom Christ the Mediator is the High Priest; which people the Apostle called an holy nation and a royal priesthood.'[1]

Similarly it was Benedict's aim and desire that the brethren should render all work, inside and outside the monastery, as a service to God.

So he laid it down that in his 'school of divine servitude' six hours each day should be given to manual toil and two to reading. The sons of Benedict, freemen be it remembered, often men of high degree, as they laboured in the field clad in the dress familiar to the pagan world as the dress of slaves, or took their share in the work of the house, cooking the meals or cleaning the rooms, sanctified industry by consecrating it to the lowliest tasks.[2]

The same truth was reiterated by John Tauler many centuries later:

Let us common Christians look to see what is our office to which our Lord has called and bidden us, and what is the gift of which our Lord has made us vessels. For every art or work, however unimportant it may seem, is a gift of God, and all these gifts are bestowed by the Holy Spirit for the profit and welfare of mankind.[3]

The significance of these statements is that they are typical of the kind of observation which has been made repeatedly and by many different writers during the centuries covered by our study. They are all anxious to stress that whatever service God appoints is an opportunity for a man to exercise his God-given priesthood, and that every form of daily toil is a medium through which his priesthood may be expressed. The situation calls loudly for the witness of Christian laymen, inspired and empowered by the Holy Ghost. For there is no doubt that Christians who do not express their priesthood in practical ways have a Christianity that is weak and starved. Let every Christian fulfil his vocation, realize his priesthood, and consecrate the whole of his life, including his daily toil, as a service to God and for the glory of God, and we shall see that this dynamic formula will again become a living instrument of reform.

[1] *De civ. Dei*, XVII. 5.
[2] H. B. Workman, *The Evolution of the Monastic Ideal*, p. 155.
[3] S. Winkworth, *Tauler's Life and Sermons*, p. 368.

Priestly fulfilment through the world

There have been many occasions in history when Christian pioneers have visited remote parts of the world and have had reason to say with some astonishment that they found the Church there. It is not, perhaps, as astonishing as it seems when it is remembered that the stage of Christian witness is God's world. It is both dangerous and untrue to suppose that outside the boundaries of the Christian Faith there is nothing but a hostile and intractable world. This is not to deny the truth of the Johannine concept that the world 'lieth in the evil one', and is waiting to be redeemed. But we should not preclude the idea of continuous redemptive activity in a world which is God's creation. There is a divine outreach which exceeds the reach of the Church, and God uses many ways and means of fulfilling His redemptive purpose which are not always obvious to men.

In the Old Testament as well as in the New, in the writings of Augustine, in the dream of Dante and the vision of Hildebrand, we find evidence of an all-transcending and all-inclusive purpose which is universal in its scope. It is a purpose which is not confined to Judaism or Christendom but which outspans those barriers which have often been erected by human blindness and ignorance. Perhaps the divine plan is being worked out in ways the Church does not recognize and does not wish to recognize. The crucial question is: Are we justified in approaching the outside world with the assumption that its attitude will inevitably be hostile and intransigent? And is there any hope that the mission or priesthood of the Christian Church may be fulfilled *through* the world?

It is our contention that this view of the hostility and intransigence of the world is based on certain fallacies. First, it is based on the fallacy that the activity of the Spirit of God is nowhere to be found except within the orbit of the Christian Faith. Because this fallacy leads to many misunderstandings, it must be examined. The ground on which the seed of the Gospel is scattered is never wholly unprepared. Whether we consider non-Christian institutions, religions, organizations, movements, or indeed any secular agency, we should not make the erroneous assumption that they are never the ally of the Christian religion. Unless we discard the doctrines of Creation, the divine image in man, prevenient grace, and the universal operation of the Holy Spirit, we must admit that the minds and hearts of men are never wholly unprepared. The Scriptures take this for granted: 'There was the light, the true light, which lighteth every man,—coming into the world' (John i. 9). Always it is coming into the world, and always it enlightens every man alive in his reason and conscience. Moreover, 'the wind—the Spirit—bloweth where it listeth, and thou hearest its voice, but thou knowest not whence it cometh or whither it goeth' (John iii. 8). And although we may not know how the Spirit works, we can see the effect of His work in human lives. But we must be careful lest when we look for the activity of the Spirit we look only in one direction; there is evidence of His presence in unexpected places.

Although it is true that the Spirit is pre-eminently active through the Church, it cannot be denied that He also guides and inspires other movements and institutions. We are aware that everywhere society is taking new forms, and these are in many cases not directed by Christian men. We hesitate to say that these are not directed by the Spirit of God, for oft-times God has used instruments other than Christian to do His will. It is the action of God in history and through history, as well as reflection on Holy Scripture, that makes us believe that God finds His servants in every land and fulfils His purpose in characteristic ways in any environment. Sometimes the Church does not recognize this, and artificial barriers are created. But even when this happens the working of the divine Spirit is not thwarted, for God finds other ways of reaching men and uses whom He will. The point is aptly made by Dr Maltby:

> Those vast tracts of the unbaptized human life we make over to poets and novelists and dramatists who explore them with inexhaustible interest and sympathy. Yet that interest and sympathy come from God who loves this human life of ours, not only as a moralist approving where it is good and disapproving where it is bad, but as a poet or artist loves it, because he cannot help loving a thing so strange, so piteous and enthralling as the story of every human soul must be.[1]

It follows that Christians should not take refuge in their sanctuaries and in the traditional forms of piety, if by so doing they

[1] Cited in E. G. Rupp, *Worldmanship and Churchmanship*, p. 27.

forget to perceive the dynamic love of God in many unexpected areas and in all His children. Wherever the Divine Spirit is active, there the Church must recognize that an opportunity is given for the fulfilment of her priesthood.

The second misapprehension is closely related to the first: it is the reluctance to recognize or even expect signs of response. Far too often the initial signs of response to God are overlooked and regarded as no response at all. Of course there is always the hope and desire that a full response will be made, but this may take time, and meanwhile the Spirit's initial activity should be recognized, for it invariably provides the opportunity for the Christian to be a priest—to draw a man nearer to Christ by reminding him that the wistfulness and questionings in his mind are the work of God. The Church should always be alert to the signs of spiritual response wherever they are to be seen. These signs of spiritual awakening are often evident in the readiness to hear the Gospel, the desire for a Bible, the request for prayer, the offer of service, the desire to be tolerant and understanding. These are frequently the early stages in a man's spiritual pilgrimage, and while these virtues do not make a man a Christian, they at least point to the fact that some response has been made to the love of God. An alert Church will expect and recognize and use such opportunities knowing that in such ways there is a priesthood waiting to be fulfilled. The Scriptures lend support to this view: 'But while he was yet afar off, his father saw him' (Luke xv. 20). The Church must follow up the compassion of the Father, and even when the son is still a great way off recognize the moment of return and show him the way. 'Before Philip called thee, I saw thee' (John i. 48), said Jesus to Nathanael. Spiritual activity had already begun as no doubt it had begun in the heart of Saul of Tarsus when Stephen was being stoned. But in each case something was left for God's servants to do. In this way there are opportunities to be explored by every Christian, and a priesthood to be fulfilled. And while it is true that much can be done by example and word and witness, there is also something to be done by an alert recognition of the Spirit's activity, an appreciation of the teachable moments in other lives, and a sanctified opportunism for the sake of the kingdom of God. While it is true that the Church must always be in advance of the world, always pointing the way, yet it will be successful in doing this only if it contrives in some measure to enter into the world's life and appreciate its highest moods, to meet it as a real friend on that level, and then lead it nearer to Christ. So through the problems and perplexities, the searchings and questionings of a bewildered world, the Church's priesthood will be fulfilled.

This may be done in another way also. For instance, Christians minister to starving refugees, to victims of catastrophe, to the necessitous, the sick and imprisoned, and in so doing they exercise their priesthood. But others also are engaged in this noble work, and even if their ideas are different their aim is the same. They are fulfilling a sacred vocation even if they do so unwittingly. Again, Wilberforce, Clarkson and Shaftesbury could not have brought their reforms to fruition unless they had received the support of many who may not have shared their Christian convictions but whose hearts nevertheless were stirred by a noble desire. Perhaps it is not sufficiently recognized that men often act in the spirit of Christ even while they do not acknowledge His authority. We do not often look for Saul among the prophets although frequently he is to be found there. This is not a plea for compromise but for a frank recognition that we live in a world where everywhere men and movements are being moved, actuated and guided by the Spirit of God and that this very fact offers to Christians opportunities and challenges through which their priesthood may be fulfilled.

In any case, all human institutions, achievements and pretensions are under the judgment of God. All are instruments which God may use if He chooses to do so. Many are not aware that God is continually inspiring, guiding and redeeming the existing order. One of the tasks of the Church is to awaken the minds of men to this awareness. But it is not the world only that is under judgment, but the Church also. And hers is a sterner judgment just because she has a greater responsibility. It behoves us all, therefore, to grasp afresh this dynamic formula of reform, and to realize more fully that we have a priestly mission to the world, a priestly service for the world, a priestly vocation in the world, and the opportunity to fulfil our priesthood through the world. A final and decisive argument in favour of reviving and understanding the doctrine of the priesthood of all believers is that in the sixteenth century it brought new life and strength and reformation to the Christian Church. In fresh circumstances, and in a different though not less needy world, its message, believed and applied, may yet do the same again.

BIBLIOGRAPHY

ADAM, K., *The Spirit of Catholicism.*
ADDIS, W. E., and ARNOLD, T., *A Catholic Dictionary.*
À KEMPIS, THOS. (Collins's Edition).
AQUINAS, T., *Summa Theologica.*
ATHANASIUS, *De Incarnatione,* (ed.) A ROBERTSON.
ATTWATER, D., *Catholic Encyclopaedic Dictionary.*
AUGUSTINE, *De civitate Dei* (trans. JOHN HEALEY 1610).
  Confessions. De Trinitate (trans.) SIR TOBY MATTHEW, 1620, ed. by DOM ROGER HUDLESTON, O.S.B.
BACKHOUSE, E., and TYLOR, C., *Early Church History. Witnesses for Christ.*
BARCLAY, W., *A New Testament Wordbook.*
BARMBY, J., *Gregory the Great.*
BARRY, F. R., *Vocation and Ministry.*
BARTH, K., *Church and State.*
BEET, W. E., *The Medieval Papacy.*
BENEDICTINE OF STANBROOK, *Medieval Mystical Tradition.*
BENSON, E. W., *Cyprian.*
BETT, H., *Studies in Religion.*
BETTENSEN, H. (ed.), *The Early Christian Fathers.*
  Documents of the Christian Church.
BOUQUET, A. C., *The Christian Faith and Non-Christian Religions.*
BOUYER, L., *The Cistercian Heritage.*
BUTTERFIELD, H., *Christianity and History.*
CHESTERTON, G. K., *St Francis of Assisi.*
CHRYSOSTOM (trans. R. S. MOXON), *On the Priesthood.*
CLEMENT OF ALEXANDRIA, *Stromata.*
CLEMENT OF ROME, *Epistle I (to Corinthians).*
CONGAR, Y., *Lay People in the Church.*
CONNOLLY, R. H., *The Liturgical Homilies.*
COULTON, G. G., *Five Centuries of Religion, Vol. II.*
CUNNINGHAM, W., *St Austin.*
CYPRIAN (trans. O. R. VASSALL-PHILLIPS), *On the Unity of the Catholic Church.*
  The Writings of Cyprian (Ante-Nicene Christian Library, ed. A. ROBERTS and J. DONALDSON).
DABIN, P., *Le Sacerdoce Royal Des Fidèles.*
DANTE, *Paradiso* (trans. C. L. SHADWELL).
  De Monarchia.
  Divina Commedia (trans. M. B. ANDERSON).
DAVIDSON, A. B., *The Theology of the Old Testament.*
DAVIS, H., *Gregory's Pastoral Care.*

DAWSON, C., *Medieval Religion.*
D'AYGALLIERS, A. W., *Ruysbroeck the Admirable.*
DEANESLY, M., *A History of the Medieval Church.*
DE FAYE, E., *Origen and his Work.*
DE LA BEDOYERE, M., *The Layman in the Church.*
DE LUBAC, H., *Catholicism.*
DOBSCHÜTZ, E. VON, *The Eschatalogy of the Gospels.*
DODD, C. H., *The Apostolic Preaching and its Developments.*
The Bible Today.
DOLLINGER, J. J. I., *The First Age of Christianity.*
DORNER, J. A., *A System of Christian Doctrine.*
DUDDEN, F. H., *Gregory the Great.*
DUNKERLEY, R., and HEADLAM, A. C. (ed.), *The Ministry and the Sacraments.*
DURELL, J. C. V., *The Historic Church.*
Epistle to Diognetus.
Expository Times, Vol. LXVII, No. 8, LXVII, No. 9.
FAIRWEATHER, W., *Origen and Greek Patristic Theology.*
FLEMING, W. K., *Mysticism in Christianity.*
FLEW, R. N., *Jesus and His Church.*
(ed.) *The Nature of the Church.*
FOSTER, J., *World Church.*
After the Apostles.
GAYFORD, S. C., *Sacrifice and Priesthood.*
GERMANUS (ed. HARDUIN), *Letter to Thomas, Bishop of Claudiopolis.*
GILBY, T. (ed.), *St Thomas Aquinas; Theological Texts.*
GREGORY THE GREAT, *The Morals.*
GWATKIN, H. M., *Selections from Early Christian Writers.*
HAGENBACH, K. R., *History of Doctrines, Vol. II.*
HAMILTON, K., *The Protestant Way.*
HARDWICK, C., *A History of the Christian Church during the Reformation.*
HARNACK, A., *The Mission and Expansion of Christianity.*
Monasticism, its Ideals and its History.
HASTINGS, J., (ed.), *Dictionary of the Bible.*
Encyclopedia of Religion and Ethics.
HEBERT, W. G., *The Throne of David.*
HERMAS (Shepherd of), *Similitudes.*
HODGSON, G. E., *English Mystic.*
HOOKER, M. D., *Jesus and the Servant.*
HORT, F. J. A., *Six Lectures on the Ante-Nicene Fathers.*
The Christian Ecclesia.
HOSKYNS, E. C., *The Fourth Gospel.*
HUGHES, P., *The Reformation in England, Vol. I.*
HUGHES, T. P., *A Dictionary of Islam.*
HUNTER, A. M., *Design for Life.*
HUTTON, W. H., *The Church and the Barbarians.*

IGNATIUS, *Epistle to Polycarp.*
INGE, W. R., *Christian Mysticism.*
International Review of Missions, Vol.XL, No. 159.
IRENAEUS, *Against Heresies.*
IVES, E. J. (ed.), *Eleven Christians.*
JUSTIN MARTYR, *Apology.*
Dialogue with Trypho (Ante-Nicene Christian Library).
KETTLEWELL, S., *Thomas à Kempis and the Brothers of the Common Life.*
KIDD, B. J., *Documents Illustrative of the History of the Church.*
KIRK, K. E. (ed.), *The Apostolic Ministry.*
KRAEMER, H., *A Theology of the Laity.*
The Christian Message in a non-Christian World.
LEWIS, J., *The Life of Wyclif.*
LIDDON, H. P., *University Sermons.*
LIGHTFOOT, R. H., 'A Dissertation on the Christian Ministry' in his *Commentary on Philippians.*
LINDSAY, T. M., *The Church and the Ministry in the Early Centuries.*
MACDONALD, D. B., *Encyclopedia of Islam, Vol. I.*
MANSON, T. W., *Ministry and Priesthood; Christ's and Ours.*
The Church's Ministry.
(ed.), *A Companion to the Bible.*
MANSON, W., *Jesus the Messiah.*
MARSIGLIO of Padua, (ed.) C. W. PREVITÉ-ORTON, *Defensor Pacis.*
MASON, A. J., *The Relation of Confirmation to Baptism.*
MATTHEWS, W. R., *The Problem of Christ in the Twentieth Century.*
MCGIFFERT, A. C., *The History of Christian Thought, Vols. I and II.*
Protestant Thought before Kant.
Member of the Church of India, *The Heritage of an Indian Christian.*
MERSCH, E., *The Whole Christ.*
MILLIGAN, W., *The Ascension and Heavenly Priesthood of our Lord.*
MOBERLY, R. C., *Ministerial Priesthood.*
MOFFATT, J., *The Theology of the Gospels.*
MOMMSEN, T., *Provinces of the Roman Empire.*
NAIRNE, A., *Epistle of Priesthood.*
NEANDER, A., *Church History, Vols. I, V,* and *IX* (Bohn Edition).
NEILL, S., *The Christian Society.*
(ed.) *The Ministry of the Church.*
Christian Faith Today.
NIEBUHR, H. R. and WILLIAMS, D. D., *The Ministry in Historical Perspectives.*
NIEBUHR, R., *The Nature and Destiny of Man, Vol. II.*
NORTH, C. R., *An Outline of Islam.*
The Suffering Servant.
OERSTERLY, W. E. and ROBINSON, T. L., *Hebrew Religion; its Origin and Development.*

ORIGEN, *De Oratione* (Ante-Nicene Christian Library).
Contra Celsum.
Homilies.
Exhortation to Martyrdom.
OWST, G. R., *Preaching in Medieval England.*
PAYNE, E. A., *The Free Church Tradition in the Life of England.*
PIUS XII (Pope), *Mediator Dei.*
POOLE, R. L., *Illustrations of the History of Medieval Thought and Learning.*
POPE, W. B., *A Compendium of Christian Theology, Vol. III.*
POWICKE, F. M., *The Christian Life in the Middle Ages.*
PREVITÉ-ORTON, C. W. (ed.), *Cambridge Medieval History, Vol. VIII.*
PRZYWARA, E. (ed.), *An Augustine Synthesis.*
RADHAKRISHNAN, S., *Religion and Society.*
RICHARDSON, A., *A Theological Wordbook.*
An Introduction to the Theology of the New Testament.
The Biblical Doctrine of Work.
RICHARDSON, C. C., *The Church through the Centuries.*
RITSCHL, A., *Justification and Reconciliation.*
ROBERTS, R. E., *The Theology of Tertullian.*
ROBINSON, H. W., *The Religious Ideas of the Old Testament.*
(ed.), *The Inspiration and Revelation in the Old Testament.*
(ed.), *Record and Revelation.*
RODWELL, J. M. (trans.), *The Quran.*
ROLLE, R. (trans. H. L. HUBBARD), *The Amending of Life.*
RUPP, E. G., *Churchmanship and Worldmanship.*
Luther's Progress to the Diet of Worms.
RUYSBROECK, J., *The Mirror of Eternal Salvation.*
SALE, G. (trans.), *The Quran.*
SANDAY, W. (ed.), *Priesthood and Sacrifice.*
SARMA, D. S., *What is Hinduism?*
SCHAFF, P., *History of the Christian Church, 311-600, Vol. I; 590-1073, Vol. I.*
Scottish Journal of Theology, Vol. IX, No. 2.
SCYZINGER, E., *The Glory of God.*
SHAPLAND, C. R. B., *First Epistle of Peter.*
SMITH, K. C., *The Church and the Churches.*
SMITH, H. H., *Pre-Reformation England.*
SNAITH, N. H., *The Distinctive Ideas of the Old Testament.*
Hymns of the Temple.
STANLEY, A. P., *The History of the Eastern Church.*
STEVENS, G., *The Theology of the New Testament.*
STREETER, B. H., *The Primitive Church; Reality.*
SWETE, H. B., *The Apocalypse.*
(ed.), *The Early History of the Church and the Ministry.*
SYKES, N., *The Crisis of the Reformation.*
TAUNTON, E. L., *The English Black Monks of St Benedict.*

BIBLIOGRAPHY

TAYLOR, V., *The Atonement in New Testament Teaching*.
TENNANT, F. R., *The Origin and Propagation of Sin*.
TERTULLIAN, *De Exhortatione*.
De Oratione.
Theologia Germanica (trans. S. WINKWORTH).
TILLICH, P., *The Courage to be*.
TORRANCE, T. F., *Royal Priesthood*.
TOWNSEND, W. J., *The Great Schoolmen of the Middle Ages*.
TRENCH, R. C., *Medieval Church History*.
ULLMANN, C., *Reformers before the Reformation*.
VISSER 'T HOOFT, W. A., *Anglo-Catholicism and Orthodoxy*.
The Renewal of the Church.
WARD, M., *Our Theological Task*.
WATSON, E. W., *The Life of Bishop John Wordsworth*.
WATSON, P. S., *The Concept of Grace*.
Articles in *London Quarterly Review*, July, Oct., *1957*.
WINDGREN, G., *Theology in Conflict*.
The Christian's Calling.
WINKWORTH, S., *The Life and Sermons of John Tauler*.
WOOLF, B. L., *Reformation Writings, Vol. I*.
WORDSWORTH, J., *The Ministry of Grace*.
WORKMAN, H. B., *Christian Thought to the Reformation*.
The Dawn of the Reformation, Vol. I.
The Evolution of the Monastic Ideal.
The Place of Methodism in the Catholic Church.
Works of John Wesley (3rd edition in 14 vols. ed. THOS. JACKSON).
WYCLIF, J., (ed.) H. WINN, *Select English Writings*.
WYLIE, J., A., *The History of Protestantism*.

INDEX OF SCRIPTURE REFERENCES

OLD TESTAMENT PASSAGES

Genesis

xxii. 12	18
xxvi. 25	18

Exodus

iv. 15–16	21
vii. 1	21
xix. 6	2, 3, 7, 14, 24, 25
xxx. 15	4

Leviticus

xxvi. 12	3, 4

Numbers

vi. 2, 3–7	20
xi. 29	18
xvi. 3	18
xviii. 5	20

Deuteronomy

vii. 6	63
x. 8	20
xvii. 12	38
xxi. 5	38

Judges

vi. 26	18
xiii. 19	18
xvii. 7	18

1 Samuel

viii. 5	4
xv. 22	25

2 Chronicles

xxvi. 18	20

Psalms

ii. 7	27
xxxvii. 29	113
xl. 6–8	25
xlv	65
l. 14	25
li. 17	25
lxviii. 18	35
cxxxii. 16	25

Isaiah

i. 3	21
x. 5	17
xi. 2	15
xiv	9
xlii. 1–4	9, 15, 16, 38
xlii. 8	205
xlix. 1–7	9, 15, 16
xlix. 8	13
l. 4–9	9, 11, 17
lii. 13–15	9, 16
liii. 1–12	9, 14, 43
lix. 21	31
lxi. 1–2	14, 15
lxi. 6	25

Jeremiah

vii. 15	4
vii. 21–3	8
vii. 28	4
xi. 4	3
xv. 9	17
xxxi. 15	9
xxxi. 31	14

258 THE ROYAL PRIESTHOOD OF THE FAITHFUL

Amos		Zechariah	
ix. 7	17	iii. 1	61
		xix. 10	13
Micah		Malachi	
iii. 11	21	i. 11–14	59
vi. 6–8	24, 25	iii. 1–2	41

NEW TESTAMENT PASSAGES

Matthew		xiii. 10, 14, 16	42
x	178	xvii. 19	40
x. 25	14	Acts	
xi. 4–5	39		
xii. 17–19	38	i. 6–8	35
xxi. 5	41	ii. 18	43
xxiv. 14	35	viii. 35	43
xxvii. 32	15	xvi. 17	51
xxviii. 19	160	xxiv. 17	58
		xxvi. 7	50
Mark		xxvi. 23	35
viii. 34	96	Romans	
x. 45	38		
xiv. 25	37	i. 4	27
		iii. 24	32
Luke		vi. 3	46
		viii. 29	29
iv. 16–22	40	viii. 32	31
vii. 19–23	40	x. 17	124
xv. 20	248	xi. 13	54
xxii. 20	31	xi. 27	31
xxii. 27	38, 42	xi. 30–3	48
		xv. 16	53, 58, 242
John		1 Corinthians	
i. 9	247		
i. 11	27	i. 2	32
i. 18	28	i. 17	37
i. 48	248	iii. 21, 23	31
iii. 5	47	ix. 14	51
iii. 8	247	x. 17	129
iv. 23	65	xii. 5	54
vi. 54	128	xii. 7	232
xii. 26	39	xv. 22	10
xiii. 3	41	xvi.	51

INDEX OF SCRIPTURE REFERENCES 259

2 Corinthians

i. 24	231
iv. 5	44, 231
v. 7	124
v. 17-18	96, 243
ix. 12	53

Galatians

ii. 20	197
vi. 16	32

Ephesians

i. 1	32
i. 4	234
i. 22	37
ii. 4-10	32
ii. 14	54
ii. 15	232
ii. 21-2	32
iii. 2	96
iii. 9	234
iv. 8, 10	35
iv. 12	54
iv. 24	96
iv. 30	95
v. 26-7	47
v. 30	32

Philippians

ii. 6-8	44
ii. 17	53, 58

Colossians

i. 12	52
i. 18	29

2 Thessalonians

ii. 13	234

1 Timothy

iii	57

Titus

iii. 4-7	46

Hebrews

i. 5	27
i. 8	34
iii. 1	28
iv. 14, 15, 16	34, 141, 49
v. 5-7	27, 28
v. 8	45
v. 18	141
vi. 27	49
vii. 17	139
viii. 1	34
ix. 1	45
ix. 14	45, 49
x. 7	44
x. 19-25	40, 46
xi. 27	124
xiii. 10	58
xiii. 15	49, 58

1 Peter

ii. 5	48
ii. 9	25, 26, 32, 63, 79

1 John

ii. 20	16, 46

Revelation

i. 6	14, 25, 26, 32, 47, 50
iii. 8	29, 234
v. 9-10	48, 50
vii. 15	50
x. 9-14	36
xx. 6	34, 50, 95
xxii. 3	44

INDEX OF SUBJECTS

Atonement, 44–6, 118–19, 141–2
Authority, 57, 60, 82–4, 86–8, 131–133, 175, 177, 189, 228

Baptism, 46–7, 91–4, 148–50, 239 240
Benedictines, 183–6
Benefit of Clergy, 135
Black Death, 203
Brethren of the Common Life, 220–4

Canon Law, 132–3
Celibacy, 136
Chrism, 94–7, 237
Church and State, 131–7, 163–71
Church Government, 57, 60, 82, 131–3, 163–4
Communion of Saints, 144
Community, 32–6, 73–4
Confirmation, 97, 161, 240
Covenant, 6–9, 24, 30–2, 227

Didache, 59
Discipline, 60, 74–5, 86, 165
Divine initiative, 204–5
Dominion, 171–4

Eastern Orthodox Church, 158–62
Election, 4–6, 62–4
Episcopacy, 69–70, 87–8, 105–6
Eschatology, 33–7, 235
Eucharist, 30–1, 58, 127–30, 157–8, 228
Existentialism, 35–6, 176, 213

Faith, 197, 211–14
Fellowship, 214–17
Feudal System, 134–5, 171–2
Forgiveness, 127, 147
Franciscans, 186–93, 223
Friends of God, 199–203, 214–15

Ghibelline ideal, 167, 169–70
Good works, 147, 186, 204–5

Iconoclasm, 114, 120–5
Incarnation, 27–30, 122, 139–41
Infallibility, 131–2
Islam, 109–20, 226

Justification, 123–4, 127, 146–7, 176, 198, 212–13

Kenosis, 44
Kingdom of priests, 18–25

Laity, 56, 106–7, 161, 180–1, 193, 233
Lay Apostolate, 233
Lay Investiture, 134–5

Martyrdom, 61, 79
Ministry, 177–8, 230–1
Mission, 51–3, 65–6, 156–7, 240–250
Monasticism, 179–83
Montanism, 75
Mysticism, 195–9

Ordination, 77, 144–5, 159, 233, 240

Pelagianism, 147, 211, 228–9
Penitential System, 125–7, 141–2
Prophet, 59
Protestants, 88–9
Protology, 234–5

Quran, 112, 115

Race (high-priestly), 62–6
Restoration, 76–7
Revelation, 1–4, 26–7
Rome (supremacy of), 102–5

INDEX OF SUBJECTS

Sacrifice, sacrifices, 12–14, 22, 47–9, 58–62, 68–9, 72–3, 79–80, 97–8
Sanctification, 182–3, 198
Scholasticism, 143, 208, 211–12, 214
Scriptures, 107–8, 114–15, 143–4, 177, 199
Secular world, 246–8
Servant, 9–17, 40–1
Servant-Messiah, 38–43
Service, 62–3, 221, 230–40, 237–9, 242–3

Theocracy, 163, 167–70
Third Order, 187–8, 233
Three dispensations, 235–6

Unity, 84, 97–8, 108–9, 143–4
Universal Episcopate, 105–6
Universal Way, 99–101

Vocation, 156, 217–19, 243–5

Widows (Order of), 60
Work, 185–6, 243–5
Worship, 49–51, 64–5, 150–3

INDEX OF NAMES

Adam, K., 89, 144, 147, 156
Addis, W. E., 132, 211
Agilulph, 103
à Kempis, Thos., 221-2
Alaric, 103, 105
Alexander (of Jerusalem), 56
Angela (of Foligno), 157
Anthony, 179, 181-2
Aquinas, 138-42, 144-5, 148, 192
Arnold T., 132, 211
Athanasius, 139-40
Attila, 103, 105
Attwater, D., 138
Augustine, 44, 91-101, 103, 131, 137, 150, 163, 181, 195, 228, 235-6, 245, 247
Augustus, 81, 169

Barclay, W., 6, 31
Barmby, J., 105
Barth, K., 164
Basil (of Caesarea), 179
Beet, W. E., 182, 189
Benedict (of Nursia), 179-85, 245
Bernard (of Clairvaux), 195, 199
Bett, H., 196
Bishop, E. E., 110
Bouquet, A. C., 111, 116
Bouyer, L., 195, 199
Bultmann, R., 34
Burns, R., 242
Butterfield, H., 13

Calvin, 154
Canakyaniti, 123
Chapman, J. A., 99
Charlemagne, 103
Chesterton, G. K., 182
Chrysostom, 89
Clarkson, T., 249
Clement (of Alexandria), 71-3, 235
Clement (of Rome), 56-8, 63, 83

Clement (pseudo), 63
Confucius, 201
Congar, Y., 151, 180
Constantine, 82, 103-4, 169
Cunningham, W., 93, 98
Cyprian, 80-90, 228
Cyriacus, 105
Cyrus, 13

Dabin, P., 153-4
Damian, P., 143
Dante, 163, 167, 169-70, 192, 196, 247
Davidson, A. B., 3, 15
Davies, H., 108
Dawson, C., 163-4, 192
Deanesly, M., 175, 183, 190
de Faye, E., 76
De La Bedoyère, M., 149-50, 153
de Lubac, H., 143, 156
Diognetus, 68
Dionysius (the Areopagite), 91
Dix, G., 53, 155
Dobschütz, E. von, 36
Dodd, C. H., 34
Dollinger, J. J. I., 95
Dorner, J. A., 149-50
Dudden, F. H., 107-8
Dunkerley, R., 158-61
Durrell, J. C. V., 67

Eckhart, 216
Ellul, J., 179
Eulogius (of Alexandria), 105

Fairweather, W., 76-7
Flew, R. N., 6, 8, 31, 36, 146
Foster, J., 111, 193
Francis (of Assisi), 99, 186-94, 227-9

Gerhardt, 195
Germanus, 121-2

INDEX OF NAMES

Gilby, T., 212
Gratian, 133, 137
Greenslade, S. L., 52
Gregory I (Pope), 102, 105-9, 137, 183, 228
Groot, G., 204, 220-4

Hadewijck, 209
Hagenbach, K. R., 202, 211, 214
Haimeric (Cardinal), 195
Hamilton, K., 88
Hardwick, C., 178
Harford, G., 23
Harnack, A., 59, 64, 179, 186, 188, 193
Hastings, J., 169
Hawke, J., 242
Headlam, A. C., 30
Hebert, A. G., 155
Henry IV (of Germany), 132
Hermas, 63
Hickinbotham, J. P., 155
Hilary (of Poitiers), 181
Hildebrand (Pope), 102, 131-7, 247
Hodgson, G. E., 197
Hooker, M. D., 17
Hort, F. J. A., 71, 95
Hoskyns, E. C., 40
Hubbard, H. L., 198
Hügel, F. Baron von, 197
Hugh (of St Victor), 235-7
Hughes, J. P., 117
Hunter, A. M., 39
Hutton, W. H., 120, 122, 124

Ignatius, 67
Inge, W. R., 218
Innocent III (Pope), 188-9
Irenaeus, 66-70, 108, 227
Ives, E. J., 100

Jerome, 179, 181
Joachim (of Flora), 235-7
John (of the Cross), 157
John (of Damascus), 121-2
John IV (Patriarch), 105

John XXII (Pope), 203
Justin (Emperor), 105
Justin Martyr, 61-6, 227

Kettlewell, S., 220, 222
Kirk, K. E., 53, 155
Korah, 18
Kraemer, H., 112-13, 181

Leo I (Pope), 103
Leo III (Emperor), 120-1, 125
Leo III (Pope), 103
Licinius, 104
Liddon, H. P., 233-4
Lightfoot, R. H., 67
Lindsay, T. M., 58, 73, 85, 88
Louis (of Bavaria), 203
Luther, 89, 99, 127, 142, 147, 170-171, 180, 195-7, 200, 224-6, 230-1

MacDonald, D. B., 113
McGiffert, A. C., 76
Maltby, W. R., 247
Manson, T. W., 14, 19, 52-3
Manson, W., 16, 38
Marsiglio, 135, 137, 163-70, 229
Martin (of Tours), 179
Mason, A. J., 96
Matthews, W. R., 33
Mersch, E., 143, 146
Methodius (of Olympus), 157
Milligan, W., 232
Moberley, R. C., 49
Moffatt, J., 38, 42-3
Mommsen, T., 70
Muhammad, 102, 109-20

Narsai, 70
Neander, A., 93, 166, 168, 200-1, 206-12
Neill, S., 114, 124-5, 155, 184, 197-8
Nicholas (of Basle), 199-200
Niebuhr, H. R., 129
Niebuhr, R., 182
North, C. R., 17, 117

Parsons, R. G., 116
Payne, E. A., 174
Peake, A. S., 116
Phillips, J. B., 35
Pius XII (Pope), 146, 148, 151
Polycarp, 59–61, 67
Poole, R. L., 164–5, 167, 173
Pope, W. B., 214
Previté-Orton, C. W., 170

Radbert, 128–9
Radhakrishnan, S., 123
Ramsey, A. M., 162
Ratramnus, 128
Richardson, C. C., 86, 90, 184, 197–8, 193, 201, 245
Ritschl, A., 177
Roberts, R. E., 74
Robinson, H. Wheeler, 14, 19
Robinson, T. L., 16
Rodwell, J. M., 112
Rohrbach, B. von, 199
Rolle, R., 198
Rupp, E. G., 231, 247
Ruysbroeck, 204, 209–20, 224

Sale, G., 112
Sanday, W., 30
Sarma, D. S., 122–3
Schaff, P., 96, 106, 181
Scyzinger, E., 144
Shaftesbury, Lord, 249
Shapland, C. R. B., 48
Smith, H. H., 174, 178, 238
Smith, K. L. Carrick, 145
Snaith, N. H., 5, 7, 11, 19
Stanley, A. P., 158–60
Stevenson, M., 23
Streeter, B. H., 123

Swete, H. B., 48, 50
Sykes, N., 204
Sylvester I (Pope), 104
Syncletius, 184

Tauler, 199–219, 224, 245
Taunton, E. L., 185
Taylor, V., 31, 37, 45
Tennant, F. R., 100
Tertullian, 73–5, 83, 181, 228
Theodore (Archimandrite), 123
Tillich, P., 213
Torrance, T. F., 15, 28, 37
Trench, R. C., 136, 201

Ullmann, C., 221–3
Upland, J., 191

Vann, G., 157
Vincent (of Lerins), 82
Visser 'T Hooft, W. A., 88–9, 179

Ward, A. M., 117
Watson, E. W., 97
Watson, P. S., 30
Watts, D. J., 5
Wesley, Charles, 36, 45, 129, 155
Wesley, John, 99, 195–6, 200
Wilberforce, W., 249
William (of Orange), 132
Williams, D. D., 129
Windgren, G., 35, 185–6, 218
Winkworth, S., 200 ff., 245
Woolf, B. L., 195
Wordsworth, J., 56
Workman, H. B., 88, 165, 173 ff., 245
Wyclif, 137, 170–8, 226, 229, 238
Wylie, J. A., 177

www.ingramcontent.com/pod-product-compliance
Lightning Source LLC
Chambersburg PA
CBHW050435240426
43661CB00055B/2397